Desserts To Die For

"I feel the end approaching. Quick, bring me my dessert, coffee and liqueur."
—BRILLAT-SAVARIN'S GREAT AUNT PIERETTE

Desserts To Die For

MARCEL DESAULNIERS

PHOTOGRAPHY BY MICHAEL GRAND

RECIPES WITH JON PIERRE PEAVEY

SIMON & SCHUSTER

New York   London   Toronto   Sydney   Tokyo   Singapore

SIMON & SCHUSTER
Rockefeller Center
1230 Avenue of the Americas
New York, New York 10020

A KENAN BOOK

DESSERTS TO DIE FOR
was prepared and produced by
Kenan Books
15 West 26th Street
New York, New York 10010

Editor: Nathaniel Marunas
Art Director/Designer: Jeff Batzli
Photography Director: Christopher C. Bain
Production Director: Karen Matsu Greenberg
Cover Photograph: Props courtesy Takashimaya;
Surface by Nancy Arner

Color separations by Ocean Graphic International Company Ltd.
Printed in Singapore

1 3 5 7 9 10 8 6 4 2

Library of Congress Cataloging-in-Publication Data

Desaulniers, Marcel.
    Desserts to die for / Marcel Desaulniers ; photography by Michael Grand
        p.   cm.
    "A Kenan book."
    Includes bibliographical references and index.
    ISBN 0-684-81139-1 : $30.00
    1. Dessert.   I. Title.
TX773.D383   1995
641.8'6--dc20   95–1152
                                                                      CIP

DEDICATION

For the Desaulniers,
especially my mother, Victoire,
and my sisters, Jeannine, Suzanne, Denise,
Paulette, and Giselle.

Also for my son Marc,
gone but not forgotten.

CONFECTIONERY ALPHABET OF ACKNOWLEDGMENTS

As the guru of ganache, I hereby bestow the following honorary titles to all the friends, colleagues, and accomplices who made *Desserts To Die For* possible:

Angel of Anglaise—Connie Desaulniers (innamorata)

Bard of Bar-le-Duc—Dan Green (literary agent)

Captain of Caramel—Jon Pierre Peavey (assistant)

Dean of Delectation—John Curtis (partner)

Empress of Ecstasy—Penny Seu (editorial advisor)

Father of Fondant—Andrew O'Connell (chef of the Trellis)

General of Genoise—Tim O'Connor (pastry chef of the Trellis)

High Priest of Hard Sauce—Michael Grand (photographer)

Impresario of Ice Cream—Nathaniel Marunas (editor)

Jester of Jelly Rolls—Jeff Batzli (art director)

King of Kirschwasser—Chris Bain (photography editor)

Lady of Linzertorte—Karen Matsu-Greenberg (production director)

Mothers of Meringue—Lisa Ekus and Merrilyn Siciak (publicists)

Nabob of Nesselrode—Simon Green (electronic media agent)

Oracles of Opulence—The kitchen staff at the Trellis

Pooh-bahs of Petit Fours—The front of the house staff at the Trellis

Quarterbacks of Quaff—Ed Digilio and Bill Valois (semper fi)

Raja of Raspberries—Michael Friedman (The Michael Friedman Publishing Group)

Swinging Sultans of Sugar—Everyone at Simon & Schuster

Temptress of Truffles—Rose Levy Beranbaum (advisor)

Usurper of Upside-Down Cakes—Danielle Desaulniers-Shepherd (beautiful daughter and budding culinarian)

Viceroy of Vanilla—Rod Stoner (mentor for more than thirty years)

Warlord of Whipped Cream—John Twichell (former Trellis pastry chef)

Xenophobe of Xylose—Jim Seu (advisor)

Yogis of Yum—Everyone at the Culinary Institute of America

Zombies of Zabaglione—Did I forget anyone?

ALSO BY MARCEL DESAULNIERS

The Trellis Cookbook (1988)

The Trellis Cookbook
(expanded edition 1992)

Death by Chocolate (1992)

The Burger Meisters (1994)

CONTENTS

INTRODUCTION

"Excess on occasion is exhilarating; it keeps moderation from becoming a habit."
—W. Somerset Maugham

Wretched excess? Is that what Desserts To Die For *is all about? The answer is an unequivocal, enthusiastic yes. With no apologies from me, this book is not for the faint of heart. Who, then, can benefit from this book?*

Desserts To Die For is for anyone with a sweet tooth. It is also for anyone who loves the occasional indulgence, or enjoys creating a special dessert with or for a loved one. If you drool over Michael Grand's photographs and think they look so edible you need to loosen your belt, this book is for you. If sharing a piece of buttercream-swathed cake seems like a sensual experience, this book is your next step toward paradise.

If you have heard the call, follow me into the confectionery arena, where multilayered and textured cakes flourish, where you will find some startlingly chilling sorbets and uncommon ice creams, where the crispiest cookies await your bite, where comforting favorites are given new vitality and flavor, where refreshing fruit concoctions wait to tantalize your palate, and where the most deadly delectations abound.

Join me if you dare on an outrageous and uncensored excursion. Remember, you only live once, and I can't think of a better way to go.

—Marcel Desaulniers
Williamsburg, Virginia

NOTES FROM THE TEST KITCHEN

ABOUT THE TEST KITCHEN

In the last eight years, I have tested recipes for several cookbooks in the home I share with my wife, Connie, in Williamsburg. For me, testing at home is an important process in writing a cookbook, since I feel I should test the recipes myself in a setting that approximates the average home kitchen.

I have spent most of my waking hours over the last thirty years in commercial kitchens, surrounded by stainless steel. So when Connie and I built our home ten years ago, we designed an intimate and cozy kitchen devoid of commercial equipment. The one exception is a large stainless steel table which works well as a space both for food preparation and for eating casual meals.

My favorite aspect of putting together a cookbook is testing the recipes, usually with an assistant manipulating the ingredients while I volley between mixing bowl and word processor. For *Desserts To Die For* I was assisted by the remarkable, enduring, creative, and always supportive Jon Pierre Peavey. A testing day began with Jon Pierre gathering the recipe ingredients from local supermarkets. We would meet at my house, which is a little more than half a mile from the Trellis. Typically we would test two to three recipes a day, unless the recipe was more involved, such as Chocolate Caramel Hazelnut Damnation (see page 43).

I should mention that Jon Pierre has worked at the Trellis for the last five years. A graduate of the Culinary Institute of America, Jon Pierre also assisted me with *The Burger Meisters* (Simon & Schuster, 1994). When he works with me on a book, Jon Pierre pretests recipes at the Trellis before we test them in my home kitchen. Sometimes this means breaking down a restaurant quantity recipe from the Trellis' repertoire; at other times he works with an agreed-upon concept and essentially creates a recipe. Jon Pierre has proved invaluable at mastering this very time-consuming and exacting work.

With recipe testing at the Trellis, Jon Pierre uses consumer equipment, from pots and pans to a Maytag range. By the time we test a recipe in my home kitchen, Jon Pierre will have prepared it three or four times at the Trellis. Quite often we finalize a recipe, working together in my home kitchen, after just one attempt. Hopefully all of our testing rewards you with easy-to-follow recipes that enable you to prepare *Desserts To Die For* just like we do at the Trellis—and at my house.

PLEASE READ ME

Oh, horrors, Marcel. You mean I actually have to read your recipes to create these extraordinary desserts?

Yes you do. But I tried to make the reading fun and informative. It always makes good sense to read a recipe completely before preparation, since it may contain an ingredient you do not like (I hope it's not chocolate) or a necessary piece of equipment that you don't have in the cupboard.

Perhaps around kitchen equipment you are like I am around electronics. That is, I purchase a new VCR, plug it into the TV set and a convenient electrical socket, and expect it to do everything it was supposed to do with little other attention. Whether fiddling with electronics or baking cakes, ignoring instructions can lead to disappointment. So just read through the recipe at least once to get a feeling about the flavors, textures, and techniques—all of which will ultimately help you produce a dessert to die for.

ORGANIZING EQUIPMENT AND INGREDIENTS

If it is your passion to explore a world of melted chocolate, crispy meringues, towering cakes, silken ice creams, tantalizing sorbets, and other confectionery miracles, then read on.

Before you prepare a dessert, first gather all the ingredients in the recipe and organize them as listed. For example, for the Fallen Angel Cake (see page 38), envision that on your kitchen counter you have already arranged in individual, appropriately sized containers:

½ pound unsalted butter
8 ounces semisweet chocolate, broken into
    ½-ounce pieces
6 large egg yolks
¾ cup granulated sugar
8 large egg whites
2 tablespoons unsweetened cocoa
2 tablespoons confectioners' sugar

With all these ingredients directly in front of you, the process of preparing the cake is more manageable. Additionally, because timing is essential when combining ingredients, you minimize the opportunities for failed desserts.

Regarding equipment, be sure to get your act together. Do you need all the paraphernalia listed in every equipment section of each recipe? For the most part, yes, but certain substitutions can be made. A sharp knife can achieve some of the same results as a food processor, provided you have the extra time and stamina. Although a handheld mixer can whip heavy cream to the same volume as a table model, it will not do the job of a table model when incorporating butter into the Buttery Bun Dough (see page 102). So I suggest gathering the listed equipment before beginning your sweet journey.

INGREDIENTS

When a professional chef authors a cookbook for use in the home kitchen, perhaps the most important requirement is to use the same ingredients and equipment available to the nonprofessional. Many food products are manufactured differently for the food-service industry than they are for the supermarket. For instance, a well-known brand of cream cheese has a higher fat content in the food-service package than in the supermarket package.

In that light, my assistant Jon Pierre Peavey shopped in local Williamsburg, Virginia, supermarkets for all the ingredients we melted, whisked, simmered, baked, cooled, decorated, and, yes, eventually consumed right in my home kitchen. A few products were obtained in specialty shops or through mail order (for information on these items, refer to the "Sources" section, page 142).

The following is additional information on some key components frequently used in *Desserts To Die For.*

BAKING POWDER AND BAKING SODA

Without getting into Chemistry 101 (especially since I failed high school chemistry at Mount Saint Charles Academy), anyone who bakes needs an elemental grasp of what happens when using bicarbonate of soda (a.k.a. baking soda) and baking powder (a blend of baking soda, cream of tartar, and cornstarch). Both the soda and the powder are leaveners that are activated by contact with a liquid. In the case of baking soda, this liquid must be acidic, such as buttermilk. Baking powder, on the other hand, can be mixed with water, milk, or other nonacidic liquids since it already contains acid in the form of cream of tartar.

Be sure to look at the expiration date on the container, since baking powder and baking soda do not improve with age. Also, be certain to measure very accurately. Improperly measured, these ingredients can seriously alter the simplest recipe. Lastly, move quickly. Once bicarbonate of soda is added to a batter, the chemical action of creating carbon dioxide gas bubbles begins. Any time lost placing the finished batter in the oven will almost certainly affect the end result (usually a collapse of the batter during baking).

BUTTER

There is no substitution for the flavor of real butter. Although margarine and vegetable shortening can be substituted in many recipes that call for butter, the dessert will not have the same smooth, rich flavor. And other aspects, such as moisture and crumb texture, may be adversely affected as well.

For best results, select butter that is specifically labeled "U.S. Grade AA unsalted butter." Without salt, butter can become rancid in a matter of days, especially if your refrigerator is overloaded and not cooling properly. So, if you are not going to use it within a few days, store the butter in the freezer.

When recipes specify softened butter, allow refrigerated or frozen butter to come to room temperature before using. Otherwise, all butter should be at refrigerator temperature (not frozen).

CHOCOLATE

Nothing treats the palate like the sumptuous, sensual, and stimulating sensation of chocolate melting in your mouth. That is the exact reason that chocolate is so beloved.

PURCHASING

When it comes to purchasing chocolate, *caveat emptor* ("let the buyer beware"). Read the ingredient label prior to purchasing and be sure to select real chocolate, that is, chocolate that contains cocoa butter rather than such fat additives as partially hydrogenated palm kernel oil or palm oil. Unsweetened chocolate, also known as chocolate liquor, is the purest form of chocolate you can purchase. It has more than 50% cocoa butter by volume; the remaining ingredient is cocoa solids.

STORING

Chocolate is very susceptible to temperature variances. If improperly stored in a warm environment—above 78 degrees Fahrenheit—the cocoa butter may separate from the cocoa solids, causing discoloration. If stored in a cold and damp environment, the sugar in the chocolate may crystalize.

Purchase chocolate from a retail establishment that sells a lot of chocolate, and stay away from dusty boxes. You should store the chocolate in a cool, dry place or well wrapped in the refrigerator (allow chocolate to come to air-conditioned room temperature—68 to 78 degrees Fahrenheit—before using in a recipe). My advice is to purchase chocolate only as you need it.

CHOOSING

I will avoid suggesting specific brands of chocolate. However, I will go on record as saying that many American chocolates are of the necessary quality to produce excellent results. It is true that many European chocolates have a higher content of chocolate liquor, making them darker and less sweet. Some European chocolate also goes through an extended manufacturing process that creates a smoother, silkier texture when eaten directly out of the box. But remember that the price does not always correspond with the quality. You are better off purchasing a product that is real, is fresh, and has been properly stored, rather than an overpriced chocolate that has been gathering dust.

UNSWEETENED CHOCOLATE

Also called chocolate liquor, unsweetened chocolate is the product yielded from the crushing of cocoa nibs (the nibs come from roasted cocoa beans). As mentioned, this is the pure form of chocolate, that is, it contains only cocoa butter and cocoa solids, without sugar or additives. Since unsweetened chocolate contains no sugar, it is too bitter to consume as is.

We purchased American-manufactured unsweetened chocolate for testing.

Semisweet Chocolate

This chocolate is an amalgam of chocolate liquor, cocoa butter, sugar, vanilla or vanillin, and an emulsifier known as lecithin. Take a good look at the label and bypass any chocolate that contains any fat other than cocoa butter. Semisweet is interchangeable with bittersweet, although the bittersweet has a higher percentage of unsweetened chocolate, giving a more pronounced flavor and darker color.

We purchased both American and European semisweet chocolate (usually the European is called bittersweet) for testing.

White Chocolate

This one gets tricky. In the United States, a product must contain chocolate liquor to be labeled as chocolate. So-called white chocolate contains sugar, cocoa butter, milk, and vanilla but no chocolate liquor, and therefore, it is not technically chocolate. So, look for white chocolate under such manufacturers' labels as "white coating." Most importantly, check the label to be certain that the only fat listed is cocoa butter, since that is the ingredient that supplies the flavor. We purchased only European white chocolate for testing. (As we go to press with *Desserts To Die For,* Baker's Chocolate has been given a temporary license to market a product called white chocolate; it lists cocoa butter as its only fat. Stay tuned for further developments.)

Cocoa

When unsweetened chocolate is pressed to remove the cocoa butter, the resulting solids are ground into cocoa powder. We tested the recipes in this book using both American and European unsweetened cocoa.

Chocolate Chips

Use chips only when specified. Many manufacturers claim that their chocolate chips have the same ingredient formulation as their baking chocolate. The fact is that some chips are formulated differently than baking chocolate (to keep their shape during baking), and in my opinion are not interchangeable with semisweet or unsweetened chocolate. As with other chocolate, look at the label and choose only those chips that have cocoa butter as the only fat. We used only American manufactured chips for testing.

Eggs

Grade AA large eggs were purchased in a supermarket for testing the recipes in *Desserts To Die For.* For best results, I recommend using this grade and size egg. For more and important information about eggs, refer to "Handling Eggs" in the "Techniques and Equipment" section (see page 139).

Flour

I recommend purchasing quality flours from such well-known manufacturers as Gold Medal (although don't overlook lesser-known, yet high-quality, regional brands such as White Lily). Major brands move faster off the supermarket shelves, making them less susceptible to problems from improper storage.

Cup of Pleasure

To enjoy a dessert completely, you need an appropriate beverage. Your choice may be as prosaic as a steaming cup of java or as indulgent as a fine vintage port. However, pairing desserts with a proper drink should not cause angst. You can break away from tradition if you like, but remember, the only rule is don't allow the dessert to overwhelm the beverage or vice versa. For instance, the flavor of a delicate champagne would be lost if served with a dark and intense chocolate dessert. Likewise, a late harvest zinfandel would steal the show from a dish of Strawberry and Banana Yin Yang Sorbet (see page 83).

Almost every recipe in this book offers a beverage suggestion. Whether it is a shot of apple jack, a tall glass of milk, or an effervescent Bellini, make sure you enjoy it. After all, enjoyment is the underlying theme of this book.

CHAPTER ONE

LET THEM EAT CAKE

"I am a staunch believer in having one's cake and eating it, a principle I have followed greedily throughout my life."
—ANNE SCOTT-JAMES

TUXEDO TRUFFLE TORTE

BUTTERSCOTCH WALNUT PUMPKIN CAKE

FOR CHOCOLATE LOVERS ONLY

LEMON BLUEBERRY CHEESECAKE

RED RASPBERRY ALMOND PASSION CAKE

CHOCOLATE VOODOO CAKE

MOCHA ALMOND PRALINE SNAP

CHOCOLATE PECAN SOUR MASH BASH

GOOEY CHOCOLATE PEANUT BUTTER BROWNIE CAKE

FALLEN ANGEL CAKE WITH GOLDEN HALOS AND SINFUL CREAM

WHITE AND DARK CHOCOLATE PATTY CAKE

CHOCOLATE CARAMEL HAZELNUT DAMNATION

TUXEDO TRUFFLE TORTE

SERVES 16

INGREDIENTS

CHOCOLATE TRUFFLE CAKE

¾ pound unsalted butter, cut into 12 1-ounce pieces (½ piece melted)

1½ pounds semisweet chocolate, broken into ½-ounce pieces

4 large eggs

4 large egg yolks

WHITE CHOCOLATE MOUSSE

6 ounces white chocolate, broken into ½-ounce pieces

2 tablespoons water

1 tablespoon Myers's dark rum

½ cup heavy cream

WHITE CHOCOLATE GANACHE

¾ cup heavy cream

1 tablespoon unsalted butter

12 ounces white chocolate, broken into ½-ounce pieces

DARK CHOCOLATE GANACHE

¾ cup heavy cream

1 tablespoon unsalted butter

9 ounces semisweet chocolate, broken into ½-ounce pieces

EQUIPMENT

Cook's knife, cutting board, measuring cup, measuring spoons, small nonstick pan, pastry brush, 9- by 3-inch springform pan, double boiler, plastic wrap, whisk, 5-quart stainless steel bowl, rubber spatula, instant-read test thermometer, electric mixer with balloon whip, baking sheet, 2 3-quart stainless steel bowls, 1½-quart saucepan, cake spatula, 2 pastry bags, 2 medium star tips, serrated slicer

PREPARE THE CHOCOLATE TRUFFLE CAKE

Preheat the oven to 300 degrees Fahrenheit.

Lightly coat the insides of a 9- by 3-inch springform pan with the melted butter. Set aside.

Heat 1 inch of water in the bottom half of a double boiler over medium heat. Place 1½ pounds semisweet chocolate and the remaining butter in the top half of the double boiler. Tightly cover the top with plastic wrap. Allow to heat for 15 minutes. Remove from the heat and stir until smooth. Transfer the chocolate to a 5-quart stainless steel bowl, using a rubber spatula to remove all the chocolate from the double boiler. Keep at room temperature until needed.

Heat 1 inch of water in the bottom half of a double boiler over medium heat. Place 4 eggs and 4 egg yolks in the top half of the double boiler. Whisk the eggs until they reach a temperature of 110 degrees Fahrenheit, about 2 to 3 minutes. Transfer the heated eggs to the bowl of an electric mixer fitted with a balloon whip. Whisk on high until the eggs become light and pale in color, about 6 to 7 minutes. Remove the bowl from the mixer. Using a rubber spatula, gently fold one third of the eggs into the melted chocolate. Add the remaining eggs and fold together gently but thoroughly. Pour the batter into the prepared springform pan. Place the springform pan onto a baking sheet on the center rack in the preheated oven. Bake for 1 hour 10 minutes to 1 hour 15 minutes, until the internal temperature of the cake reaches 170 degrees Fahrenheit. Remove the truffle cake from the oven and allow to cool in the pan for 45 minutes. Before releasing the cake from the springform pan, use your fingertips to press down gently on the outside edges of the cake (to create as flat a surface as possible). Remove the sides (but not the bottom) of the springform pan and refrigerate the cake until needed, for at least 1 hour.

PREPARE THE WHITE CHOCOLATE MOUSSE

(This may be done while the truffle cake is baking.) Heat 1 inch of water in the bottom half of a double boiler over low heat. When the water is hot (do not allow to simmer), place 6 ounces of white chocolate, 2 tablespoons of water, and 1 tablespoon of rum in the top half of the double boiler. Using a rubber spatula, constantly stir the white chocolate, water, and rum until the chocolate has melted and the mixture is smooth, about 5 to 6 minutes. Remove from the heat and set aside.

Using a hand-held whisk, whip ½ cup heavy cream in a well-chilled 3-quart stainless steel bowl until stiff. Vigorously whisk one third of the whipped cream into the melted white chocolate (continue to whisk until smooth and thoroughly combined). Add the combined whipped cream and white chocolate to the remaining whipped cream and use a rubber spatula to fold all until smooth. Tightly cover the top of the bowl with plastic wrap and refrigerate until needed, for at least 45 minutes.

MAKE THE WHITE CHOCOLATE GANACHE

Heat ¾ cup heavy cream and 1 tablespoon of butter in a 1½-quart saucepan over medium high heat. Bring to a boil. Place 12 ounces white chocolate in a 3-quart stainless steel bowl. Pour the boiling cream over the chocolate and allow to stand for 5 minutes. Stir until smooth. Set aside until needed.

PREPARE THE DARK CHOCOLATE GANACHE

Heat ¾ cup heavy cream and 1 tablespoon of butter in a 1½-quart saucepan over medium high heat. Bring to a boil. Place 9 ounces semisweet chocolate in a 3-quart stainless steel bowl. Pour the boiling cream over the chocolate and allow to stand for 5 minutes. Stir until smooth. Refrigerate until needed, no less than 30 minutes.

BEGIN ASSEMBLING
THE CAKE

Remove the cake from the refrigerator. Using a cake spatula, spread the white chocolate mousse evenly over the top and sides of the cake. Place in the freezer for 1 hour.

Reserve and refrigerate 1 cup white chocolate ganache. Pour the remaining amount of white chocolate ganache over the top of the truffle cake. Use a cake spatula to spread the ganache evenly over the top and sides of the cake. Refrigerate the cake for 30 minutes.

Fill a pastry bag fitted with a medium star tip with the reserved white chocolate ganache. Fill another pastry bag fitted with a medium star tip with the dark chocolate ganache.

Score the top of the cake with two parallel lines 1 inch from the edge of one side of the cake and 1½ inches apart. Score a third line, intersecting the previous two, across the bottom third of the cake. Pipe white chocolate stars (each star touching the other) along the scored lines. Refrigerate the cake for 10 minutes. Pipe dark chocolate stars over the remaining areas on the top of the cake. Refrigerate the cake for at least 1 hour before cutting and serving.

TO SERVE

Heat the blade of the serrated slicer under hot running water and wipe the blade dry before cutting each slice. Allow the slices to stand at room temperature for 15 to 20 minutes before serving.

THE CHEF'S TOUCH

On Monday, March 20, 1989, the Trellis dedicated its seasonal preview dinner to celebrate the publication of Rose Levy Beranbaum's **The Cake Bible.** *Rose and pastry chef John Twichell collaborated on selecting several desserts from Rose's book that we would offer as a "Cake Bible sampler" for dessert to the 180 guests who had gathered to honor Rose that evening. The hit was her Chocolate Oblivion Truffle Torte. In the days that followed, John decided to experiment with Rose's torte—not to embellish on her recipe, but to use it as the basis for a Trellis-style dessert (known in our kitchen as going for the throat). The result is a gâteau of such divine rich chocolate flavor and silky texture that its effect on the palate is both lasting and fleeting—a true chocolate dichotomy.*

Although the preparation of this dessert may seem daunting due to the four separate recipes, it is actually quite manageable.

For same-day preparation of the torte, make the mousse and the two ganaches while the truffle cake is baking. Follow the recipe directions for refrigerating or setting aside these items.

If the heat of the cream for the white and dark chocolate ganaches is not sufficient to melt the chocolate thoroughly or if the chocolate does not completely dissolve while you are stirring the mixture, place the bowls of ganache over some very hot water (not simmering or boiling) and continue to stir to a smooth texture.

When removing the truffle cake from the springform pan, remove the sides only; allow the cake to remain on the bottom of the springform pan until it has been sliced and served.

Covering the truffle cake with a layer of white chocolate mousse also serves to mask the dark chocolate.

If your kitchen is warm, refrigerate the ganache so that it is firm enough to pipe the stars. Conversely, if the ganache is too firm to pipe from the pastry bag, warm it by massaging the pastry bag with your hands for a few moments.

The torte must be refrigerated as directed in the recipe during the different phases of assembly or the components will meld and you will lose the sharp-dressed look of the torte.

To spread the production of this dessert over two days, I recommend baking the chocolate truffle cake on day 1. After the cake has cooled to room temperature, cover with film wrap and refrigerate until you have made the mousse and ganache on day 2.

After assembly, you may keep this cake in the refrigerator for two to three days before serving. Do not forget to allow the slices to stand at room temperature for 15 to 20 minutes before serving.

Such an exquisite confection should be accompanied by a long flute of tantalizing effervescence—champagne. A crisp, intensely flavored vintage wine would complement this gâteau du soiré perfectly. I recommend a 1985 Bollinger Brut Grande Année.

Score the top of the cake with two parallel lines, 1½ inches apart 1 inch from the edge of one side of the cake. Score a third line, intersecting the previous two, across the bottom third of the cake.

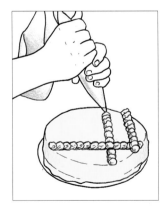

Pipe white chocolate stars (each star touching the other) along the scored lines.

Pipe dark chocolate stars over the remaining areas on the top of the cake.

BUTTERSCOTCH WALNUT
PUMPKIN CAKE

SERVES 10 TO 12

INGREDIENTS

WALNUT CAKE

½ pound plus 2 tablespoons unsalted butter (2 tablespoons melted)

1½ cups all purpose flour

2 teaspoons baking soda

¼ teaspoon salt

1 cup tightly packed light brown sugar

6 ounces cream cheese, softened

3 large eggs

½ teaspoon pure vanilla extract

1 cup finely chopped toasted walnuts

PUMPKIN CAKE

¼ pound plus 1 tablespoon unsalted butter (1 tablespoon melted)

1 cup all purpose flour

1 teaspoon baking soda

½ teaspoon ground cinnamon

½ teaspoon ground cloves

½ teaspoon ground nutmeg

¼ teaspoon salt

¾ cup 100% natural solid pack pumpkin

½ cup nonfat buttermilk

½ cup tightly packed light brown sugar

½ cup granulated sugar

2 large eggs

½ teaspoon pure vanilla extract

BUTTERSCOTCH WALNUT FILLING

¾ cup heavy cream

¾ cup granulated sugar

¼ teaspoon fresh lemon juice

¼ pound unsalted butter, cut into 4 1-ounce pieces

1 cup walnuts, chopped into ⅛-inch pieces

GLAZED WALNUTS

1 cup granulated sugar

⅓ cup water

¼ teaspoon fresh lemon juice

20 walnut halves

BROWN SUGAR ICING

2 cups tightly packed light brown sugar

1 cup heavy cream

½ pound unsalted butter, cut into 8 1-ounce pieces

¼ teaspoon cream of tartar

EQUIPMENT

Measuring cup, measuring spoons, small nonstick pan, baking sheet with sides, food processor with metal blade, cook's knife, cutting board, pastry brush, 2 9- by 1½-inch round cake pans, parchment paper, sifter, wax paper, electric mixer with paddle, rubber spatula, toothpick, 3 cardboard cake circles, 1-quart bowl, 2 1½-quart saucepans, whisk, serrated slicer, cake spatula, fork, cooling rack, small plastic container with lid, 3-quart saucepan, 3-quart stainless steel bowl, pastry bag, large star tip

MAKE THE WALNUT CAKE

Preheat the oven to 325 degrees Fahrenheit. Lightly coat the insides of 2 9- by 1½-inch cake pans with melted butter. Line each pan with parchment paper, then lightly coat the parchment paper with more melted butter. Set aside.

Combine together in a sifter 1½ cups all purpose flour, 2 teaspoons baking soda, and ¼ teaspoon salt. Sift onto wax paper and set aside.

Place the remaining ½ pound butter, 1 cup light brown sugar, and 6 ounces cream cheese in the bowl of an electric mixer fitted with a paddle. Beat on medium for 2 minutes. Increase the speed to high and beat for 2 additional minutes. Scrape down the sides of the bowl. Now beat on high for 30 seconds. Scrape down the sides of the bowl. Add the 3 eggs, one at a time, beating on medium for 30 seconds and scraping down the sides of the bowl after each addition. Add ½ teaspoon vanilla extract and beat on high for 30 seconds. Operate the mixer on low, while gradually adding the sifted dry ingredients. Once all the dry ingredients have been incorporated, turn off the mixer and add the finely chopped walnuts and mix on medium for 20 seconds.

Remove the bowl from the mixer and use a rubber spatula to finish mixing the batter, until smooth and thoroughly combined.

Immediately divide the cake batter between the prepared pans, spreading evenly, and bake on the center rack in the preheated oven, until a toothpick inserted in the center of the cakes comes out clean, about 28 to 30 minutes. Remove the cakes from the oven and cool in the pans for 15 minutes at room temperature. Invert the cakes onto cake circles. Carefully remove the parchment paper. Refrigerate the cakes until needed.

MAKE THE PUMPKIN CAKE

Lightly coat the insides of a 9- by 1½-inch cake pan with melted butter. Line the pan with parchment paper, then lightly coat the parchment paper with more melted butter. Set aside.

Combine together in a sifter 1 cup all purpose flour, 1 teaspoon baking soda, ½ teaspoon cinnamon, ½ teaspoon cloves, ½ teaspoon nutmeg, and ¼ teaspoon salt. Sift onto wax paper and set aside.

Place ¾ cup solid pack pumpkin and ½ cup buttermilk in a small bowl. Combine thoroughly. Set aside.

Place the remaining ¼ pound butter, ½ cup light brown sugar, and ½ cup granulated sugar in the bowl of an electric mixer fitted with a paddle. Beat on medium for 2 minutes. Scrape down the sides of the bowl. Increase the speed to high and beat for 2 additional minutes. Scrape down the sides of the bowl. Add the 2 eggs and beat on medium for 30 seconds. Scrape down the sides of the bowl. Add ½ teaspoon vanilla extract and beat on high for 30 seconds. Operate the mixer on low while gradually adding the sifted dry ingredients. Once all the dry ingredients have been incorporated, turn off the mixer, add the pumpkin-and-buttermilk mixture, and mix on medium for 20 seconds. Remove the bowl from the mixer and use a rubber spatula to finish mixing the batter, until smooth and thoroughly combined.

Immediately pour the cake batter in the prepared pan, spreading evenly. Bake on the center rack in the preheated oven until a toothpick inserted in the center of the cake comes out clean, about 45 minutes. Remove the cake from the oven and cool in the pan for 15 minutes at room temperature. Invert the cake onto a cake circle. Carefully remove the parchment paper. Turn the cake upright and refrigerate until needed.

MAKE THE BUTTERSCOTCH WALNUT FILLING

Heat ¾ cup heavy cream in a 1½-quart saucepan over medium low heat, until hot (do not allow to simmer or boil). Combine ¾ cup sugar and ¼ teaspoon lemon juice in a separate 1½-quart saucepan. Stir with a whisk to combine (the sugar will resem-

ble moist sand). Caramelize the sugar for 4 to 5 minutes over medium high heat, stirring constantly with a whisk to break up any lumps (the sugar will first turn clear as it liquefies, then light brown as it caramelizes). Remove the saucepan from the heat. Add the hot cream, one half at a time, stirring vigorously after each addition (the cream will bubble and hiss when added). Add the butter, one piece at a time, stirring to incorporate before adding the next piece. Cool in the refrigerator for 45 minutes before placing in the bowl of an electric mixer fitted with a paddle. Beat on high for 2 minutes, until light (*but not fluffy*). Add the walnuts and stir to incorporate. Set aside for a few moments.

BEGIN ASSEMBLING THE CAKE

Remove the cakes from the refrigerator. Use a slicer to trim off just enough of the top of the pumpkin cake to create an even surface. Divide the butterscotch filling and use one portion to cover one of the walnut cake layers and one portion to cover the pumpkin cake layer. Evenly spread the filling to the edges. Place the pumpkin cake layer on top of the butterscotch-coated walnut cake. Now top the pumpkin cake with the remaining walnut cake. Press down gently but firmly to level the layers. Refrigerate the cake while preparing the glazed walnuts and the brown sugar icing.

MAKE THE GLAZED WALNUTS

Heat 1 cup sugar, ⅓ cup water, and ¼ teaspoon lemon juice in a 1½-quart saucepan over medium high heat. Bring to a boil. Adjust the heat and allow to simmer slowly, stirring frequently with a whisk until the mixture thickens and turns golden, about 15 minutes. Remove the saucepan from the heat. Using a dinner fork, dip the walnuts one at a time into the golden sugar. Place the glazed walnuts on a cooling rack, spaced so that they are not touching. Allow the glaze on the walnuts to harden, about 1 minute. Transfer the glazed walnuts to a sealed plastic container and store in the freezer until needed (stored in this fashion the walnuts will keep for eons).

PREPARE THE BROWN SUGAR ICING

Heat 2 cups brown sugar, 1 cup heavy cream, 2 1-ounce pieces of butter, and ¼ teaspoon cream of tartar in a 3-quart saucepan over medium high heat, stirring frequently while bringing the mixture to a boil. Allow the mixture to continue boiling while stirring constantly, for 2 minutes. Transfer the bubbly hot mixture to a 3-quart stainless steel bowl and allow to stand at room temperature for 1 hour before proceeding (the mixture needs to be cool enough so it does not melt the additional butter, yet not so tacky that it will not blend with the butter). Place the cooled mixture in the bowl of an electric mixer fitted with a paddle. Beat on low for 30 seconds. Then beat on medium for 2 minutes, while adding the remaining 6 pieces of butter, one at a time, until incorporated. Scrape down the sides of the bowl. Increase the speed to high and beat for an additional 2 minutes. Scrape down the sides of the bowl, then beat on high for 1 additional minute until light and fluffy. Transfer 1 cup of icing to a pastry bag fitted with a large star tip, and place in the refrigerator until needed.

FINISH ASSEMBLING THE CAKE

Remove the cake from the refrigerator and use a cake spatula to coat the top and sides of the cake evenly with the brown sugar icing. Pipe a circle of twenty brown sugar icing stars along the outside edge of the top of the cake. Top each star with a glazed walnut. Refrigerate the cake for 30 minutes before cutting and serving.

TO SERVE

Heat the blade of the serrated slicer under hot running water and wipe the blade dry before cutting each slice. Allow the cake to stand at room temperature for 10 minutes before serving.

THE CHEF'S TOUCH

Pumpkin's availability ties it to the autumn season. To encourage you to make this dessert anytime, however, I suggest the use of canned 100% natural solid pack pumpkin (look at the ingredient statement on the label—it should list only pumpkin). If fresh pumpkins are available, use 1 pound of peeled pumpkin meat, cut into ½-inch pieces. Steam the pumpkin in a 3-quart saucepan with ½ cup water. Allow to cook for 25 minutes, stirring occasionally to prevent sticking and burning. Cool the cooked pumpkin to room temperature, then puree. This may yield slightly more than the suggested amount, so measure the required ¾ cup and snack on the bit that remains.

The walnuts should be toasted before they are chopped. Toasting will both improve flavor and eliminate any moisture the nuts may have acquired in storage. Toast the walnuts on a baking sheet in a 325 degree Fahrenheit oven for 12 to 14 minutes. Allow the nuts to cool thoroughly before chopping. I suggest using a food processor for finely chopping the walnuts. You may use a cook's knife to chop the nuts into ⅛-inch pieces.

You may wish to prepare the butterscotch walnut pumpkin cake over a couple of days or more. The glazed walnuts can be prepared anytime and kept frozen indefinitely. Bake the walnut cakes and the pumpkin cake on day 1 (cool and refrigerate until the next day), then make the butterscotch filling and the brown sugar icing on day 2. Assemble the cake as directed in the recipe.

After assembly, you may keep the butterscotch walnut pumpkin cake in the refrigerator for up to two to three days before serving. Allow the slices to stand at room temperature for 10 to 15 minutes before serving.

Although this dessert is delicious year-round it obviously has an autumnal tone. Whether or not you have falling leaves in mind, an excellent seasonally inspired beverage accompaniment would be a glass of hot apple cider, and for those who want a bit of "enhancement" for their cider, a shot of apple jack is a treat.

FOR CHOCOLATE LOVERS ONLY

SERVES 12

INGREDIENTS

CHOCOLATE CAKE

½ pound plus 2 tablespoons unsalted butter
(2 tablespoons melted)

8 ounces semisweet chocolate, broken into
½-ounce pieces

10 large egg yolks

½ cup granulated sugar

8 large egg whites

CHOCOLATE MOUSSE

6 ounces semisweet chocolate, broken into
½-ounce pieces

1½ cups heavy cream

3 large egg whites

2 tablespoons granulated sugar

CHOCOLATE LOVERS GANACHE

1½ cups heavy cream

18 ounces semisweet chocolate, broken into
½-ounce pieces

2 cups toasted hazelnuts, chopped into ¼-inch
pieces (see page 22 for tips on toasting
hazelnuts)

EQUIPMENT

Measuring cup, measuring spoons, small nonstick
pan, pastry brush, baking sheet with sides, 2 100%
cotton kitchen towels, cook's knife, cutting board,
2 9- by 1½-inch round cake pans, parchment
paper, double boiler, plastic wrap, whisk, electric
mixer with paddle and balloon whip, rubber
spatula, 5-quart stainless steel bowl, toothpick,
2 9-inch cake circles, 2 3-quart stainless steel
bowls, 1-quart container, 1½-quart saucepan, cake
spatula, serrated knife, pastry bag, large star tip,
serrated slicer

START THE CHOCOLATE LOVE FEAST

Preheat the oven to 325 degrees Fahrenheit.
Lightly coat the insides of 2 9- by 1½-inch cake
pans with melted butter. Line each pan with parchment paper, then lightly coat the parchment with
more melted butter. Set aside.

Heat 1 inch of water in the bottom half of a
double boiler over medium heat. Place remaining
butter and 8 ounces semisweet chocolate in the top
half of the double boiler. Tightly cover the top with
plastic wrap. Allow to heat for 10 to 12 minutes.
Remove from heat, stir until smooth, and set aside
until needed.

Place 10 egg yolks and ½ cup sugar in the bowl
of an electric mixer fitted with a paddle. Beat on
high until slightly thickened and lemon colored,
about 4 minutes. Scrape down the sides of the bowl
and beat on high for 2 additional minutes.

While the egg yolks are beating, whisk 8 egg
whites in a 5-quart stainless steel bowl until stiff but
not dry, about 5 to 6 minutes (use a handy cordless
beater and this task will take about 3 minutes).

Using a rubber spatula, fold the melted chocolate mixture into the beaten egg yolk mixture.
Add one quarter of the beaten egg whites and stir
to incorporate, then gently fold in the remaining
egg whites.

Divide the batter between the prepared pans,
spreading evenly, and bake on the center rack in
the preheated oven, until a toothpick inserted in the
center of the cake comes out clean, about 32 to 35
minutes. Remove the cakes from the oven and
allow to cool in the pans for 15 minutes. (During
baking, the surface of the cakes will form a crust;
this crust will normally collapse when the cakes are
removed from the oven.) Invert the cakes onto cake
circles. Remove parchment paper and refrigerate
cakes for 1 hour.

PREPARE THE CHOCOLATE MOUSSE

Heat 1 inch of water in the bottom half of a double boiler over medium heat. Place 6 ounces of
semisweet chocolate in the top half of the double
boiler. Tightly cover the top with plastic wrap.
Allow to heat for 10 to 12 minutes. Remove from
heat and stir until smooth. Transfer the melted
chocolate to a 5-quart stainless steel bowl and set
aside until needed.

Place 1½ cups heavy cream in the well-chilled
bowl of an electric mixer fitted with a well-chilled
balloon whip. Whisk on high for 1 minute, until
peaks form. Set aside for a few moments until needed.

Whisk 3 egg whites in a 3-quart stainless steel
bowl until soft peaks form, about 2½ to 3 minutes.
Add 2 tablespoons sugar and continue to whisk
until stiff peaks form, 1 to 1½ minutes. Add a
quarter of the whipped cream to the chocolate and
whisk quickly and vigorously, then add the choco-
late-and-cream mixture to the egg whites, followed
by the remaining whipped cream. Fold all together
gently but thoroughly. Refrigerate the chocolate
mousse until needed.

PREPARE THE CHOCOLATE LOVERS GANACHE

Heat 1½ cups heavy cream in a 1½-quart saucepan over medium high heat. Bring to a boil. Place
18 ounces of semisweet chocolate in a 3-quart
stainless steel bowl. Pour the boiling cream over
the chocolate. Tightly cover the top with plastic
wrap and allow to stand for 5 minutes, then stir
until smooth.

Combine 1½ cups chocolate ganache with
1 cup chopped hazelnuts, and hold this mixture
at room temperature to use for the filling. Keep the
remaining chocolate ganache at room temperature
until needed.

ASSEMBLE AND DECORATE THE CAKE

Remove cakes from the refrigerator. Using a cake spatula, spread the chocolate hazelnut ganache mixture over the top of one cake. Spread evenly to the edges. Invert the other cake layer on top of the ganache-covered cake. Gently press the cakes together. Using a very sharp serrated knife, trim the outside edges of the top layer to create a more uniform shape. At this point the cake must be refrigerated for 30 minutes.

Evenly spread ¾ cup of the chocolate mousse over the sides of the cake. Chill the cake in the freezer for 30 minutes, or refrigerate for 1 hour.

Remove the cake from the freezer and pour the room-temperature chocolate ganache over the cake, spreading with a spatula to create an even coating of ganache on both the top and the sides of the cake. Refrigerate cake for 20 to 25 minutes to set ganache.

Remove the cake from the refrigerator. Press the remaining cup chopped hazelnuts into the ganache on the sides of the cake, distributing them evenly. Transfer the chocolate mousse to a pastry bag fitted with a large star tip. Pipe mousse stars over the entire top of the cake. Refrigerate the cake for at least 1 hour before cutting and serving.

PREPARE FOR LOVE AT FIRST BITE

Heat the blade of the serrated slicer under hot running water and wipe the blade dry before cutting each slice. Allow the slices of For Chocolate Lovers Only to stand at room temperature for 15 to 20 minutes before serving.

THE CHEF'S TOUCH

For Chocolate Lovers Only seems to have entered the confectioner's vernacular in much the same way as Death by Chocolate. Although our version is different from others, I would wager that all versions share a measure of tender loving care.

This cake is leavened with egg whites. To ensure that your cakes attain the appropriate volume (and reach the same heights as ours do at the Trellis), make sure the whites are whisked in an immaculately clean bowl and that the whites are incorporated into the batter exactly as stated in the recipe. (One quarter of the whites is stirred into the batter to lighten it so it will easily accept the remaining whites). The crust on the surface of the cakes will usually be smooth upon their removal from the oven, though sometimes slight cracks will be obvious. Do not be appalled by what happens next: the cake will collapse and the surface will resemble that of an earthquake-torn landscape (a bit hyperbolic perhaps, but when you see it happen you will get my point). It is supposed to look like that.

At the Trellis, we are fond of accompanying For Chocolate Lovers Only with Double Chocolate Sauce (see page 130) or with two scoops of Blackberry Chocolate Praline Ice Cream (see page 80).

After assembly, you may keep this cake in the refrigerator for one to two days before serving. Allow the slices to stand at room temperature for 15 to 20 minutes before serving.

If the hazelnuts purchased have not been skinned, you can skin them yourself. First, toast the nuts on a baking sheet at 325 degrees Fahrenheit for 18 to 20 minutes (be certain not to overtoast the nuts as they have a tendency to become bitter). Remove the toasted nuts from the oven and immediately cover with a damp 100% cotton kitchen towel. Invert another baking sheet over the first one to hold in the steam (this makes the nuts easier to skin). After 5 minutes, remove the skins from the nuts by placing them, a few at a time, inside a folded dry kitchen towel and rubbing vigorously between your hands. If skinned hazelnuts are purchased, toast at 325 degrees Fahrenheit for 10 to 12 minutes, then allow the nuts to cool before using. Chop the cooled hazelnuts, by hand using a cook's knife or in a food processor fitted with a metal blade, into ¼-inch pieces.

To complete the loving experience, I suggest sipping a 1977 Fonseca vintage port.

LEMON BLUEBERRY CHEESECAKE

SERVES 10 TO 12

INGREDIENTS

CITRUS SHORTBREAD
COOKIE CRUST

3 tablespoons unsalted butter, melted
12 Citrus Shortbread Cookies (see page 133)

LEMON BLUEBERRY CHEESECAKE

1½ pounds cream cheese, softened
2 cups granulated sugar
2 teaspoons minced lemon zest
¼ cup all purpose flour
2 tablespoons cornstarch
1 teaspoon pure vanilla extract
½ teaspoon salt
6 large eggs
½ cup fresh lemon juice
1 cup fresh blueberries, stemmed and washed

SOUR CREAM AND
BLUEBERRY TOPPING

¼ cup sour cream
2 teaspoons granulated sugar
2 cups fresh blueberries, stemmed and washed

EQUIPMENT

Measuring cup, measuring spoons, small nonstick pan, vegetable peeler, cook's knife, cutting board, 9- by 1½-inch cake pan, pastry brush, 9- by 3-inch springform pan, food processor with metal blade, 2-quart bowl, electric mixer with paddle, rubber spatula, baking sheet with sides, instant-read test thermometer, whisk, serrated knife, cake spatula, serrated slicer

PREPARE THE CITRUS SHORTBREAD COOKIE CRUST

Preheat the oven to 250 degrees Fahrenheit. Place a 9- by 1½-inch cake pan partially filled with 4 cups of hot water on the bottom rack of the oven (the bottom rack should be at least 3 inches below the center rack).

Coat the inside of a 9- by 3-inch springform pan with 1 tablespoon melted butter. Set aside.

In a food processor fitted with a metal blade, chop the cookies in two batches. Pulse each batch until all the cookies are in crumbs (the total should yield 2 cups crumbs). Transfer the crumbs to a 2-quart bowl. Combine the cookie crumbs with 2 tablespoons melted butter. Mix by hand until the crumbs bind together. Press the crumbs around the buttered sides of the springform pan, then onto the buttered bottom of the pan. Place the pan in the freezer until needed.

MAKE THE LEMON BLUEBERRY CHEESECAKE

Place 1½ pounds cream cheese, 2 cups sugar, and 2 teaspoons minced lemon zest in the bowl of an electric mixer fitted with a paddle. Beat on low until smooth, about 3 minutes. Scrape down the sides of the bowl. Add ¼ cup flour, 2 tablespoons cornstarch, 1 teaspoon vanilla extract, and ½ teaspoon salt. Beat on medium for 2 minutes. Scrape down the sides of the bowl. Add 2 eggs and beat on low for 2 minutes. Scrape down the sides of the bowl. Add the remaining 4 eggs and beat on medium for 2 minutes. Once again, scrape down the sides of the bowl (all this mixing and scraping creates a beautifully smooth cheesecake). Add ½ cup lemon juice and mix on low for 1 minute. Remove the bowl from the mixer. Use a rubber spatula to finish mixing the batter until it is smooth and thoroughly combined. Pour the cheesecake batter into the prepared springform pan, spreading evenly. Place the springform pan onto a baking sheet with sides (the pan will remain on the baking sheet throughout baking and cooling).

Sprinkle 1 cup blueberries over the top of the batter. The weight of the blueberries should cause them to sink to various depths in the batter (if the berries do not sink, distribute them with a little more force—somewhere between a sprinkle and a pitch).

Place the baking sheet with the springform pan on the center rack of the preheated oven and bake for 1 hour. Lower the oven temperature to 225 degrees Fahrenheit and bake for 1 hour. Reduce the temperature to 200 degrees Fahrenheit and bake the cheesecake until the internal temperature of the cheesecake filling reaches 175 degrees, about 1½ hours. (The timing depends on how frequently you peek at the cheesecake. If you open the oven door more often than necessary, it may take an additional 30 minutes or more for the filling to reach the desired temperature.) Remove the cheesecake from the oven and cool on the baking sheet at room temperature for 1 hour. Refrigerate the cheesecake for 12 hours (do not remove the cake from the pan) before proceeding.

PREPARE THE SOUR CREAM AND BLUEBERRY TOPPING

Combine ¼ cup sour cream and 2 teaspoons granulated sugar in a small bowl and whisk until smooth.

Release the cheesecake from the sides of the springform pan. (If the cake does not immediately separate, wrap a damp, hot cotton towel around the sides of the pan. Make sure the towel covers the sides completely. Hold the towel around the pan for about 1 minute, then carefully release and remove the springform pan.) If top crust of the cake is not level, trim with a serrated knife.

Use a cake spatula to spread the sour cream mixture over the top of the cake, spreading evenly to the edges. Neatly arrange the blueberries on top of the sour cream. Refrigerate for 30 minutes before cutting and serving.

TO SERVE

Heat the blade of the serrated slicer under hot running water and wipe the blade dry before cutting each slice. Serve immediately.

THE CHEF'S TOUCH

A cheesecake dessert is an indulgence that even the most health-conscious people seem to justify. My theory is that cheesecake lovers are a bit like chocolate lovers—they are easily seduced. And this Lemon Blueberry Cheesecake is worth falling for. The balance of sweetness and acidity combined with the textural contrast between the velvety batter and the sprightly berry produces extraordinary sensations in your mouth.

One whole medium-size lemon should yield 2 to 2½ teaspoons of minced lemon zest. Use a sharp vegetable peeler to zest the lemon. Be careful to remove only the colored skin and not the bitter white pith, which lies directly beneath the skin. After removing the colored skin with a vegetable peeler, cut it into thin strips and then mince the strips with a very sharp cook's knife.

Preparation of the cheesecake may be spread out over two days or more. The cookies may be baked and kept in the freezer for several days before using. For an even quicker start out of the gate, set up the springform pan with the cookie crumbs, cover the pan with plastic wrap, and keep it in the freezer for one to two days before using.

After assembly, the cheesecake may be kept in the refrigerator for two to three days.

If you love fresh blueberries as much as I do, you may want to sprinkle additional berries onto each dessert plate before serving. Otherwise I suggest no other accompaniment.

Once you have tasted this dessert you will understand why it needs no embellishment, although with a little coaxing, I could enjoy a rich and lively Château Rieussec sauterne.

RED RASPBERRY ALMOND PASSION CAKE

SERVES 10 TO 12

INGREDIENTS

RASPBERRY ALMOND CAKE

¾ pound plus 2 tablespoons unsalted butter (2 tablespoons melted)

3 cups cake flour

2 teaspoons baking soda

½ teaspoon salt

2 cups granulated sugar

1½ cups toasted sliced almonds, finely chopped

5 large eggs

2 teaspoons almond extract

1 teaspoon pure vanilla extract

1 cup sour cream

1 cup hot water

RED RASPBERRY CRUSH

2 8-ounce packages frozen whole red raspberries in light syrup, thawed

2 tablespoons granulated sugar

1 teaspoon fresh lemon juice

BITTER CHOCOLATE ALMOND BUTTERCREAM

6 ounces semisweet chocolate, broken into ½-ounce pieces

4 ounces unsweetened chocolate, broken into ½-ounce pieces

1 pound unsalted butter, cut into 16 1-ounce pieces

2 teaspoons almond extract

4 large egg whites

1 cup granulated sugar

EQUIPMENT

Measuring cup, measuring spoons, small nonstick pan, baking sheet, food processor with metal blade, cook's knife, cutting board, pastry brush, 2 9- by 1½-inch round cake pans, parchment paper, sifter, wax paper, electric mixer with paddle and balloon whip, rubber spatula, toothpick, 4 cardboard cake circles, serrated slicer, medium gauge strainer, 2 3-quart stainless steel bowls, double boiler, plastic wrap, whisk, 5-quart stainless steel bowl, instant-read test thermometer, cake spatula, pastry bag, medium star tip

PREPARE THE RASPBERRY ALMOND CAKE

Preheat the oven to 325 degrees Fahrenheit.

Lightly coat the insides of 2 9- by 1½-inch cake pans with melted butter. Line each pan with parchment paper, then lightly coat the parchment paper with more melted butter. Set aside.

Combine together in a sifter 3 cups cake flour, 2 teaspoons baking soda, and ½ teaspoon salt. Sift onto wax paper and set aside.

Place the remaining ¾ pound butter and 2 cups granulated sugar in the bowl of an electric mixer fitted with a paddle. Beat on low for 3 minutes. Scrape down the sides of the bowl and beat on medium for 3 minutes. Scrape down the sides of the bowl, add the chopped almonds, and beat on medium for an additional 30 seconds. Add 5 eggs, one at a time, beating on medium for 30 seconds and scraping down the bowl after each addition. Add 2 teaspoons almond extract and 1 teaspoon vanilla and beat on high for 2 more minutes. While operating the mixer on low, add half of the sifted dry ingredients and allow to mix for 15 seconds. Add ½ cup sour cream followed by the remaining dry ingredients, then add the remaining ½ cup sour cream and mix for another 30 seconds.

Add 1 cup hot water and mix for 15 seconds. Increase speed to medium and beat for an additional 20 seconds before removing the bowl from the mixer. Use a rubber spatula to finish mixing the batter until it is smooth and thoroughly combined.

Immediately divide the batter between the prepared pans, spreading evenly. Bake on the center rack in the preheated oven until a toothpick inserted in the center of the cake comes out clean, 35 to 40 minutes. Remove the cakes from the oven and cool in the pans for 15 minutes at room temperature. Invert onto the cake circles. Carefully remove the parchment paper, then allow to cool at room temperature for an additional 30 minutes. Turn the cakes over. Using a slicer, trim off just enough of the top of each cake to make an even surface. Slice each cake horizontally into 2 equal layers. Place each layer onto a cake circle. Refrigerate uncovered while preparing the red raspberry crush.

MAKE THE RED RASPBERRY CRUSH

In the bowl of a food processor fitted with a metal blade, process the raspberries, 2 tablespoons granulated sugar, and the lemon juice until smooth, about 15 to 20 seconds. Strain the puree through a strainer, using a rubber spatula to press down on the seeds and pulp (discard the seeds and pulp). This should yield about 1 cup of red raspberry crush.

Remove the cake layers from the refrigerator. Drizzle 3 to 4 tablespoons red raspberry crush (even if you have extracted more than 1 cup of puree, do not drizzle more than 4 tablespoons on each cake; otherwise the cake will become sodden) over each cake layer. Use a rubber spatula to evenly spread to the edges. Refrigerate the raspberry-soaked cake layers.

PREPARE THE BITTER CHOCOLATE ALMOND BUTTERCREAM

Heat 1 inch of water in the bottom half of a double boiler over medium heat. Place 6 ounces semisweet chocolate and 4 ounces unsweetened chocolate in the top half of the double boiler. Tightly cover the top with plastic wrap. Allow to heat for 8 to 10 minutes. Remove from the heat and stir until smooth. Transfer to a small bowl and set aside until needed.

Place 1 pound butter pieces in the bowl of an electric mixer fitted with a paddle. Beat the butter on low for 2 minutes, then on medium for 3 minutes. Scrape down the sides of the bowl. Beat on high until light and fluffy, about 4 to 5 minutes. Add 2 teaspoons almond extract and beat on high for 1 minute. Remove about one quarter of the butter mixture and whisk it into the melted chocolate (this makes it easier to incorporate the chocolate into the remaining butter; if you do not first introduce a little butter into the chocolate you may end up with a marbleized icing). Place the chocolate-and-butter mixture into the mixing bowl with the remaining butter and beat on medium until the chocolate and butter are thoroughly combined, about 1 minute. Scrape down the sides of the bowl. Now one last time: beat on high for 2 minutes, until light and fluffy. Transfer the mixture to a 5-quart stainless steel bowl and set aside until needed.

Heat 1 inch of water in the bottom half of a double boiler over medium heat. Place 4 egg whites and 1 cup sugar in the top half of the double boiler. Gently whisk the egg whites until they reach a temperature of 120 degrees Fahrenheit, about 2 to 3 minutes. Transfer the heated egg whites to the bowl of an electric mixer fitted with a balloon whip. Whisk on high until stiff peaks form, about 6 minutes. Remove the bowl from the mixer. Use a rubber spatula to gently but thoroughly fold the whipped egg whites into the chocolate-and-butter mixture. Hold at room temperature until needed.

ASSEMBLE THE PASSION CAKE

Remove the cake layers from the refrigerator. Use a cake spatula to evenly spread ¾ cup of bitter chocolate almond buttercream over 3 of the cake layers. Stack these 3 layers one on top of the other. Invert the last cake layer onto the stacked layers, pressing down gently but firmly to level the layers. Smoothly spread 2 more cups of buttercream onto the top and sides of the cake (1 cup on top and 1 cup on the sides). Refrigerate the cake for 15 minutes.

Fill a pastry bag fitted with a medium star tip with the remaining buttercream. Remove the cake from the refrigerator. Pipe a circle of stars (each touching the other) along the outside edge of the top of the cake. Continue to pipe out the stars until the top is covered. Refrigerate the cake for 30 minutes before cutting and serving.

TO SERVE

Heat the blade of the serrated slicer under hot running water and wipe the blade dry before making each slice. Allow the cake to stand at room temperature 10 to 15 minutes before serving.

THE CHEF'S TOUCH

As soon as you cut into this confection you will come to understand why it was named Red Raspberry Almond Passion Cake; the author assumes no responsibility for what happens after the first bite.

Toast the almonds for 10 minutes in a 325 degree Fahrenheit oven before using them. This will improve the flavor as well as eliminate any moisture the nuts may have acquired in storage.

The red raspberry crush may be prepared using 1 pint of fresh red raspberries or 2 cups of IQF (individually quick frozen) red raspberries (thaw the IQF berries before pureeing).

Be sure to remove the melted chocolate from the top half of the double boiler after melting so that the chocolate can cool to room temperature before it is added to the whipped butter. If the chocolate is too warm (more than 80 degrees Fahrenheit), it may melt the butter.

I strongly urge using an electric mixer with a balloon whip to prepare the buttercream. Using a hand-held whisk (be it manual or electric) will not create the desired texture.

One additional caveat about the buttercream: be certain that the mixing bowl is impeccably clean before whisking the egg whites. Any grease or soap residue will reduce the volume of the egg whites, spoil the taste, and—alas—cool the flames of passion.

The final touches: garnish the outside ring of buttercream stars with fresh red raspberries, then gently and evenly press 1 cup of toasted almonds into the sides of the cake.

As we all know, well-chilled champagne certainly can induce passion. Choose a 1985 Veuve Cliquot La Grande Dame and discover how far this pairing of sweet and bubbly can take you.

CHOCOLATE VOODOO CAKE

SERVES 10 TO 12

INGREDIENTS

DRUNKEN ZOMBIE CAKE

1 cup raisins

½ cup Myers's dark rum

½ pound plus 2 tablespoons unsalted butter
    (2 tablespoons melted)

1 cup all purpose flour

¼ cup unsweetened cocoa

2 teaspoons baking powder

½ teaspoon ground cinnamon

½ teaspoon ground allspice

⅛ teaspoon salt

10 ounces semisweet chocolate, broken into
    ½-ounce pieces

1 cup tightly packed light brown sugar

4 large eggs

1 teaspoon pure vanilla extract

MOCHA RUM MOUSSE

8 ounces semisweet chocolate, broken into
    ½-ounce pieces

¼ cup brewed full-strength coffee

2 tablespoons Myers's dark rum

1 cup heavy cream

3 large egg whites

2 tablespoons granulated sugar

BLACKENED MOLASSES GLAZE

¾ cup heavy cream

3 tablespoons unsalted butter

2 tablespoons blackstrap molasses

6 ounces semisweet chocolate, broken into
    ½-ounce pieces

CHOCOLATE CARAMEL
VOODOO NEEDLES

1 cup granulated sugar

¼ teaspoon lemon juice

½ ounce semisweet chocolate

EQUIPMENT

Measuring cup, measuring spoons, small nonstick pan, 1-quart plastic container with tight-fitting lid, pastry brush, 2 9- by 1½-inch round cake pans, parchment paper, sifter, wax paper, double boiler, plastic wrap, whisk, electric mixer with paddle and balloon whip, rubber spatula, toothpick, 2 cardboard cake circles, 5-quart stainless steel bowl, 1½-quart saucepan, cake spatula, 3-quart stainless steel bowl, 4 nonstick baking sheets, plastic container with lid, serrated slicer

WHY WE CALL IT DRUNKEN

Combine 1 cup raisins and ½ cup dark rum in a plastic container with a tight-fitting lid. Allow to stand at room temperature for 6 hours or overnight.

MAKE THE DRUNKEN ZOMBIE CAKE

Preheat the oven to 325 degrees Fahrenheit.

Lightly coat the insides of 2 9- by 1½-inch cake pans with melted butter. Line each pan with parchment paper, then lightly coat the parchment paper with more melted butter. Set aside.

Combine together in a sifter 1 cup flour, ¼ cup cocoa, 2 teaspoons baking powder, ½ teaspoon ground cinnamon, ½ teaspoon allspice, and ⅛ teaspoon salt. Sift onto wax paper and set aside.

Heat 1 inch of water in the bottom half of a double boiler over medium heat. Place 10 ounces semisweet chocolate in the top half of the double boiler. Tightly cover the top with plastic wrap. Allow to heat for 8 minutes. Remove from the heat and stir until smooth. Keep at room temperature until ready to use.

Place the remaining ½ pound butter and 1 cup brown sugar in the bowl of an electric mixer fitted with a paddle. Beat on medium for 2 minutes. Use a rubber spatula to scrape down the sides of the bowl. Beat on high for 2 minutes. Scrape down the sides of the bowl. Add the 4 eggs, one at a time,

beating on medium for 30 seconds and scraping down the sides of the bowl after each addition. Add 1 teaspoon vanilla extract and beat on high for 30 seconds. Add the melted chocolate and beat on medium for 30 seconds. Operate the mixer on low while gradually adding the sifted dry ingredients. Once all the dry ingredients have been incorporated, turn off the mixer, add the rum-infused raisins, and mix on medium for 30 seconds (at this point, the aromas wafting up from the mixing bowl are quite extraordinary). Remove the bowl from the mixer and use a rubber spatula to finish mixing the batter until smooth and thoroughly combined.

Immediately divide the cake batter between the prepared pans, spreading evenly. Bake on the center rack in the preheated oven until a toothpick inserted in the center of the cakes comes out clean, about 32 to 35 minutes. Remove the cakes from the oven and cool in the pans for 15 minutes at room temperature. Invert the cakes onto cake circles. Carefully remove the parchment paper. Place the cakes in the freezer for 1 hour or in the refrigerator for at least 2 hours (the cakes must be thoroughly cooled before adding the mousse, as described later).

MAKE THE MOCHA RUM MOUSSE

Heat 1 inch of water in the bottom half of a double boiler over medium heat. Place 8 ounces semisweet chocolate, ¼ cup coffee, and 2 tablespoons dark rum in the top half of the double boiler. Tightly cover the top with plastic wrap. Allow to heat for 5 to 6 minutes. Remove from the heat and stir until smooth. Transfer the chocolate mixture to a 5-quart stainless steel bowl and keep at room temperature until ready to use.

Place 1 cup heavy cream in the well-chilled bowl of an electric mixer fitted with a well-chilled balloon whip. Whisk on high for 1 minute until peaks form. Set aside for a few moments.

Whisk 3 egg whites in a 3-quart stainless steel bowl until soft peaks form, about 2½ to 3 minutes. Add 2 tablespoons sugar and continue to whisk until stiff peaks form, 1 to 1½ minutes. Use a rubber spatula to quickly fold one third of the whisked egg whites into the melted chocolate. Then place the whipped cream and the remaining egg whites on top of the chocolate and use a rubber spatula to fold together until smooth and completely combined. Refrigerate the mocha rum mousse for 30 to 45 minutes (the mousse must be refrigerated until slightly firm before beginning to assemble the cake).

BEGIN ASSEMBLING THE CAKE

Remove the cake layers from the freezer or refrigerator and the mousse from the refrigerator. Reserve 1 cup of mousse and set aside in the refrigerator for a few moments. Spoon the remaining mousse onto one of the inverted cake layers, using a cake spatula to spread evenly to the edges. Place the other inverted cake layer on top of the mousse and press gently into place. Use a cake spatula to coat the top and sides of the cake with the reserved cup of mousse. Place the cake in the freezer while preparing the blackened molasses glaze and the voodoo needles.

PREPARE THE BLACKENED MOLASSES GLAZE

Heat ¾ cup heavy cream, 3 tablespoons butter, and 2 tablespoons molasses in a 1½-quart saucepan. Stir to dissolve the molasses, then bring to a boil. Place 6 ounces semisweet chocolate in a 3-quart stainless steel bowl. Pour the boiling cream mixture over the chocolate and allow to stand for 5 minutes. Stir until smooth. Keep the glaze at room temperature for 1 hour before using (the glaze will thicken to the desired texture during that time period).

PREPARE THE CHOCOLATE CARAMEL VOODOO NEEDLES

Combine 1 cup sugar and ¼ teaspoon lemon juice in a 1½-quart saucepan. Stir with a whisk to combine (the sugar will resemble moist sand). Caramelize the sugar for 5½ to 6 minutes over medium high heat, stirring constantly with a whisk to break up

any lumps (the sugar will first turn clear as it liquefies, then light brown as it caramelizes). Remove the saucepan from the heat, add the chocolate, and stir to dissolve. Dip a wire whisk into the chocolate caramel and drizzle the hot caramel, in long thin lines, onto 4 nonstick baking sheets, one sheet at a time (move the whisk back and forth over the length of the baking sheets). Continue drizzling—making an effort to create as many individual long, thin, and separate chocolate caramel strips as possible—until all the caramel is used. Allow the strips to harden at room temperature, about 15 minutes. Break the strips into the desired size voodoo needles (3- to 4-inch needles make for delightful sticking). The voodoo needles may be stored in a tightly sealed plastic container in the freezer until needed (which may be sooner than you think, especially if an intruder sticks a finger into the glaze).

FINISH ASSEMBLING THE CAKE

Remove the cake from the freezer. Pour the glaze over the top of the cake. Use a cake spatula to spread a smooth coating of glaze over the top and sides of the voodoo cake. Refrigerate the cake for 1 hour to set the glaze.

TO SERVE

Heat the blade of a serrated slicer under hot running water and wipe the blade dry before cutting each slice. Place a piece of Chocolate Voodoo Cake in the center of each serving plate. Randomly stick the chocolate caramel voodoo needles into the cake slices (avoid thinking about your enemies at this time, if at all possible). Dispatch immediately.

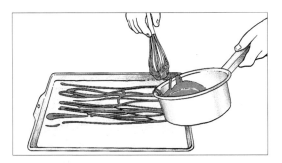

Dip a wire whisk into the chocolate caramel and drizzle the hot caramel, in long thin lines, onto the nonstick baking sheet.

Randomly stick the chocolate caramel voodoo needles into the cake slices.

MOCHA ALMOND PRALINE SNAP

SERVES 10

INGREDIENTS

ESPRESSO ALMOND MERINGUE

1 cup sliced toasted almonds

1¼ cups granulated sugar

3 tablespoons cornstarch

10 large egg whites

1 tablespoon instant espresso powder

¼ teaspoon cream of tartar

⅛ teaspoon salt

1 teaspoon almond extract

ALMOND PRALINE

2 cups sliced toasted almonds

3 cups granulated sugar

1½ teaspoons fresh lemon juice

EXQUISITE CHOCOLATE BUTTERCREAM

10 ounces semisweet chocolate, broken into
    ½-ounce pieces

2 ounces unsweetened chocolate, broken into
    ½-ounce pieces

1 pound unsalted butter, cut into 16 1-ounce pieces

6 large egg whites

1 cup granulated sugar

EQUIPMENT

Measuring cup, measuring spoons, 9- by 3-inch springform pan, 4 10- by 15-inch baking sheets, cook's knife, cutting board, parchment paper, food processor with metal blade, double boiler, whisk, instant-read test thermometer, electric mixer with balloon whip and paddle, rubber spatula, pastry bag, 2 9- by 13-inch nonstick baking sheets, 3-quart saucepan, 3 small plastic containers with lids, small bowl, plastic wrap, 5-quart stainless steel bowl, large star tip, 3-quart stainless steel bowl, serrated knife, large metal kitchen spoon, cake spatula, serrated slicer

PREPARE THE ESPRESSO ALMOND MERINGUE LAYERS

Preheat the oven to 250 degrees Fahrenheit. Using the removable bottom of a 9- by 3-inch springform pan as a guide, trace a circle on each of 4 sheets of parchment paper (cut to fit the baking sheets) with a pencil. Place each sheet of parchment paper, with the trace mark face down, on a baking sheet.

Place 1 cup sliced almonds, ¼ cup sugar, and 3 tablespoons cornstarch in the bowl of a food processor fitted with a metal blade. Pulse the mixture until finely chopped. Set aside.

Heat 1 inch of water in the bottom half of a double boiler over medium high heat. Place 10 egg whites, 1 cup sugar, 1 tablespoon espresso powder, ¼ teaspoon cream of tartar, and ⅛ teaspoon salt in the top half of the double boiler. Heat the egg white mixture to a temperature of 120 degrees Fahrenheit while gently and constantly whisking, about 2½ to 3 minutes. Transfer the mixture to the bowl of an electric mixer fitted with a balloon whip. Whisk on high until stiff but not dry, about 3 to 3½ minutes. Add 1 teaspoon almond extract and whisk on high for 15 seconds. Remove the bowl from the mixer and use a rubber spatula to fold in the finely chopped almond mixture.

Fill a pastry bag (with no tip) with about one quarter of the meringue. Fill a traced circle with meringue: start in the center and pipe a ½-inch wide spiral toward the outside of the circle. Fill the pastry bag again and repeat this procedure with each of the 3 remaining circles (each circle should be filled with about one quarter of the original amount of meringue). Place the meringues on the center and bottom racks of the preheated oven and bake for 1 hour (rotate the meringues from center to bottom after 30 minutes). Reduce the oven temperature to 225 degrees Fahrenheit and bake for an additional 2 hours. Remove from the oven and allow to cool on the baking sheets for 30 minutes before handling.

MAKE THE ALMOND PRALINE

Evenly divide and spread 2 cups of almonds over the surface of 2 9- by 13-inch nonstick baking sheets with sides. Set aside.

Place 3 cups sugar and 1½ teaspoons lemon juice in a 3-quart saucepan. Stir with a whisk to combine (the sugar will resemble moist sand).

Caramelize the sugar for about 10 minutes over medium high heat, stirring constantly with a whisk to break up any lumps (the sugar will first turn clear as it liquefies, then light brown as it caramelizes). Remove the saucepan from the heat. Carefully pour the caramelized sugar over the almonds, evenly dividing it between the 2 baking sheets, covering as many of the nuts as possible (the more nuts covered the better). Pick up the baking sheets by the handles and gently rock them to allow the caramelized sugar to flow over the almonds; move quickly but carefully because the sugar will stop flowing as it cools. Allow the praline to harden at room temperature, about 15 minutes.

Place the praline from 1 baking sheet on a cutting board. Use a sharp cook's knife to chop the praline into ⅛-inch pieces (later this praline will be incorporated with some of the exquisite chocolate buttercream), which can be stored in a tightly sealed plastic container in the freezer until needed. Break 10 irregular 1½-inch pieces from the remaining sheet of praline (these will be used to garnish the top of the snap). Store in a tightly sealed plastic container in the freezer until needed.

The remaining praline should be broken into 2- to 3-inch pieces. Place these pieces in the bowl of a food processor fitted with a metal blade. Pulse until very finely chopped (the finely chopped praline will be used to decorate the sides of the snap) and store in a tightly sealed plastic container in the freezer until needed.

PREPARE THE EXQUISITE CHOCOLATE BUTTERCREAM

Heat 1 inch of water in the bottom half of a double boiler over medium heat. Place 10 ounces semisweet chocolate and 2 ounces unsweetened chocolate in the top half of the double boiler. Tightly cover the top with plastic wrap and allow to heat for 8 to 10 minutes. Remove from heat and stir until smooth. Transfer to a small bowl and set aside until needed. (This is done to dissipate the heat in the chocolate. If the chocolate is too warm it may melt the butter when the two are combined.)

Place 1 pound butter in the bowl of an electric mixer fitted with a paddle. Beat the butter on low for 2 minutes, then on medium for 3 minutes. Scrape down the sides of the bowl. Beat on high until light and fluffy, about 5 minutes. Transfer whipped butter to a 5-quart stainless steel bowl and set aside during the next step.

Heat 1 inch of water in the bottom half of a double boiler over medium heat. Place 6 egg whites and 1 cup sugar in the top half of the double boiler. Heat the egg white mixture to a temperature of 120 degrees Fahrenheit while gently and constantly whisking, about 2½ to 3 minutes. Transfer the mixture to the bowl of an electric mixer fitted with a balloon whip. Whisk on high until stiff peaks form, about 4 to 4½ minutes. Remove the bowl from the mixer. Fold the melted chocolate into the whipped butter, using a rubber spatula to combine thoroughly. Fold in the whipped egg whites until thoroughly combined. Transfer 1 cup buttercream to a pastry bag fitted with a large star tip. Refrigerate until needed. Transfer 3 cups of buttercream to a 3-quart stainless steel bowl. Combine the ⅛-inch chopped pralines with the 3 cups buttercream (this becomes 4 cups of almond praline brittle buttercream). Hold remaining 3 cups of buttercream until needed.

BEGIN ASSEMBLING THE MOCHA ALMOND PRALINE SNAP

Trim each meringue with a serrated knife so that it fits perfectly inside a closed 9- by 3-inch springform pan. Place a trimmed meringue, top side up, inside the pan. Spoon 1⅓ cups almond praline brittle buttercream on top of the meringue, spreading evenly to the edges. Place another meringue inside the pan on top of the first layer of buttercream, gently pressing into place. Spoon 1⅓ cups almond praline buttercream on top of the meringue in the pan and spread evenly to the edges. Top the buttercream layer with the third meringue, gently pressing into place. Spoon the remaining 1⅓ cups almond praline buttercream over the meringue in the pan, spreading evenly to the edges. Top the last layer of almond praline buttercream with the last meringue, placing it bottom side up (so the smoothest surface is facing up). Press down gently on the last layer to level it into place. Chill in the freezer for 1 hour.

FINISH ASSEMBLING THE CAKE

Remove the springform pan from the freezer. Release the sides of the springform pan. Use a cake spatula to cover evenly the top and sides of the layered meringue and almond praline buttercream with the remaining exquisite chocolate buttercream. Press a thick coating of finely chopped almond praline on the sides of the cake, coating evenly. Pipe a circle of 10 buttercream stars along the outside edge of the top of the cake. Decorate each star with an irregular piece of almond praline. Refrigerate for 30 minutes before cutting and serving.

TO SERVE

Heat the blade of the serrated slicer under hot running water and wipe the blade dry before cutting each slice. Serve immediately.

CHOCOLATE PECAN SOUR MASH BASH

SERVES 12

INGREDIENTS

PECAN CAKE

½ pound plus 1 tablespoon unsalted butter
   (1 tablespoon melted)

3 cups finely chopped toasted pecans

2 cups cake flour

1½ teaspoons baking soda

½ teaspoon salt

1½ cups tightly packed light brown sugar

3 large eggs

8 tablespoons sour mash whiskey

1 teaspoon pure vanilla extract

¾ cup hot water

CHOCOLATE GANACHE

2 cups heavy cream

4 tablespoons unsalted butter

4 tablespoons granulated sugar

18 ounces semisweet chocolate, broken into
   ½-ounce pieces

4 ounces unsweetened chocolate, broken into
   ½-ounce pieces

1 cup toasted pecans, chopped into ⅛-inch pieces

CHOCOLATE SOUR MASH MOUSSE

12 ounces semisweet chocolate, broken into
   ½-ounce pieces

2 ounces unsweetened chocolate, broken into
   ½-ounce pieces

¾ cup heavy cream

3 tablespoons sour mash whiskey

5 large egg whites

2 tablespoons granulated sugar

CHOCOLATE SOUR MASH SAUCE

Chocolate Sour Mash Sauce (see page 131), warm

EQUIPMENT

Measuring cup, measuring spoons, baking sheet with sides, food processor with metal blade, cook's knife, cutting board, small nonstick pan, pastry brush, 9- by 3-inch springform pan, sifter, wax paper, electric mixer with paddle, rubber spatula, toothpick, 3-quart saucepan, 3 3-quart stainless steel bowls, whisk, serrated slicer, cake spatula, cardboard cake circle, double boiler, plastic wrap, 5-quart stainless steel bowl, large metal kitchen spoon, serrated knife

MAKE THE PECAN CAKE

Preheat the oven to 300 degrees Fahrenheit.

Lightly coat the insides of a 9- by 3-inch springform pan with melted butter. Press a thin coating of ½ cup finely chopped pecans onto the buttered bottom of the pan. Set aside.

Combine together in a sifter 2 cups cake flour, 1½ teaspoons baking soda, and ½ teaspoon salt. Sift onto wax paper and set aside.

Place the remaining ½ pound butter and 1½ cups light brown sugar in the bowl of an electric mixer fitted with a paddle. Beat on low for 2 minutes. Scrape down the sides of the bowl. Add the remaining 2½ cups finely chopped pecans and mix on low for 1 minute. Add the 3 eggs, 4 tablespoons sour mash whiskey, and 1 teaspoon vanilla extract and beat on medium for 2 minutes. Scrape down the sides of the bowl. Operate the mixer on low, while slowly adding the sifted dry ingredients; allow to mix for 15 seconds. Add ¾ cup hot water, increase the speed to medium, and beat for an additional 10 seconds before removing the bowl from the mixer. Use a rubber spatula to finish mixing the batter, until it is smooth and thoroughly combined.

Immediately pour the batter into the prepared springform pan, spreading evenly. Place the pan on a baking sheet with sides. Put the baking sheet on the center rack in the preheated oven. Bake until a toothpick inserted in the center of the cake comes out clean, 1 hour and 10 minutes to 1 hour and 15 minutes. Remove the cake from the oven and cool in the pan for 30 minutes at room temperature. Remove the sides of the pan (wash and dry the sides for use later) and refrigerate the cake for 30 minutes.

PREPARE THE CHOCOLATE GANACHE

While the cake is cooling, heat 2 cups heavy cream, 4 tablespoons butter, and 4 tablespoons sugar in a 3-quart saucepan over medium high heat. When hot, stir to dissolve the sugar. Bring to a boil. Place 18 ounces semisweet chocolate and 4 ounces unsweetened chocolate in a 3-quart stainless steel bowl. Pour the boiling cream over the chocolate, allow to stand for 5 minutes, and then stir until smooth.

Remove 1 cup ganache and combine with 1 cup chopped pecans. Hold this mixture at room temperature to use for the filling. Also hold the remaining ganache at room temperature until needed.

Remove the chilled cake from the refrigerator. Use a slicer to trim off just enough of the top of the cake to make an even surface. Slice the cake horizontally into 3 equal layers, leaving the bottom layer on the bottom of the springform pan. Sprinkle 2 tablespoons of sour mash whiskey on both the bottom and the center layer. Reassemble the springform pan. Pour the ganache-and-pecan mixture over the cake layer in the bottom of the pan. Use a cake spatula to spread the ganache evenly over the surface of the cake. Top with the center cake layer and press down gently but firmly to level the cake. Place the top layer on a cardboard cake circle, then place the cake layers in the freezer for at least 30 minutes.

PREPARE THE CHOCOLATE SOUR MASH MOUSSE

Heat 1 inch of water in the bottom half of a double boiler over medium heat. Place 12 ounces semi-sweet chocolate and 2 ounces unsweetened chocolate in the top half of the double boiler. Tightly cover the top with plastic wrap. Heat for 7 to 8 minutes, remove from the heat, and stir until smooth. Transfer to a 5-quart stainless steel bowl and set aside until needed.

Using a hand-held whisk, whip ¾ cup heavy cream and 3 tablespoons sour mash whiskey in a well-chilled stainless steel bowl until stiff. In a separate bowl, whisk 5 egg whites until soft peaks form, add 2 tablespoons sugar, and continue to whisk until stiff peaks form. Place one third of the whipped cream into the melted chocolate and whisk vigorously until smooth. Place the remaining whipped cream and the whisked egg whites on top of the chocolate and use a rubber spatula to fold together until smooth and completely combined.

Remove the cake layers from the freezer. Spoon the mousse on top of the center cake layer in the springform pan, spreading evenly to the edges. Place the remaining cake layer on top of the mousse and press gently to level. Place the cake in the freezer for 20 minutes.

ASSEMBLE THE BASH

Remove the cake from the freezer and cut around the edges to release the cake from the sides of the springform pan. Spoon 1 cup of ganache onto the cake and smooth it over the top and sides of the cake. Refrigerate the cake for 15 to 20 minutes to set the ganache. Pour the remaining ganache over the cake, once again using a cake spatula to evenly spread the ganache over the top and sides. (If the ganache has become too firm to pour, place the bowl of ganache over a pan of hot tap water or place the bowl onto a warm heating pad. It should take less than a minute or two for the ganache to attain "pourable" consistency.) Refrigerate the cake for 1 hour before serving.

TO SERVE

Heat the blade of the serrated slicer under hot running water and wipe the blade dry before cutting each slice. Allow the slices to stand at room temperature for 15 to 20 minutes before serving. Before placing the Chocolate Pecan Sour Mash Bash slices onto (10-inch diameter) plates, flood the base of each plate with 3 to 4 tablespoons warm Chocolate Sour Mash Sauce, then place a slice of bash in the center of each plate. Serve immediately.

THE CHEF'S TOUCH

If you are a teetotaler then you should probably refer to some other recipe. For those who do enjoy "a taste" every now and then, however, this is one bash you do not want to miss. There should be no substitutions for the sour mash whiskey in this case. Go with the flow or flip to another page.

Toasting the pecans improves their flavor and eliminates any moisture the nuts may have acquired in storage. Toast the nuts on a baking sheet in a 325 degree Fahrenheit oven for 10 to 12 minutes. Be certain to allow the nuts to cool thoroughly before chopping. Use a food processor with a metal blade to finely chop the nuts. A cook's knife will work well for chopping the pecans into ⅛-inch pieces.

The bash certainly can be prepared in one afternoon; however, you may want to spread the production over two days. On day 1, bake and cool the pecan cake. After the whole cake is thoroughly cooled, wrap with plastic wrap and refrigerate until the next day. On day 2, prepare the ganache, the mousse, and the sauce, then complete the assembly of the cake.

After assembly, you may keep the bash in the refrigerator for two to three days before serving. Allow the slices to stand at room temperature for 15 to 20 minutes before serving.

In keeping with the Bacchanalian nature of this dessert, add a final touch of sour mash whiskey–infused whipped cream. I suggest a dollop or two—or even three. (Whisk 1½ cups heavy cream and 6 tablespoons sour mash whiskey in a well-chilled stainless steel bowl until stiff.) And if you reach this part of the recipe, I am certain that suggesting a shot of good sour mash whiskey to accompany this cake will not be taken amiss.

GOOEY CHOCOLATE PEANUT BUTTER BROWNIE CAKE

SERVES 12

INGREDIENTS

GOOEY BROWNIE CAKES

½ pound plus 2 tablespoons unsalted butter (2 tablespoons melted)

12 ounces semisweet chocolate, broken into ½-ounce pieces

1 cup granulated sugar

3 large eggs

1 tablespoon pure vanilla extract

½ cup all purpose flour

1 teaspoon baking powder

1 cup creamy peanut butter

CHOCOLATE PEANUT BUTTER GANACHE

1½ cups heavy cream

3 tablespoons granulated sugar

2 tablespoons creamy peanut butter

18 ounces semisweet chocolate, broken into ½-ounce pieces

1½ cups toasted unsalted peanuts, chopped into ⅛-inch pieces

EQUIPMENT

Measuring cup, measuring spoons, 3 9- by 1½-inch cake pans, pastry brush, parchment paper, double boiler, plastic wrap, whisk, electric mixer with paddle, rubber spatula, 3 cardboard cake circles, serrated knife, cake spatula, 3-quart saucepan, 3-quart stainless steel bowl, serrated slicer

MAKE THE GOOEY BROWNIE CAKES

Preheat the oven to 300 degrees Fahrenheit.

Lightly coat the insides of 3 9- by 1½-inch cake pans with melted butter. Line each pan with parchment paper, then lightly coat the paper with more melted butter. Set aside.

Heat 1 inch of water in the bottom half of a double boiler over medium heat. Place 12 ounces of semisweet chocolate and the remaining ½ pound butter in the top half. Tightly cover the top with plastic wrap. Allow to heat for 8 to 10 minutes. Remove from the heat and stir until smooth. Set aside until needed.

Place 1 cup of sugar, 3 eggs, and 1 tablespoon vanilla in the bowl of an electric mixer fitted with a paddle. Beat on medium for 2 minutes. Use a rubber spatula to scrape down the sides of the bowl. Beat on high for 2 minutes. Scrape down the bowl. Add the melted chocolate and beat on medium until the chocolate is thoroughly incorporated, about 15 seconds. Add ½ cup flour and 1 teaspoon baking powder and beat on low for 1 minute. Remove the bowl from the mixer and use a rubber spatula to thoroughly combine.

Divide the batter between the prepared pans, spreading evenly. Place 1 of the pans on the center rack and the remaining 2 pans on the bottom rack of the preheated oven. Bake until the batter is set but not dry (a toothpick inserted in the center of the cakes should hold some residual batter), about 20 to 22 minutes (rotate the brownie cakes from top to bottom about halfway through the baking time).

Remove the brownie cakes from the oven and allow to cool in the pans at room temperature for 10 to 15 minutes. Invert each brownie cake onto an individual cake circle. (These baked brownie cake layers are very delicate, so use a knife to cut around the edges of the cake layers inside the pans; this will ensure that the cake layers do not tear when removed from their respective pans.) Remove the parchment paper from each brownie cake. Place the brownie cakes in the refrigerator to cool for 10 minutes. Remove 2 of the brownie cakes from the refrigerator and use a cake spatula to spread ½ cup of peanut butter in an even layer over each cake. Place these 2 brownie cake layers in the freezer while preparing the ganache.

PREPARE THE CHOCOLATE PEANUT BUTTER GANACHE

Heat the heavy cream, 3 tablespoons sugar, and 2 tablespoons creamy peanut butter in a 3-quart saucepan over medium high heat. When hot, stir to dissolve the sugar and blend in the peanut butter. Bring to a boil. Place 18 ounces semisweet chocolate in a 3-quart stainless steel bowl. Pour the boiling cream over the chocolate and allow to stand for 5 minutes. Stir until smooth.

ASSEMBLE THE CAKE

Remove the two brownie cakes from the freezer and pour 1 cup of ganache onto each of these layers, using a cake spatula to spread the ganache to the edges. Refrigerate the ganache-covered cake layers for 10 minutes (to allow the ganache to become firm). Remove all the brownie cake layers from the refrigerator. Stack the 2 ganache-coated layers on top of each other, then top with the uncoated layer and gently press into place. Place the assembled brownie cake layers in the freezer for 10 minutes (lacking freezer space, you may opt to place the cake in the refrigerator for about 30 minutes).

Using a cake spatula, evenly spread ½ cup ganache around the sides of the cake. Pour the remaining ganache onto the top of the cake and

use a cake spatula to spread the ganache to the edges. If your kitchen is cool, the ganache may become firm and difficult to pour. If this happens, warm the bowl of ganache over a pan of hot tap water or place the bowl onto a warm heating pad. The ganache should attain the proper viscosity in a minute or two. Use a whisk to gently stir the ganache until smooth.

Press the chopped peanuts into the ganache on the sides of the cake, coating evenly. Refrigerate the cake for 10 minutes before cutting and serving.

TO SERVE

Heat the blade of the serrated slicer under hot running water and wipe the blade dry before making each slice. Allow the slices to stand at room temperature for at least 1 hour before serving. The longer the cake is held at room temperature the gooier the texture will be. The cake may be refrigerated for two to three days after assembly. Remember, the gooier the better.

FALLEN ANGEL CAKE WITH GOLDEN HALOS AND SINFUL CREAM

SERVES 6 TO 10

INGREDIENTS

FALLEN ANGEL CAKE

½ pound plus 3 teaspoons unsalted butter (3 teaspoons melted)

8 ounces semisweet chocolate, broken into ½-ounce pieces

6 large egg yolks

¾ cup granulated sugar

8 large egg whites

2 tablespoons unsweetened cocoa

2 tablespoons confectioners' sugar

GOLDEN HALOS

1 cup granulated sugar

⅓ cup warm water

SINFUL CREAM

2 cups heavy cream

1 tablespoon granulated sugar

3 tablespoons sour mash whiskey

EQUIPMENT

Measuring cup, measuring spoons, 9- by 3-inch springform pan, pastry brush, parchment paper, double boiler, plastic wrap, electric mixer with paddle and balloon whip, rubber spatula, 3-quart stainless steel bowl, whisk, 3 baking sheets, toothpick, 6-quart saucepan, 1½-quart saucepan, 9-inch stainless steel kitchen spoon, sifter, serrated slicer

PREPARE THE FALLEN ANGEL CAKE

Preheat the oven to 325 degrees Fahrenheit.

Coat the inside of a 9- by 3-inch springform pan with 2 teaspoons melted butter. Line the pan with parchment paper. Coat the parchment paper with the remaining teaspoon of melted butter. Set aside.

Heat 1 inch of water in the bottom half of a double boiler over medium heat. Place 8 ounces semisweet chocolate and the remaining ½ pound butter in the top half. Tightly cover the top with plastic wrap. Heat for 10 to 12 minutes. Remove from the heat and stir until smooth. Set aside until needed.

Place 6 egg yolks and ¾ cup sugar in the bowl of an electric mixer fitted with a paddle. Beat the mixture on high until it becomes lemon-colored and slightly thickened, about 3 minutes. Scrape down the sides of the bowl. Set the mixer on medium and continue to mix the yolks while whipping 8 egg whites.

Whisk the egg whites in a 3-quart stainless steel bowl until stiff but not dry (about 4 minutes if whisking by hand and less time if using an electric hand-held beater).

Remove the bowl with the egg yolks from the mixer. Use a rubber spatula to fold in the melted chocolate. Add one third of the beaten egg whites and stir to incorporate, then gently fold in the remaining egg whites. Pour the mixture into the springform pan, spreading evenly. Place on a baking sheet (this is insurance against batter spills) on the center rack of the preheated oven. Bake for 52 to 54 minutes, until a long toothpick or wooden skewer inserted in the center of the cake comes out fairly clean. (The toothpick should hold some residual batter, but should not be wet. Traditionally cakes are baked until a toothpick inserted in the center of the cake is clean and dry when removed. Our fallen angel cake is pulled from the oven about 10 to 15 minutes before that point in order to maintain a heightened degree of moisture.) Remove the baked cake from the oven and allow to cool in the springform pan for 15 minutes. Release the cake from the springform pan and invert it onto a cake circle. Remove the parchment paper and hold the cake at room temperature.

PREPARE THE GOLDEN HALOS

Line two baking sheets with parchment paper. Fill a 6-quart saucepan one third full with water. Heat the water and hold at a simmer while preparing the syrup.

Heat 1 cup granulated sugar and ⅓ cup water in a 1½-quart saucepan over medium high heat. Use a 9-inch-long stainless steel kitchen spoon to stir the sugar mixture while it is heating. Intermittently, use a water-dampened pastry brush to "wash" the inside of the saucepan at the edge of the liquefied sugar (this deters crystal formation around the inside of the pan). Heat the sugar syrup until it acquires a light golden color, about 16 minutes. Remove the saucepan from the heat and carefully place it in the pan of simmering water (expect a bit of sizzling at this moment). Working quickly, drizzle a spoonful (using the same spoon used to stir the sugar) of sugar syrup in a circular motion onto the parchment paper to create each halo. The halos will harden at air-conditioned room temperature in a matter of minutes. Hold the halos at room temperature until ready to serve the completed dessert. If the weather is hot and humid, I recommend placing the halos in the freezer.

MAKE THE SINFUL CREAM

Place 2 cups heavy cream, 1 tablespoon granulated sugar, and 3 tablespoons sour mash whiskey in the well-chilled bowl of an electric mixer fitted with a well-chilled balloon whip. Whisk on high until soft peaks are formed, about 45 to 60 seconds.

THE FINISHING TOUCHES

Place 2 tablespoons each of the unsweetened cocoa and the confectioners' sugar in a sifter. Lightly and evenly dust the cake with the cocoa and sugar.

TO SERVE

Heat the blade of the serrated slicer under hot running water and wipe the blade dry before cutting each slice.

For each serving of cake, portion a heaping kitchen spoonful of sinful cream into the center of a 10-inch plate. Nestle a slice of cake onto each cloud of cream, and crown the cake with a golden halo.

THE CHEF'S TOUCH

Our Fallen Angel Cake is named for the precipitous fall it undergoes after being removed from the oven. Do not despair when this happens—it gives the cake its interesting appearance and dense texture.

The preparation of the sugar halos may seem a bit daunting if you have never worked with cooked sugar. I recommend a little practice—you are sure to be rewarded for your effort.

Work quickly when preparing the halos. If the sugar becomes too stiff to spoon onto the parchment paper, remove the pot of sugar from the simmering water. Heat the pot of sugar over medium high heat until the sugar is viscous enough to drizzle.

The halos may be prepared several days in advance. Store the halos in a sealed plastic container in your freezer. Place a piece of parchment paper in between each halo to prevent sticking. Remove the halos from the freezer immediately before serving the fallen angel cake.

The cake is at its best when served within an hour or so after being removed from the oven. Once the cake has cooled to room temperature, you can store it in the refrigerator for two to three days. Before serving bring the cake to room temperature for at least an hour.

I would not discourage a sip or two of your favorite Tennessee whiskey to help dispatch this dessert.

WHITE AND DARK CHOCOLATE PATTY CAKE

SERVES 12

INGREDIENTS

WHITE CHOCOLATE PATTY CAKE

6 tablespoons unsalted butter (2 tablespoons melted)

12 ounces white chocolate, broken into ½-ounce pieces

2 tablespoons water

10 large egg yolks

¾ cup granulated sugar

6 large egg whites

½ cup cake flour, sifted

DARK CHOCOLATE MOUSSE

14 ounces semisweet chocolate, broken into ½-ounce pieces

4 ounces unsweetened chocolate, broken into ½-ounce pieces

½ cup brewed full-strength coffee

2 ounces white chocolate, broken into ½-ounce pieces

2 cups heavy cream

4 large egg whites

2 tablespoons granulated sugar

WHITE AND DARK CHOCOLATE GANACHES

8 ounces white chocolate, broken into ½-ounce pieces

1¼ cups heavy cream

8 ounces semisweet chocolate, chopped into ¼-inch pieces

EQUIPMENT

Measuring cup, measuring spoons, small nonstick pan, sifter, wax paper, cook's knife, cutting board, pastry brush, 2 9- by 1½-inch round cake pans, parchment paper, double boiler, plastic wrap, 2 whisks, electric mixer with paddle and balloon whip, rubber spatula, 5-quart stainless steel bowl, toothpick, 2 cardboard cake circles, 3-quart stainless steel bowl, 9- by 3-inch springform pan, large metal kitchen spoon, 1-quart bowl, serrated knife, cake spatula, pastry bag, medium star tip, serrated slicer

BEGIN PREPARING THE WHITE CHOCOLATE PATTY CAKE

Preheat the oven to 325 degrees Fahrenheit.

Lightly coat the insides of 2 9- by 1½-inch cake pans with melted butter. Line each pan with parchment paper, then lightly coat the parchment paper with more melted butter. Set aside.

Heat 1 inch of water in the bottom half of a double boiler over medium heat. Place the remaining 4 tablespoons butter, 12 ounces white chocolate, and 2 tablespoons water in the top half of the double boiler. Tightly cover the top with plastic wrap. Allow to heat for 10 to 12 minutes. Remove from heat, discard the plastic wrap, stir until smooth, and set aside until needed.

Place 10 egg yolks and ½ cup sugar in the bowl of an electric mixer fitted with a paddle. Beat on high for 2 minutes. Use a rubber spatula to scrape down the sides of the bowl. Continue to beat on high for 2 minutes, until slightly thickened and lemon-colored. Adjust the mixer speed to low and continue to mix the yolks while whisking the egg whites (if this is not done, the yolks will develop undesirable lumps).

Whisk 6 egg whites in a 5-quart stainless steel bowl until soft peaks form, about 3 minutes. Gradually add the remaining ¼ cup sugar while continuing to whisk the egg whites until stiff but not dry, about 2 to 3 more minutes.

Add the melted chocolate to the beaten egg yolks and beat on medium until completely incorporated, about 30 seconds. Remove the bowl from the mixer. Using a rubber spatula, fold the sifted cake flour into the beaten egg yolk and chocolate mixture. Add a third of the whisked egg whites and stir to incorporate, then gently fold in the remaining egg whites.

Divide the batter between the prepared pans, spreading evenly, and bake on the center rack in the preheated oven until a toothpick inserted in the center of the cake comes out clean, about 26 to 30 minutes. Remove the cakes from the oven and allow to cool in the pans for 20 minutes. Invert the cakes onto cake circles and cool to room temperature, about 20 minutes. Remove the parchment paper and refrigerate the cakes, on the cake circles, until needed.

PREPARE THE DARK CHOCOLATE MOUSSE

Heat 1 inch of water in the bottom half of a double boiler over medium heat. Place 14 ounces semisweet chocolate, 4 ounces unsweetened chocolate, ½ cup brewed coffee, and 2 ounces white chocolate in the top half of the double boiler. Tightly cover the top with plastic wrap. Allow to heat for 12 to 14 minutes. Remove from heat and stir until smooth. Transfer to a 3-quart stainless steel bowl, then set aside at room temperature until needed.

Place 2 cups heavy cream in the well-chilled bowl of an electric mixer fitted with a well-chilled balloon whip. Whisk on high until stiff, about 1 minute. Set aside in refrigerator until needed.

Whisk 4 egg whites in a 5-quart stainless steel bowl until soft peaks form, about 3 minutes. Add 2 tablespoons sugar and continue to whisk until stiff but not dry, 1½ to 2 minutes. Fold a quarter of the egg whites into the melted chocolate mixture. Then add egg white–and–chocolate mixture to the remaining egg whites, followed by the remaining whipped cream. Fold all together gently but thoroughly. Refrigerate the chocolate mousse until needed.

BEGIN ASSEMBLING THE PATTY CAKE

Place one of the inverted white chocolate patty cake layers inside a closed 9- by 3-inch springform pan. Use your fingers to gently pat down the edges of the cake (to create as flat a surface as possible).

Spoon the dark chocolate mousse on top of the cake, spreading evenly. Place the remaining cake layer on top of the cake, and once again gently pat down the edges to create a flat surface. Wrap the entire cake (pan and all) with plastic wrap and place in the freezer for 2 hours.

MAKE THE WHITE AND DARK CHOCOLATE GANACHES

Heat 1 inch of water in a double boiler over medium heat. Place 8 ounces white chocolate in the top half of the double boiler. Tightly cover the top with plastic wrap. Allow to heat for 6 minutes, then remove from heat and stir until smooth. Heat 1¼ cups heavy cream in a 1½ quart saucepan over medium heat. Bring to a boil. Place 8 ounces of chopped semisweet chocolate in a 1-quart bowl. Pour ½ cup boiling cream over the melted white chocolate and the remaining ¾ cup over the chopped semisweet chocolate. Stir both until smooth. Refrigerate the white chocolate ganache for at least 1 hour. Set aside the dark chocolate ganache at room temperature until needed.

FINISH ASSEMBLING THE PATTY CAKE

Remove the cake from the freezer. Remove the plastic wrap. Cut around the edges to release the cake from the sides of the springform pan. Using a cake spatula, smooth 3 to 4 tablespoons dark chocolate ganache on the top and sides of the cake (consider this the primer coat of ganache). Refrigerate the cake for 10 minutes to firm the ganache.

Pour the remaining ganache over the cake and use a cake spatula to spread the ganache over the top and sides of the cake. Refrigerate the cake for 10 to 15 minutes to set the ganache before decorating with the white chocolate ganache.

Fill a pastry bag fitted with a medium star tip with the white chocolate ganache. Pipe a circle of white chocolate stars (each touching the other) along the outside edge of the top of the cake. Then pipe a second circle of stars inside the first (once again each star touching the other). Refrigerate the cake for at least 30 minutes before cutting and serving.

TO SERVE

Heat the blade of the serrated slicer under hot running water and wipe the blade dry before cutting each slice. Allow the slices to stand at room temperature for 10 to 15 minutes before serving.

THE CHEF'S TOUCH

I happened upon pastry chef Tim O'Connor patting down the edges of a white chocolate mousse cake one day and joked in passing that we should call it a patty cake rather than a mousse cake. As they say in show business, a legend was born—or so we hope.

Be sure to use good white chocolate (Droste's is our choice) for this recipe. Look for white chocolate with cocoa butter as the second ingredient, after sugar. Lesser quality white chocolate has been manufactured with tropical oils, which impart absolutely no chocolate flavor to the product. (The U.S. government does not recognize white chocolate as a real chocolate product; consequently, it is labeled "white coating" or with some other utilitarian handle.)

When you prepare this recipe, you may notice that the melted white chocolate, butter, and water starts out smooth, then gets very grainy. Don't worry—keep stirring and it will become (and remain) smooth in just a minute or so.

After assembly, you may keep the patty cake in the refrigerator for up to two days before serving.

A cup of French roast coffee would be my choice for a beverage to accompany the winsome patty cake. This robust coffee works well with the particular sweetness of the dessert.

CHOCOLATE CARAMEL HAZELNUT DAMNATION

SERVES 12 TO 16

INGREDIENTS

CARAMEL SAUCE

1 cup heavy cream
2 tablespoons unsalted butter
¼ teaspoon salt
2 cups granulated sugar
½ teaspoon fresh lemon juice

CARAMEL CHOCOLATE CHEESECAKE

1 teaspoon melted unsalted butter
1 cup finely chopped toasted hazelnuts
½ cup hot brewed coffee
½ cup caramel sauce
4 ounces semisweet chocolate, broken into ½-ounce pieces
2 ounces unsweetened chocolate, broken into ½-ounce pieces
1 pound cream cheese, softened
½ cup granulated sugar
¼ teaspoon salt
3 large eggs
½ teaspoon pure vanilla extract

HAZELNUT PRALINE

½ cup whole toasted hazelnuts
½ cup granulated sugar
¼ teaspoon fresh lemon juice

CHOCOLATE FUDGE CAKE

8 tablespoons plus 1 teaspoon unsalted butter
1½ cups plus 1 tablespoon cake flour
1 teaspoon baking soda
¼ teaspoon salt
2 ounces unsweetened chocolate, broken into ½-ounce pieces
1½ cups tightly packed light brown sugar

2 large eggs
½ teaspoon pure vanilla extract
½ cup sour cream
½ cup hot water

CHOCOLATE CARAMEL GANACHE

1 cup heavy cream
12 ounces semisweet chocolate, broken into ½-ounce pieces
½ cup caramel sauce
1 cup finely chopped toasted hazelnuts

CHOCOLATE CARAMEL MOUSSE

4 ounces semisweet chocolate, broken into ½-ounce pieces
1 ounce unsweetened chocolate, broken into ½-ounce pieces
3 tablespoons caramel sauce
¾ cup heavy cream
4 large egg whites
2 tablespoons granulated sugar

EQUIPMENT

Measuring cup, measuring spoons, baking sheet with sides, 2 large 100% cotton kitchen towels, food processor with metal blade, 1½-quart saucepan, 3-quart saucepan, whisk, 9- by 1½-inch round cake pan, 9- by 3-inch springform pan, double boiler, plastic wrap, electric mixer with paddle, rubber spatula, instant-read test thermometer, pie tin, sifter, wax paper, toothpick, cardboard cake circle, 4 3-quart stainless steel bowls, 1-quart plastic container, large metal kitchen spoon, serrated knife, cake spatula, serrated slicer

PREPARE THE CARAMEL SAUCE

Heat 1 cup cream, 2 tablespoons butter, and ¼ teaspoon salt in a 1½-quart saucepan over medium heat. Bring to a simmer, then adjust heat to keep cream hot until needed. Combine 2 cups sugar and the lemon juice in a 3-quart saucepan. Stir with a whisk to combine (the sugar will resemble moist sand). Caramelize the sugar for 7 to 8 minutes over medium high heat, stirring constantly with a whisk to break up any lumps (the sugar will first turn clear as it liquefies, then light brown as it caramelizes). Remove the saucepan from the heat. Carefully pour one third of the hot cream mixture into the caramelized sugar (this will cause frenetic bubbling); use a whisk to stir the caramel until the bubbling has subsided. Add the remaining cream and stir until smooth. This recipe should yield 2 cups of caramel sauce. Set aside until needed during the preparation of the other components in the damnation cake.

Preheat the oven to 300 degrees Fahrenheit.

Place a 9- by 1½-inch cake pan partially filled with 4 cups of water on the bottom rack of the oven (the bottom rack should be at least 3 inches below the center rack). This creates the desired moist baking environment for the cheesecake.

PREPARE THE CARAMEL CHOCOLATE CHEESECAKE

Lightly coat the bottom of a 9- by 3-inch spring-form pan with 1 teaspoon melted butter. Press 1 cup finely chopped hazelnuts into the buttered bottom of the pan. Set aside.

Heat 1 inch of water in the bottom half of a double boiler over medium heat. Place the coffee, ½ cup caramel sauce, 4 ounces semisweet chocolate, and 2 ounces unsweetened chocolate in the top half of the double boiler. Tightly cover the top with plastic wrap. Heat for 6 minutes, then remove from the heat and stir until smooth. Set aside until needed.

Place the softened cream cheese, ½ cup sugar, and ¼ teaspoon salt in the bowl of an electric mixer fitted with a paddle. Beat on low for 1 minute. Scrape down the sides of the bowl, then beat on medium for an additional 2 minutes. Scrape down the bowl. Add the 3 eggs, one at a time, beating on medium for 15 seconds after each addition. Scrape down the bowl after each addition. Add ½ teaspoon vanilla extract and the melted chocolate mixture and beat on medium for 10 seconds. Remove the bowl from the mixer. Use a rubber spatula to finish mixing the batter, until it is smooth and thoroughly combined. (This repetitive beating, alternated by scraping down the bowl, will give the cake a silky smooth texture.) Pour the cheesecake mixture into the prepared springform pan, spreading evenly.

Place the springform pan on the center rack of the preheated oven and bake the cheesecake until the internal temperature of the cheesecake filling reaches 170 degrees Fahrenheit, about 1 hour. Turn off the oven and allow the cheesecake to remain in the oven for an additional 30 minutes. Remove from the oven and cool at room temperature for 30 minutes. (Don't forget to remove the cake pan with the water from the oven.) Refrigerate the cheesecake in the springform pan for at least 1 hour before assembling the cake.

PREPARE THE HAZELNUT PRALINE

While the cheesecake is baking, place ½ cup whole hazelnuts into a pie tin, grouping the nuts together, side by side. Combine ½ cup sugar and ¼ teaspoon lemon juice in a 1½-quart saucepan. Stir with a whisk to combine (the sugar will resemble moist sand). Caramelize the sugar for 4 to 4½ minutes over medium high heat, stirring constantly with a whisk to break up any lumps (the sugar will first turn clear as it liquefies, then light brown as it caramelizes). Remove the saucepan from the heat. Carefully pour the caramelized sugar over the hazelnuts, covering as many of the nuts as possible. Place the pie tin in the freezer to harden the praline, about 15 minutes.

Remove the praline from the freezer and break into 2- to 2½-inch pieces. Place the broken praline pieces into the bowl of a food processor fitted with a metal blade. Finely chop the praline. This should yield 1½ cups finely chopped praline. Keep the praline in a tightly sealed plastic container in the freezer until needed.

Adjust the oven temperature to 325 degrees Fahrenheit.

PREPARE THE CHOCOLATE FUDGE CAKE

Coat the inside of a 9- by 2-inch cake pan with 1 teaspoon butter, then flour the pan with 1 tablespoon cake flour, shaking out the excess. Set aside.

Sift together the remaining 1½ cups cake flour, the baking soda, and ¼ teaspoon salt onto wax paper. Set aside.

Heat 1 inch of water in the bottom half of a double boiler over medium heat. Place 2 ounces unsweetened chocolate in the top half of the double boiler. Tightly cover the top with plastic wrap and allow to heat for 4 to 5 minutes. Remove from the heat and stir until smooth.

Place 1½ cups brown sugar and the remaining 8 tablespoons butter in the bowl of an electric mixer fitted with a paddle. Beat on low for 2 minutes and then on medium for 2 minutes. Scrape down the sides of the bowl, then beat on high for 2 additional minutes. Add the 2 eggs, one at a time, scraping down the bowl and beating on medium for 30 seconds after each addition. Add the melted chocolate and ½ teaspoon vanilla extract and beat on low for 30 seconds. Scrape down the bowl. While operating the mixer on low, add a third of the sifted dry ingredients and ¼ cup sour cream. Allow to mix for 30 seconds. Add another third of the dry ingredients and the remaining ¼ cup of sour cream and mix for another 30 seconds. Add the remaining sifted dry ingredients and ½ cup hot water. Increase the mixer speed to medium and beat for 10 seconds. Remove the bowl from the mixer. Use a rubber spatula to finish mixing the batter, until it is smooth and thoroughly combined. Immediately pour the cake batter into the prepared pan, spreading evenly. (Move quickly—once the hot water is added to the batter, the leavening action of the baking soda will be activated. If you take too long getting the pan in the oven, the baking soda will lose its "punch.") Bake in the center rack in the preheated oven for 45 minutes, until a toothpick inserted in the center of the cake comes out clean. Remove from the oven and allow to cool in the pan for 15 minutes at room temperature. Turn out onto a cake circle and refrigerate for 30 minutes.

PREPARE THE CHOCOLATE CARAMEL GANACHE

Heat 1 cup heavy cream in a 1½-quart saucepan over medium high heat. Bring to a boil. Place 12 ounces semisweet chocolate and ½ cup caramel sauce in a 3-quart stainless steel bowl. Pour the boiling cream over the chocolate-and-caramel sauce and allow to stand for 5 minutes. Stir until smooth.

Remove 1 cup chocolate caramel ganache and combine with 1 cup finely chopped hazelnuts. Hold this mixture at room temperature to use for the filling. The remaining ganache should also be kept at room temperature until needed.

PREPARE THE CHOCOLATE CARAMEL MOUSSE

Heat 1 inch of water in the bottom half of a double boiler over medium heat. Place 4 ounces semisweet chocolate, 1 ounce unsweetened chocolate, and 3 tablespoons caramel sauce in the top half of the double boiler. Tightly cover the top with plastic wrap. Allow to heat for 6 to 8 minutes. Remove from heat and stir until smooth. Transfer to a 3-quart stainless steel bowl and set aside until needed.

Using a hand-held whisk, whip ¾ cup heavy cream in a well-chilled 3-quart stainless steel bowl until stiff. In a separate bowl, whisk 4 egg whites until soft peaks form. Add 2 tablespoons sugar and continue to whisk until stiff peaks form. Use a rubber spatula to fold one third of the egg whites into the chocolate-and-caramel mixture. Spoon the whipped cream and then the remaining egg whites on top of the mixture and fold together until smooth and completely combined.

BEGIN ASSEMBLING THE CHOCOLATE CARAMEL HAZELNUT DAMNATION

Remove the chocolate fudge cake from the refrigerator. Turn the cake over. Using a slicer, trim off just enough of the top of the cake to make an even surface. Slice the cake horizontally into two equal layers. Remove the cheesecake from the refrigerator. Do not remove the cheesecake from the springform pan (it will be used to build the damnation cake, layer upon layer). Use your fingertips to gently press down on the outside edges of the cheesecake (to create as flat a surface as possible). Pour the ganache-and-hazelnut mixture over the cheesecake. Use a cake spatula to spread the ganache evenly over the surface of the cheesecake. Then invert the top half of the fudge cake onto this ganache layer, pressing down gently to level the cake layer.

Spoon the chocolate caramel mousse onto the inverted cake layer and spread evenly. Place the bottom half of the fudge cake on the mousse layer, pressing down gently to level the cake layer. Place the entire cake in the freezer for 30 minutes or refrigerate for 1 hour.

COMPLETE THE ASSEMBLY

Remove the cake from the refrigerator. Using a knife, cut around the inside edges of the pan, then release the cake from the sides of the springform pan (leave the cake on the bottom of the pan). Use a cake spatula to smooth the top and sides of the cake with 3 to 4 tablespoons ganache. Pour the remaining ganache over the cake. Using a cake spatula, evenly spread the ganache over the top and sides of the cake. (If the ganache has become too firm to pour, place the bowl of ganache over a pan of hot tap water or set the bowl on a warm heating pad. The ganache will become "pourable" in a minute or two. Stir until smooth.) Press the reserved chopped praline into the sides of the cake, coating evenly. Refrigerate the cake for 1 hour before serving.

TO SERVE

Heat the blade of the serrated slicer under hot running water and wipe the blade dry before cutting each slice. Allow the slices to stand at room temperature for 30 minutes before serving.

Use the remaining ⅔ cup caramel sauce to decorate the dessert plates. Warm the sauce to a "pourable" consistency, then use a spoon and eclectically drizzle caramel sauce over each plate.

THE CHEF'S TOUCH
Our first pastry chef at the Trellis, Don Mack, shared my fondness for tagging desserts with wicked appellations. For Don, naming this dessert was (as we say in our kitchen) a "no brainer." The name makes sense because a lot of damn hard work goes into the preparation. However, the pleasure that will be your reward for making Damnation is certain to be heavenly.

This recipe calls for 2½ cups of whole toasted hazelnuts. To skin the nuts (if not done already), first toast them on a baking sheet at 325 degrees Fahrenheit for 18 to 20 minutes (be certain not to overtoast or they will become bitter). Remove the toasted nuts from the oven and immediately cover with a damp 100% cotton kitchen towel. Invert another baking sheet over the first one to hold in the steam (this makes the nuts easier to skin). After 5 minutes, remove the skins from the nuts by placing small quantities inside a folded dry kitchen towel and rubbing vigorously between the hands. If skinned hazelnuts are purchased, toast at 325 degrees Fahrenheit for 10 to 12 minutes, then allow the nuts to cool before using. Place 2 cups of cooled hazelnuts in the bowl of a food processor fitted with a metal blade; process until *finely chopped. The remaining ½ cup of nuts will be used whole.*

Consider preparing Damnation over a period of two or three days. The hazelnut praline may be prepared several days in advance. Keep the chopped praline in a tightly sealed plastic container in the freezer until needed. The cheesecake and fudge cake may be prepared up to two days in advance. (Don't forget that the caramel sauce needs to be prepared before doing the cheesecake. The remaining sauce may be kept, covered with plastic wrap, in the refrigerator until needed for the chocolate caramel ganache and the chocolate caramel mousse. Be sure to bring the refrigerated caramel sauce to room temperature before using.) On the chosen day, prepare the chocolate caramel ganache and the chocolate caramel mousse. Assemble the cake as directed in the recipe.

Use several toothpicks inserted in the sides of the chocolate fudge cake as guides to accurately halve the cake horizontally.

After assembly, the Damnation may be held in the refrigerator for two or three days before serving. Allow the slices to stand at room temperature for 30 minutes before serving.

I suggest a glass of deep purple vintage port to ensure your salvation.

CHAPTER TWO

FRUITFUL FINALES

"How sweet it is."

—JACKIE GLEASON, THE GREAT ONE

CHILLED FRUIT SOUP WITH POACHED APPLES, CRISPY CROUTONS,
AND JONNY'S HARD CIDER ICE CREAM

MY CHERRY CLAFOUTI

CHOCOLATE DRENCHED FRUIT

LEMON AND FRESH BERRY "SHORTCAKE" WITH ROSE'S LEMON LUSCIOUS ICE CREAM

WARM ORANGE SEGMENTS AND SLICED STRAWBERRIES WITH CINNAMON HONEY
BISCUITS AND VANILLA CUSTARD SAUCE

OVEN-ROASTED PEACHES WITH VERY BERRY YOGURT

CRANBERRY AND TOASTED WALNUT CROSTATA

STRAWBERRY RHUBARB VANILLA CUSTARD TART

CHILLED FRUIT SOUP
WITH POACHED APPLES, CRISPY CROUTONS, AND JONNY'S HARD CIDER ICE CREAM

SERVES 6

INGREDIENTS

POACHED APPLES

2 cups cranberry juice cocktail
1 cup granulated sugar
1 cup port wine
3 3-inch cinnamon sticks
8 whole cloves
3 Granny Smith apples

FRUIT SOUP

2 Granny Smith apples
½ pint blueberries, stemmed and washed
½ pint strawberries, stemmed
1 cup cranberry juice cocktail
¼ cup granulated sugar
⅛ cup fresh lemon juice

CRISPY APPLE CAKE CROUTONS

¼ pound plus 1 teaspoon unsalted butter
1½ cups plus 1 teaspoon all purpose flour
½ teaspoon fresh lemon juice
1 Granny Smith apple
¾ teaspoon baking powder
½ teaspoon baking soda
½ teaspoon ground cinnamon
¼ teaspoon salt
1 cup granulated sugar
2 large eggs
½ teaspoon pure vanilla extract

JONNY'S HARD CIDER ICE CREAM

Jonny's Hard Cider Ice Cream (see page 79)

EQUIPMENT

Measuring cup, measuring spoons, 3-quart saucepan, kitchen spoon, paring knife, corer, cutting board, medium gauge strainer, 3-quart stainless steel bowl, plastic wrap, 5-quart stainless steel bowl, food processor with metal blade, 1-quart noncorrosive container, 9- by 5- by 3-inch loaf pan, sifter, wax paper, electric mixer with paddle, rubber spatula, nonstick baking sheet, toothpick, serrated slicer, slotted kitchen spoon, ice cream scoop

POACH THE APPLES

Heat 2 cups cranberry juice cocktail, 1 cup sugar, port wine, cinnamon sticks, and cloves in a 3-quart saucepan over medium high heat. When hot, stir to dissolve the sugar. Bring to a boil, then adjust the heat and allow to simmer for 15 minutes.

While the cranberry juice mixture is simmering, peel, core, and halve 3 Granny Smith apples. Place the peeled apple halves into the simmering liquid. Adjust the heat as necessary to allow the apple halves to poach slowly for 30 minutes, turning them after 15 minutes (a spicy potpourri aroma will fill your kitchen during the simmering of the apples). Remove from the heat and allow the apples to steep in the poaching liquid for 1 hour at room temperature. Transfer the apples to a 3-quart stainless steel bowl. Strain the poaching liquid over the apples (discard the cinnamon sticks and whole cloves). Cover the top with plastic wrap and refrigerate for at least 3 hours before serving.

PREPARE THE FRUIT SOUP

Peel, core, quarter, and chop 2 Granny Smith apples into ¼-inch pieces. Heat the chopped apples, blueberries, strawberries, 1 cup cranberry juice cocktail, ¼ cup sugar, and ⅛ cup lemon juice in a 3-quart saucepan over medium high heat. When hot, stir to dissolve the sugar.

Bring the fruit and juice mixture to a boil, then adjust the heat and allow to simmer for 20 to 22 minutes, until the liquid is slightly thickened. Remove from the heat and cool in an ice-water bath to a temperature of 40 to 45 degrees Fahrenheit. Place the cooled mixture in the bowl of a food processor fitted with a metal blade. Process until smooth and frothy, about 2 minutes (this should yield 3 cups). Transfer the fruit soup to a noncorrosive container, cover with plastic wrap, and refrigerate until ready to serve.

PREPARE THE CRISPY APPLE CAKE CROUTONS

Preheat the oven to 350 degrees Fahrenheit.

Lightly coat the insides of a 9- by 5- by 3-inch loaf pan with 1 teaspoon butter. Flour the pan with 1 teaspoon flour and shake out the excess. Set aside.

In a stainless steel bowl, acidulate 1 cup of water with the lemon juice. Peel, core, quarter, and chop 1 Granny Smith apple into ¼-inch pieces and immediately place in the acidulated water. Set aside.

Combine together in a sifter 1½ cups all purpose flour, baking powder, baking soda, cinnamon, and salt. Sift onto wax paper and set aside.

Place the remaining ¼ pound butter and 1 cup sugar in the bowl of an electric mixer fitted with a paddle. Mix on medium for 3 minutes. Scrape down the sides of the bowl. Mix on high for an additional 2 minutes. Scrape down the sides of the bowl. Add the eggs, one at a time, beating on high for 30 seconds and scraping down the bowl after each addition. Add the vanilla extract and beat on high for 30 seconds. Drain and rinse the chopped apples. Add the chopped apples and beat on medium for 30 seconds. Add the sifted dry ingredients and mix on low for 30 seconds. Remove the bowl from the mixer and use a rubber spatula to finish mixing the batter until smooth and thoroughly combined.

Immediately pour the apple cake batter into the prepared loaf pan. Place the loaf pan on a baking sheet on the center rack of the preheated oven and bake until a toothpick inserted in the center of the cake comes out clean, about 40 to 42 minutes. Remove the cake from the oven. Allow the cake to cool in the pan for 30 minutes. Remove from the pan and allow to cool to room temperature before slicing.

TO SERVE

Cut the cake into 1-inch-thick slices. Trim the crust from the cake slices. Cut the slices into 1-inch cubes. Toast the cake cubes on a nonstick baking sheet in a preheated 350 degree Fahrenheit oven until golden brown, about 15 to 18 minutes. Keep the croutons warm while assembling the dessert.

Portion ½ cup chilled fruit soup into each of six 9- to 10-inch soup plates.

Remove the poached apples from the refrigerator. Use a slotted spoon to remove the apples from the poaching liquid (discard the liquid). Cut each half into a quarter. Make a fan out of each quarter: cut ¼-inch slices from end to end, then gently press down on the slices to produce a fan effect.

Place a fan of sliced apples to the left and right of the center of the plate, then place a large scoop of Jonny's Hard Cider Ice Cream into the center, between the apples. Sprinkle a few croutons onto each portion. Serve immediately.

THE CHEF'S TOUCH

My first encounter with the diverting concept of soup as dessert occurred a few years ago at Cakebread Cellars in Napa Valley. Invited by vintner Jack Cakebread and his wife Dolores, I joined four other chefs in a wine country culinary exposition called An American Harvest Workshop. We spent our days gathering the best foods of Napa and Sonoma county farms, returning in the evening to the winery's kitchen to prepare dinner for sixty to eighty people. On one night, noted Atlanta chef Guenter Seeger of the Ritz-Carlton Buckhead intrigued the diners with a grape soup with cabernet and cognac parfait. It was an extraordinary dessert. Later, I encouraged our pastry chef to develop a dessert soup for one of the Trellis' preview dinners.

This particular recipe for Chilled Fruit Soup with Poached Apples and Crispy Croutons was developed specifically for this book by my assistant Jon Pierre Peavey. Jon Pierre has, I believe, brought together an amalgam of tastes and textures that play off each other like the players in a good string quartet do.

The poached apples may be prepared several days in advance of serving the Chilled Fruit Soup. Keep the apples, covered by the strained poaching liquid, refrigerated in a noncorrosive container.

The Chilled Fruit Soup is best served within forty-eight hours of preparation.

Although the apple cake may be baked several hours (even a day) ahead, it is best to wait until just a few minutes before serving the dessert to cut the apple cake and bake the croutons. To make life simpler, the cake can be baked, allowed to cool, and then covered with plastic wrap and refrigerated until ready to serve the dessert. At that time, the croutons can be cut and toasted as described in the recipe.

A rather subjective beverage choice to accompany the Chilled Fruit Soup would be a 1984 Cakebread Cellars Rutherford Reserve. (Good luck finding this wine. You may need to give Jack a call at Cakebread—he may still have a bottle or two on hand.) A late harvest zinfandel would also do nicely.

MY CHERRY CLAFOUTI

SERVES 8

INGREDIENTS

CITRUS SHORTBREAD COOKIE CRUST

3 tablespoons unsalted butter, melted
12 Citrus Shortbread Cookies (see page 133), broken into quarters

MY CHERRY FILLING

1 cup dried cherries
¼ cup cherry brandy
1 cup heavy cream
½ cup granulated sugar
3 large eggs

MY, MY CHERRY TOPPING

½ cup dried cherries, chopped
1 cup heavy cream

EQUIPMENT

Measuring cup, measuring spoons, small nonstick pan, cook's knife, cutting board, pastry brush, 9½- by ¾-inch false-bottom tart pan, food processor with metal blade, 3-quart stainless steel bowl, small stainless steel bowl, small saucepan, plastic wrap, 3-quart saucepan, whisk, medium gauge strainer, rubber spatula, baking sheet, electric mixer with balloon whip, serrated slicer

ASSEMBLE THE CITRUS SHORTBREAD COOKIE CRUST

Lightly coat the inside of a 9½- by ¾-inch false-bottom tart pan with 1 tablespoon melted butter. Set aside.

In a food processor fitted with a metal blade, chop the cookies in two batches, until they are crumbs (to yield 2 cups of crumbs), about 20 to 25 seconds per batch. Transfer the crumbs to a 3-quart stainless steel bowl. Combine the cookie crumbs with the remaining 2 tablespoons melted butter. Mix by hand until the crumbs bind together. Press the crumbs around the buttered sides of the tart pan, then onto the buttered bottom. Place the pan in the freezer until needed.

PREPARE MY CHERRY FILLING

Preheat the oven to 325 degrees Fahrenheit.

Place 1 cup dried cherries in a small stainless steel bowl. Heat the cherry brandy in a small saucepan over medium high heat. When hot, immediately pour over the dried cherries. Cover with plastic wrap and allow to stand at room temperature until needed.

Heat 1 cup heavy cream and ¼ cup sugar in a 3-quart saucepan over medium heat. When hot, stir to dissolve the sugar. Bring to a boil.

While the cream is heating to a boil, whisk the eggs and remaining ¼ cup sugar in a 3-quart stainless steel bowl (to prevent lumps, continue to whisk the eggs until the cream boils). As soon as the cream mixture begins to boil, pour it into the egg and sugar mixture and stir to combine. Set aside for a few moments.

Thoroughly drain the brandy-steeped cherries (save this liquid for the cherry topping). Sprinkle the cherries over the surface of the shortbread cookie crust. Pour the cream and egg mixture over the cherries in the tart pan and use a rubber spatula to spread the cherries evenly throughout the surface of the crust. Place the pan on a baking sheet on the center shelf of the preheated oven and bake until the filling has set, about 30 minutes. Remove the clafouti from the oven and allow to cool at room temperature for 30 minutes. Loosely cover the cooled clafouti with plastic wrap and refrigerate for 2 hours before serving.

PREPARE MY, MY CHERRY TOPPING

In a small bowl, toss the chopped dried cherries with the reserved brandy liquid. Set aside.

Place 1 cup heavy cream in the well-chilled bowl of an electric mixer fitted with a well-chilled balloon whip. Mix on high until stiff, about 1 minute. Remove the bowl from the mixer and use a rubber spatula to fold in the brandy-marinated chopped cherries. Refrigerate the topping until ready to cut and serve the clafouti.

TO SERVE

Heat the blade of the serrated slicer under hot running water and wipe the blade dry before cutting each slice. Serve with a dollop or two—or three—of My, My Cherry Topping.

THE CHEF'S TOUCH

This is not your traditional clafouti. I must admit that for some time I thought a clafouti less than worthy, even if it is a classic French dessert. Invigorating what I considered a wimpy dessert with a funny name involved little more, however, than adding brandy and a surfeit of whipped cream.

The dried cherries for the filling may be steeped in other brandies; even grappa (why not be iconoclastic?) would work.

The cherry topping may be prepared using a hand-held electric mixer, or by hand using a wire whisk (preparation time may increase slightly).

After assembly, My Cherry Clafouti may be held in the refrigerator for twenty-four hours.

I would feel very content if I were offered a shot of cherry brandy to accompany My Cherry Clafouti.

CHOCOLATE DRENCHED FRUIT

SERVES 12

INGREDIENTS

2½ pounds semisweet chocolate, broken into
½-ounce pieces

1 pound red seedless grapes, stemmed, washed,
and dried

¾ pound dried pineapple slices

¾ pound dried peach halves

¾ pound dried pear halves

2 pints strawberries with stems, lightly rinsed
and dried

EQUIPMENT

Cook's knife, paper towels, double boiler, plastic
wrap, rubber spatula or whisk, instant-read test
thermometer, 3-quart stainless steel bowl, fork,
2 baking sheets, parchment paper, large circular
serving platter

COMMENCE THE DELUGE OF CHOCOLATE

Heat 1 inch of water in the bottom half of a double
boiler over medium heat. Place 1 pound of semisweet chocolate in the top half of the double boiler.
Tightly cover the top with plastic wrap. Allow to
heat for 12 minutes. Remove from the heat and
allow to stand for 5 minutes before removing the
plastic wrap. Use a rubber spatula or whisk to stir
the chocolate until smooth, and continue to stir
until the temperature of the chocolate is reduced
to 90 degrees Fahrenheit.

Line 2 baking sheets with parchment paper.
Place the grapes in a stainless steel bowl. Pour the
melted chocolate over the grapes. Use a fork to
transfer the chocolate-drenched grapes, one at a
time, onto the parchment paper–lined baking
sheets. Refrigerate the chocolate-drenched grapes
for 10 to 15 minutes, until the chocolate has hardened. Transfer the chocolate-covered grapes to the
center of a large serving platter and refrigerate.

Heat 1 inch of water in the bottom half of a
double boiler over medium heat. Place 1 pound of
semisweet chocolate in the top half of the double
boiler. Tightly cover the top with plastic wrap.
Allow to heat for 12 minutes. Remove from the
heat and allow to stand for 5 minutes before
removing the plastic wrap. Use a rubber spatula or
whisk to stir the chocolate until smooth, and continue to stir until the temperature of the chocolate
is reduced to 90 degrees Fahrenheit.

One at a time, dip ¾ to 1 inch of each dried
fruit into the melted chocolate. Allow excess
chocolate to drip into the top half of the double
boiler before placing the drenched fruit onto parchment paper–lined baking sheets. Refrigerate the
chocolate-drenched fruit for 10 to 15 minutes, until
the chocolate has hardened. Transfer the chocolate-
covered fruit to the large serving platter, arrange the
fruit near the outside edge of the platter, and return
to the refrigerator.

Heat 1 inch of water in the bottom half of a
double boiler over medium heat. Place ½ pound of
semisweet chocolate in the top half of the double
boiler. Tightly cover the top with plastic wrap.
Allow to heat for 8 minutes. Remove from the heat
and allow to stand for 5 minutes before removing
the plastic wrap. Use a rubber spatula or whisk to
stir the chocolate until smooth, and continue to stir
until the temperature of the chocolate is reduced to
90 degrees Fahrenheit.

Holding the strawberries by the stem end, dip
¾ to 1 inch of each berry, one at a time, into the
melted chocolate. Allow excess chocolate to drip
into the bowl before placing the drenched strawberries onto parchment paper–lined baking sheets.
Refrigerate the chocolate-drenched berries for 10
to 15 minutes, until the chocolate has hardened.
Transfer the chocolate-covered berries to the serving platter, placing them in between the grapes and
the dried fruit, and return to the refrigerator.

Keep the drenched fruit refrigerated until 10 to
15 minutes before serving.

LEMON AND FRESH BERRY "SHORTCAKE"

WITH ROSE'S LEMON LUSCIOUS ICE CREAM

SERVES 8

INGREDIENTS

LEMON POPPY SEED "SHORTCAKE"

¼ pound plus 1 teaspoon unsalted butter, softened

1¾ cups plus 1 teaspoon all purpose flour

½ teaspoon baking powder

½ teaspoon baking soda

¼ teaspoon salt

1¼ cups granulated sugar

3 large eggs

2 teaspoons poppy seeds

½ cup buttermilk

2 tablespoons fresh lemon juice

2 teaspoons minced lemon zest

½ teaspoon pure lemon extract

STRAWBERRY PUREE

1 pint fresh strawberries, stemmed

¼ cup granulated sugar

1 teaspoon fresh lemon juice

WHIPPED CREAM

1½ cups heavy cream

ROSE'S LEMON LUSCIOUS ICE CREAM

Rose's Lemon Luscious Ice Cream (see page 72)

FRESH BERRY GARNISH

1 pint fresh strawberries, stemmed and quartered

½ pint fresh blackberries

½ pint fresh red raspberries

3 teaspoons poppy seeds

EQUIPMENT

Measuring cup, measuring spoons, vegetable peeler, cook's knife, cutting board, pastry brush, 9- by 5- by 3-inch loaf pan, sifter, wax paper, electric mixer with paddle and balloon whip, rubber spatula, toothpick, food processor with metal blade, 2-quart stainless steel bowl, serrated slicer, ice cream scoop

PREPARE THE LEMON POPPY SEED "SHORTCAKE"

Preheat the oven to 325 degrees Fahrenheit.

Lightly coat the insides of a 9- by 5- by 3-inch loaf pan with 1 teaspoon butter. Flour the pan with 1 teaspoon flour and shake out the excess. Set aside.

Combine together in a sifter 1¾ cups all purpose flour, baking powder, baking soda, and salt. Sift onto wax paper and set aside.

Place the remaining ¼ pound butter and 1¼ cups sugar in the bowl of an electric mixer fitted with a paddle. Mix on low for 2 minutes. Scrape down the sides of the bowl. Mix on low for an additional 2 minutes (this mixing on low is necessary to dissolve the sugar). Scrape down the sides of the bowl. Increase the speed to medium and beat for 3 minutes. Scrape down the sides of the bowl. Increase mixer speed to high and beat for 3 minutes, then scrape down the bowl.

Add the eggs, one at a time, beating on medium for 2 minutes and scraping down the sides of the bowl after each addition. Now beat on medium for an additional 8 minutes. Scrape down the sides of the bowl. Add the poppy seeds. Operate the mixer on low while gradually adding the sifted dry ingredients. Once all of the dry ingredients have been incorporated, about 45 seconds, turn off the mixer, add the buttermilk, then mix on medium for 20 seconds. Add 2 tablespoons lemon juice, lemon zest, and lemon extract and mix on medium for 20 seconds. Remove the bowl from the mixer and use a rubber spatula to finish mixing this delightfully aromatic batter, until smooth and thoroughly combined.

Immediately pour the "shortcake" batter into the prepared loaf pan. Place the loaf pan on a baking sheet on the center rack of the preheated oven and bake until a toothpick inserted in the center of the "shortcake" comes out clean, about 1 hour. Remove the "shortcake" from the oven. Allow the "shortcake" to cool in the pan for 20 minutes. Remove from the pan and allow to cool to room temperature.

MAKE THE STRAWBERRY PUREE

In the bowl of a food processor fitted with a metal blade, process 1 pint of stemmed strawberries, ¼ cup sugar, and 1 teaspoon lemon juice until smooth, about 20 seconds (this should yield 1½ cups strawberry puree). Transfer the puree to a stainless steel bowl, cover with plastic wrap, and refrigerate until needed.

MAKE THE WHIPPED CREAM

Place the heavy cream in the well-chilled bowl of an electric mixer fitted with a well-chilled balloon whip. Whisk on high until stiff peaks form, about 1 minute. Cover with plastic wrap and refrigerate until needed.

TO SERVE

Use a serrated slicer to cut the "shortcake" into 16 ½-inch thick slices.

Drizzle 1 tablespoon of strawberry puree onto each dessert plate. Place a slice of "shortcake" on the sauce in the center of each plate. Top each slice of "shortcake" with 3 small scoops of Rose's Lemon Luscious Ice Cream.

Now top the ice cream with a second slice of "shortcake." Equally divide the berries onto each plate around the "shortcake." Drizzle 2 tablespoons of strawberry puree over the cake and berries on each plate. Top each "shortcake" with a heaping tablespoon of whipped cream, and for the final touch, sprinkle ½ teaspoon of poppy seeds over each portion of whipped cream. Serve immediately.

THE CHEF'S TOUCH

If you have been searching for a twist on the standard shortcake recipe, seek no more. This confluence of "shortcake," berries, and Rose's Lemon Luscious Ice Cream is a wonderful variation on a traditional theme.

The "shortcake" may be prepared two to three days before serving the dessert. Wrap the thoroughly cooled cake in plastic wrap and refrigerate until needed. For enhanced flavor, consider toasting the sliced "shortcake" before serving.

Although the suggested berries work well with the cake and ice cream, use whatever is available. Also, if you like more berries per serving, don't be bashful—serve more.

My mother loves shortcake, and often served it when we were growing up in Woonsocket, Rhode Island. Mom would probably suggest a sparkling cold glass of milk to go along with this dessert. Now that I have lived in Virginia for more than twenty-five years, my suggestion would be a tall glass of iced tea.

WARM ORANGE SEGMENTS AND SLICED STRAWBERRIES

WITH CINNAMON HONEY BISCUITS AND VANILLA CUSTARD SAUCE

SERVES 8

INGREDIENTS

CINNAMON HONEY BISCUITS

1 cup plus 2 tablespoons buttermilk

¼ cup honey

4 cups all purpose flour

1½ tablespoons baking powder

1½ tablespoons granulated sugar

1 teaspoon salt

¾ teaspoon ground cinnamon

8 tablespoons chilled unsalted butter, cut into 1-tablespoon pieces

VANILLA CUSTARD SAUCE

1½ cups heavy cream

2 large eggs

2 tablespoons granulated sugar

1 teaspoon pure vanilla extract

WARM ORANGES AND STRAWBERRIES

2 tablespoons unsalted butter

2 tablespoons granulated sugar

8 navel oranges, peeled and cut into sections

1 pint strawberries, stemmed and quartered

EQUIPMENT

Measuring cup, measuring spoons, cook's knife, paring knife, cutting board, whisk, small bowl, electric mixer with paddle, rolling pin, 2½-inch biscuit cutter, 2 nonstick baking sheets, 2-quart saucepan, 3-quart stainless steel bowl, instant-read test thermometer, 5-quart stainless steel bowl, large nonstick sauté pan, rubber spatula, aluminum foil

MAKE THE CINNAMON HONEY BISCUITS

Preheat the oven to 325 degrees Fahrenheit.

Whisk the buttermilk and honey together in a small bowl. Set aside for a few minutes.

Place 3¾ cups flour, baking powder, 1½ tablespoons sugar, salt, and cinnamon into the bowl of an electric mixer fitted with a paddle. Mix on low for 30 seconds to combine the ingredients. Add 8 individual tablespoons chilled butter and mix on low for 2 minutes, until the butter is "cut into" the flour and the mixture develops a mealy texture. Add the buttermilk-and-honey mixture and mix on low for 10 seconds. Increase the mixer speed to medium and mix until the dough comes together, about 10 seconds (for tender biscuits, avoid over-mixing). Transfer the dough from the mixing bowl to a clean, dry, lightly floured work surface.

Roll the dough (using the extra ¼ cup flour as necessary to prevent sticking) to a thickness of ¾ inch. Cut the dough into 8 biscuits using a 2½-inch biscuit cutter (if things get a little sticky, dip the cutter in flour before making each cut). Form the remaining dough into a ball. Roll the dough to a thickness of ¾ inch. Cut the dough into 4 biscuits using the biscuit cutter. Once again, form the remaining dough into a ball. Roll the dough to a thickness of ¾ inch. Cut the dough into 4 biscuits. Divide the 16 biscuits onto 2 nonstick baking sheets, about 2 inches apart. Bake the biscuits on the center rack of the preheated oven for about 13 to 14 minutes, until lightly browned (rotate the baking sheets from one side of the oven to the other about halfway through the baking time). Remove the biscuits from the oven. The biscuits may be served immediately, or allowed to cool and stored for up to three days in a resealable plastic bag. Warm the biscuits before serving.

PREPARE THE VANILLA CUSTARD SAUCE

Heat the heavy cream in a 2-quart saucepan over medium high heat. Bring to a boil. While the cream is heating, whisk the eggs and 2 tablespoons sugar in a 3-quart stainless steel bowl for 2 minutes. Pour the boiling cream into this mixture and stir gently to combine. Return the mixture to the saucepan and heat over medium high heat, stirring constantly. Bring to a temperature of 180 degrees Fahrenheit, about 1½ minutes.

Remove sauce from the heat and cool in an ice-water bath to a temperature of 40 degrees Fahrenheit, about 10 minutes. When cold, stir in the vanilla extract (this should yield about 2 cups sauce). Transfer to a plastic container. Securely cover and refrigerate until ready to use.

PREPARE THE WARM ORANGES AND STRAWBERRIES

Heat 2 tablespoons of butter and 2 tablespoons sugar in a large nonstick sauté pan over medium high heat, constantly stirring to dissolve the sugar. When the mixture begins to bubble, add the oranges and strawberries and heat until warmed through, about 2 minutes (use a rubber spatula to gently combine the fruit while heating). Remove the pan from the heat. Cover the pan with foil to keep the fruit warm for a few minutes.

TO SERVE

Split all the biscuits in half and keep warm. Portion 3 tablespoons of vanilla custard sauce onto each dessert plate. Place 2 warm biscuit halves (the bottom halves) in the center of each dessert plate. Portion 2 tablespoons of warm oranges and strawberries onto each. Then top with the remaining biscuit halves. Finish by drizzling ½ tablespoon of vanilla custard sauce onto the top of each biscuit. Serve immediately.

THE CHEF'S TOUCH

This dessert is easy to take for granted because it is so simple to prepare and the flavors and textures are so familiar that you may think you have enjoyed it before. This is comfort food at its best.

My assistant Jon Pierre Peavey made a lot of biscuits as a teenager in Wisconsin. He urged me to emphasize how important it is to handle the dough as little as possible in order to achieve tender biscuits. So, once again let me say, do not overmix the biscuit dough.

The oranges may be sectioned several hours or even the day before serving the dessert (be sure to store in a covered noncorrosive container in the refrigerator until needed). Drain the orange segments in a colander before warming them.

For a special final touch, shake some ground cinnamon over each biscuit.

Apple cider, hot or cold, works very nicely with this dessert, especially if you are inclined to lace it with apple brandy.

OVEN-ROASTED PEACHES WITH VERY BERRY YOGURT

SERVES 8

INGREDIENTS

VERY BERRY YOGURT

1 pint blueberries, stemmed and washed

1 pint strawberries, stemmed

¼ cup granulated sugar

1 pint red raspberries

3 cups plain lowfat yogurt

BRANDIED PEACH PUREE

3 medium ripe peaches, unpeeled, pitted, and cut into 8 slices each

½ cup tightly packed light brown sugar

1 cup water

¼ cup brandy

OVEN-ROASTED PEACHES

¼ pound plus 2 tablespoons unsalted butter (2 tablespoons melted)

½ cup granulated sugar

10 tablespoons tightly packed light brown sugar

2 large eggs

1 teaspoon minced orange zest

½ teaspoon pure vanilla extract

1 cup all purpose flour

¾ teaspoon baking soda

¼ cup cultured nonfat buttermilk

4 medium ripe peaches, halved and pitted

EQUIPMENT

Measuring cup, measuring spoons, stainless steel cook's knife, cutting board, small nonstick pan, vegetable peeler, 3-quart saucepan, rubber spatula, food processor with metal blade, medium gauge strainer, 2 3-quart stainless steel bowls, 5-quart stainless steel bowl, plastic wrap, 2-quart plastic container with lid, pastry brush, 8 8-ounce ovenproof soufflé cups, electric mixer with paddle, 2 baking sheets, cake spatula

MAKE THE VERY BERRY YOGURT

Heat the blueberries, strawberries, and ¼ cup granulated sugar in a 3-quart saucepan over medium heat. As the mixture gets hot, the sugar will dissolve and the berries will liquefy and begin to boil (after about 10 minutes). Allow the mixture to boil, stirring occasionally, until it becomes very thick, about 20 more minutes. Wonderful aromas will permeate your kitchen during this time. Remove the mixture from the heat and cool in an ice-water bath to a temperature of 40 to 45 degrees Fahrenheit, about 20 minutes. Transfer the cold berry mixture to the bowl of a food processor fitted with a metal blade. Process until smooth, about 30 seconds (don't overprocess or the mixture will get foamy). Strain the berry puree through a strainer into a 3-quart stainless steel bowl (this should yield 1¼ cups intensely colored berry puree). Add the whole red raspberries and the yogurt and stir to combine. Cover the bowl with plastic wrap and refrigerate until needed.

PREPARE THE BRANDIED PEACH PUREE

Heat the 3 pitted and sliced peaches, ½ cup light brown sugar, and the water in a 3-quart saucepan over medium high heat. When hot, stir to dissolve the sugar. Bring to a boil, then adjust the heat and allow the mixture to simmer until thick, about 20 minutes. Remove from the heat. Cool in an ice-water bath to a temperature of 40 to 45 degrees Fahrenheit, about 20 minutes. Transfer the cold peach mixture to the bowl of a food processor fitted with a metal blade. Add the brandy and process the mixture until smooth, about 1 minute (this should yield 1¾ cups puree). Transfer the brandied peach puree to a plastic container. Securely cover, and refrigerate until needed.

ROAST THE PEACHES

Preheat the oven to 350 degrees Fahrenheit.

Lightly coat the insides of each soufflé cup with melted butter.

Place the remaining ¼ pound butter, ½ cup granulated sugar, and 2 tablespoons light brown sugar in the bowl of an electric mixer fitted with a paddle. Beat on medium for 3 minutes. Scrape down the sides of the bowl. Once again beat on medium for 3 minutes, then scrape down the sides of the bowl. Add 1 egg and beat on high for 30 seconds, then scrape down the sides of the bowl. Add the remaining egg and beat on high for 30 seconds, then scrape down the sides of the bowl. Add the minced orange zest and the vanilla extract and beat on high for 30 seconds. Add the flour and baking soda and mix on low for 15 seconds. Add the buttermilk and continue to mix on low for an additional 30 seconds. Remove the bowl from the mixer and use a rubber spatula to finish mixing the batter until smooth and thoroughly combined.

Evenly divide the batter into the prepared soufflé cups (about 2 heaping tablespoons per cup). Place a peach half, cut side up, onto the batter in each cup, pushing down gently until the peach is even with the batter, yet still exposed. Sprinkle 1 tablespoon of light brown sugar over the cut surface of each peach. Place 4 soufflé cups on each of 2 baking sheets and bake on the center rack of the preheated oven until golden brown and bubbly on top, about 24 to 26 minutes. Remove from the oven and allow to cool for 8 to 10 minutes before removing the oven-roasted peaches from the soufflé cups.

TO SERVE

Portion ½ cup of Very Berry Yogurt into each of 8
9- to 10-inch soup plates. Drizzle 2 tablespoons of
brandied peach puree over the Very Berry Yogurt
on each plate. Using a cake spatula, remove the
oven-roasted peaches (along with the baked batter
that surrounds each peach), one at a time, from the
soufflé cups and set each in the center of the yogurt
on each plate. Serve immediately.

THE CHEF'S TOUCH

*This recipe has made a convert out of me,
since I have always scorned yogurt. Something about the word itself made it a target
of my humor for years. But since my friend
Judith Choate put together a book of yogurt
recipes (Cooking with Yogurt), I have developed more respect for the tangy and healthful
substance. It receives homage here because
this Very Berry Yogurt is flat-out delicious.*

*Preparation of this dessert can be spread
out over a couple of days. Both the Very
Berry Yogurt and the Brandied Peach Puree
can be prepared a day or two in advance.*

*Once removed from the oven, the Oven-
Roasted Peaches need to cool in the soufflé
cups for 8 to 10 minutes before handling—
otherwise the baked batter that surrounds the
peaches will fall apart when removed from
the soufflé cups. The peaches will stay warm
and delicious in the soufflé cups for up to
30 minutes after being removed from the
oven. This dessert is best served warm, but it
is also quite delicious at room temperature.*

*Although peaches may be available from
May through October in the United States,
their accessibility does not always translate
into deliciousness. They are best in the warm
months of the year when picked as ripe as
possible, from as close to your home as possible. Finally, select ripe peaches with smooth
and blemish free skins.*

*My wife, Connie, and I recently served
this dessert at our home for a small dinner
party. It was Connie's idea to accompany the
dessert with Bellinis—Italian Spumante
infused with peach nectar—a very agreeable
selection indeed.*

CRANBERRY AND TOASTED WALNUT CROSTATA

SERVES 8

INGREDIENTS

WALNUT CRUST DOUGH

1½ cups all purpose flour

1 tablespoon plus 1 teaspoon granulated sugar

½ teaspoon salt

½ cup toasted walnuts, finely chopped

4 tablespoons chilled unsalted butter, cut into 1-tablespoon pieces

2 large egg yolks

3 tablespoons ice water

CRANBERRY WALNUT FILLING

1 cup heavy cream

¼ cup granulated sugar

1 cup dried cranberries

1½ cups toasted walnuts

¼ teaspoon ground cinnamon

EQUIPMENT

Measuring cup, measuring spoons, food processor with metal blade, electric mixer with paddle, small bowl, whisk, plastic wrap, 3-quart saucepan, rubber spatula, 9-inch pie pan, parchment paper, 10- by 15-inch baking sheet with sides, pastry brush, serrated knife

MAKE THE WALNUT CRUST DOUGH

Place 1¼ cups flour, 1 teaspoon sugar, and the salt in the bowl of an electric mixer fitted with a paddle. Mix on low for 15 seconds to combine the ingredients. Add all but 2 tablespoons of the chopped walnuts (the reserved walnuts will be sprinkled on the crust just prior to baking) and combine on low for 15 seconds. Add the chilled butter and mix on low for 1½ to 2 minutes, until the mixture develops a coarse texture. In a small bowl, whisk together 1 egg yolk with the ice water. Add the egg-and-water mixture to the mixing bowl and mix on low for 1 minute, until a loose dough is formed.

Remove the dough from the mixer and form it into a smooth round ball. Wrap in plastic wrap and refrigerate for at least 2 hours. The filling should be prepared as soon as the dough is refrigerated.

PREPARE THE CRANBERRY WALNUT FILLING

Heat the heavy cream and ¼ cup sugar in a 3-quart saucepan over medium heat. When hot, stir to dissolve the sugar. Bring to a boil, then adjust the heat and allow to simmer for 6 minutes, until slightly thickened. Remove from the heat and add the cranberries, 1½ cups toasted walnuts, and the cinnamon; stir with a rubber spatula to thoroughly combine.

Line a 9-inch pie pan with plastic wrap. Transfer the hot filling to the pie pan, spreading the mixture evenly to the edges. Refrigerate until ready to assemble the crostata.

ASSEMBLE AND BAKE THE CROSTATA

Preheat the oven to 375 degrees Fahrenheit.

After the crostata dough has been refrigerated for 2 hours, transfer it to a clean, dry, lightly floured sheet of parchment paper. Roll the dough (using the remaining ¼ cup flour as necessary to prevent the dough from sticking) into a circle about 14 inches in diameter and ⅛ inch thick. Place the rolled dough (leave it on the parchment paper) on a baking sheet. Invert the chilled cranberry and walnut mixture onto the center of the rolled dough (discard the plastic wrap). Fold the edges of the dough towards the center to enclose the cranberry and walnut mixture, leaving a 3½- to 4-inch "window" of fruit and nuts. Refrigerate for 10 minutes.

In a small bowl, whisk the remaining egg yolk. Brush the top of the crostata dough with the whisked egg. Sprinkle the reserved finely chopped walnuts over the egg-washed dough, then sprinkle with the remaining tablespoon sugar.

Place the baking sheet with the crostata on the center rack of the preheated oven and bake for 30 minutes, until golden brown. Remove the baked crostata from the oven and allow to stand at room temperature for 15 minutes before cutting and serving.

TO SERVE

Heat the blade of the knife under hot running water and wipe the blade dry before cutting each slice (as you would a pie or cake). Serve immediately while warm, or better yet, serve it with a scoop of Double Cappuccino Ice Cream (see page 77).

see page 77

STRAWBERRY RHUBARB VANILLA CUSTARD TART

SERVES 8

INGREDIENTS

TART SHELL DOUGH

1¼ cups all purpose flour

1 teaspoon granulated sugar

½ teaspoon salt

8 tablespoons chilled unsalted butter, cut into
  1-tablespoon pieces

3 tablespoons ice water

4 cups uncooked rice

VANILLA CUSTARD CREAM

1 cup whole milk

½ cup heavy cream

½ cup granulated sugar

2 large eggs

⅓ cup all purpose flour

1 tablespoon unsalted butter, softened

1 teaspoon pure vanilla extract

RHUBARB FILLING

2 pounds rhubarb, chopped into ½-inch pieces

½ cup granulated sugar

2 tablespoons fresh lemon juice

STRAWBERRY GLAZE AND TOPPING

3 pints strawberries, stemmed

¼ cup granulated sugar

EQUIPMENT

Measuring cup, measuring spoons, electric mixer with paddle, plastic wrap, rolling pin, 9- by 1½-inch round cake pan with removable bottom, paring knife, aluminum foil, baking sheet, 3-quart saucepan, whisk, 3-quart stainless steel bowl, rubber spatula, 5-quart stainless steel bowl, instant-read test thermometer, 1½-quart saucepan, medium gauge strainer, small bowl, pastry brush, serrated slicer

MAKE THE TART SHELL DOUGH

Place 1 cup flour, 1 teaspoon sugar, and the salt in the bowl of an electric mixer fitted with a paddle. Mix on low for 15 seconds to combine the ingredients. Add the chilled butter and mix on low for 1½ minutes until the butter is "cut into" the flour and the mixture develops a very coarse texture. Add the ice water, 1 tablespoon at a time, while mixing on low until the dough comes together, about 30 seconds. Remove the dough from the mixer and form it into a smooth round ball. Wrap in plastic wrap and refrigerate for at least 2 hours.

Preheat the oven to 375 degrees Fahrenheit.

After the dough has relaxed in the refrigerator for 2 hours, transfer it to a clean, dry, lightly floured work surface. Roll the dough (using the remaining ¼ cup flour as necessary to prevent the dough from sticking) into a circle about 14 inches in diameter and ⅛ inch thick.

Line the cake pan with the dough, gently pressing the dough around the bottom and sides. Refrigerate for 5 to 10 minutes to firm the dough. Cut away the excess dough leaving a 1-inch border, which should be crimped around the top edge of the pan. Refrigerate for 15 minutes.

Line the dough with an 18- by 18-inch piece of aluminum foil (use 2 pieces of foil if necessary); weight down the foil with 4 cups uncooked rice. Place on a baking sheet and bake in the center of the preheated oven until the edges of the tart dough are golden brown, about 20 minutes (rotate the pan 180 degrees after 10 minutes). Remove the baked tart shell from the oven; discard the foil and rice. Return the tart shell to the oven and allow to bake for an additional 2 minutes (to allow the bottom crust to get some dry heat). Remove from the oven and allow to cool at room temperature while preparing the vanilla custard cream.

PREPARE THE VANILLA CUSTARD CREAM

Heat the milk and cream in a 3-quart saucepan over medium heat. Bring to a boil. While the milk mixture is heating, whisk ½ cup sugar and eggs in a stainless steel bowl for 3 minutes, then add ⅓ cup flour and whisk until smooth.

Pour the boiling milk mixture into the egg, sugar, and flour mixture and stir to combine. Return to the saucepan and heat over medium heat, stirring vigorously and constantly with a wire whisk for 4 minutes, until the mixture thickens and the flour has cooked through. Remove the custard from the heat, add 1 tablespoon butter and vanilla extract, and stir to combine.

Transfer the vanilla custard cream to the baked tart shell and use a rubber spatula to spread the custard evenly to the edges. Refrigerate while preparing and cooling the rhubarb filling.

MAKE THE RHUBARB FILLING

Heat the sliced rhubarb with ½ cup sugar and the lemon juice in a 3-quart saucepan over medium heat. Occasionally stir to dissolve the sugar while heating. Bring the mixture to a boil (because of the volume of rhubarb this will take about 8 to 9 minutes), then adjust the heat and allow to simmer for 40 minutes (stirring often), until the mixture is very thick, concentrated, and "rhubarby." (The yield should be 2 cups; any more means the cook became impatient and the mixture did not reduce in volume to the desired consistency.) Remove the filling from the heat and cool in an ice-water bath to a temperature of 40 to 45 degrees, about 15 to 20 minutes.

Remove the baked tart shell with the custard from the refrigerator. Transfer the rhubarb filling onto the custard using a rubber spatula to evenly spread to the edges. Refrigerate the tart while preparing the strawberry glaze and topping.

PREPARE THE STRAWBERRY GLAZE

Heat 1 pint strawberries and ¼ cup sugar in a 1½-quart saucepan over medium high heat. Occasionally stir to dissolve the sugar while heating. Bring to a boil, then adjust the heat and allow to simmer until the mixture is very thick, about 15 minutes. Remove from the heat and strain through a medium gauge strainer into a small bowl, using a rubber spatula to press down on the seeds and pulp (discard the seeds and pulp). This should yield ½ cup strawberry glaze. Set aside for a few moments until needed.

COMPLETE THE FINISHING TOUCHES

Remove the tart from the refrigerator. Arrange the whole strawberries, stem side down, onto the rhubarb filling in a ring along the outside edge of the tart. Continue to arrange rings of strawberries onto the rhubarb filling until the filling is completely covered with rings of whole berries.

Use a pastry brush to brush the strawberry glaze onto the strawberries, covering the berries as well as any rhubarb filling that may be peeking through the sides of the berries. Refrigerate the tart for 1 hour before cutting and serving.

TO SERVE

Heat the blade of the slicer under hot running water and wipe the blade dry before cutting each slice. Serve immediately.

THE CHEF'S TOUCH

I thought about naming this dessert "for rhubarb lovers only," but I did not want to frighten away those souls with timid palates. After all, rhubarb's special flavor is remarkably piquant. Personally, I love how it awakens the palate. My only trepidation when eating this fruit, however, is that it is a member of the buckwheat family; having acquired late in life an allergy to buckwheat flour, I always eat my rhubarb tart one very cautious bite at a time.

Our Strawberry Rhubarb Vanilla Custard Tart has just the right balance of flavor even for those who are a bit shy when it comes to a tart pie.

Be certain to stir the rhubarb almost constantly while it is cooking as it will spatter quite a bit; the stirring helps lessen the spattering and will make cleaning your range top a bit easier. You may also consider cooking the rhubarb filling in a larger saucepan or pot; this will also help keep the spattering down.

If you do not have any uncooked rice on hand, you may use any available dried uncooked legumes or, if you have them, commercial pie weights.

If the available strawberries are not the prettiest, or if the sizes of the berries are dramatically different, you may opt for slicing the berries and layering the sliced berries on top of the rhubarb filling in a starburst pattern.

Serve a very cold glass of milk with this strawberry rhubarb tart.

CHAPTER THREE

IRRESISTIBLE ICE CREAMS AND SORBETS

"Enjoy your ice cream while it's on your plate—that's my philosophy."

—THORNTON WILDER

TRICK OR TREAT ICE CREAM

LATE HARVEST SORBET

HOLIDAY SUNDAE—ON MONDAY

ROSE'S LEMON LUSCIOUS ICE CREAM

SWEET DREAMS ICE CREAM SANDWICHES

LONG ISLAND ICED TEA SORBET

DOUBLE CAPPUCCINO ICE CREAM

JONNY'S HARD CIDER ICE CREAM

BLACKBERRY CHOCOLATE PRALINE ICE CREAM

VERMONT MAPLE SYRUP AND TOASTED WALNUT ICE CREAM

STRAWBERRY AND BANANA YIN YANG SORBET

ESPRESSO WITH A TWIST ICE CREAM

"WHAT A CHUNK OF CHOCOLATE" ICE CREAM TERRINE

TRICK OR TREAT ICE CREAM

YIELDS 3 QUARTS

INGREDIENTS

ORANGE CUSTARD ICE CREAM

3 cups orange juice

1½ cups granulated sugar

4 tablespoons minced orange zest

2 cups heavy cream

1 cup half-and-half

5 large egg yolks

DARK CARAMEL SAUCE

1 cup heavy cream

2 tablespoons unsalted butter

½ cup granulated sugar

⅛ teaspoon fresh lemon juice

CHOCOLATE BONBON SAUCE

4 ounces semisweet chocolate, broken into
    ½-ounce pieces

½ cup heavy cream

ADDED TREATS

1 cup semisweet chocolate chips

1 cup toasted unsalted peanuts

EQUIPMENT

Measuring cup, vegetable peeler, cook's knife, cutting board, measuring spoons, 3-quart saucepan, whisk, 2 3-quart stainless steel bowls, 5-quart stainless steel bowl, plastic wrap, electric mixer with paddle, rubber spatula, instant-read test thermometer, ice cream freezer, 1½-quart saucepan, 4-quart plastic container with lid

PREPARE THE ORANGE CUSTARD ICE CREAM

Heat the orange juice, 1 cup sugar, and minced orange zest in 3-quart saucepan over medium high heat. When hot, stir to dissolve the sugar. Bring to a boil. Allow to boil for 15 minutes (this will yield 2¼ cups of slightly thickened syrup).

Cool the syrup in an ice-water bath to a temperature of 40 to 45 degrees Fahrenheit, about 15 minutes. Cover with plastic wrap and refrigerate until needed.

Heat 2 cups heavy cream and the half-and-half in a 3-quart saucepan over medium high heat. Bring to a boil.

While the cream is heating, place the egg yolks and ½ cup sugar in the bowl of an electric mixer fitted with a paddle. Beat the eggs on high for 2 to 2½ minutes. Scrape down the sides of the bowl, then beat on high until slightly thickened and lemon-colored, 2½ to 3 minutes. (At this point, the cream should be boiling. If not, adjust the mixer speed to low and continue to mix until the cream boils. If the eggs are not mixed until the point the boiling cream is added, they will develop undesirable lumps).

Pour the boiling cream into the beaten egg yolks and whisk to combine. Return to the saucepan and heat over medium high heat, stirring constantly. Bring to a temperature of 185 degrees Fahrenheit, about 1 minute. Remove from the heat and transfer to a 3-quart stainless steel bowl. Cool in an ice-water bath to a temperature of 40 to 45 degrees Fahrenheit, about 15 minutes.

When the mixture is cold, combine with the chilled orange syrup mixture, then freeze in an ice cream freezer, following the manufacturer's instructions.

While the orange custard ice cream is freezing, prepare the sauces.

PREPARE THE DARK CARAMEL SAUCE

Heat 1 cup heavy cream and the butter in a 1½-quart saucepan over low heat.

While the cream is heating, place ½ cup sugar and the lemon juice in a 3-quart saucepan. Stir with a whisk to combine (the sugar will resemble moist sand). Caramelize the sugar by heating for 4 minutes over medium high heat, stirring constantly with a wire whisk to break up any lumps (the sugar will first turn clear as it liquefies, then light brown as it caramelizes). Carefully (to avoid splattering) add the hot cream and butter, whisking briskly to combine. Remove from the heat and transfer the caramel sauce to a 3-quart stainless steel bowl. Allow to cool to room temperature.

PREPARE THE CHOCOLATE BONBON SAUCE

Place the semisweet chocolate in a 3-quart stainless steel bowl. Heat ½ cup heavy cream in a 1½-quart saucepan over medium high heat. Bring to a boil. Pour the boiling cream over the chocolate and allow to stand for 5 minutes. Stir with a whisk until smooth. Set aside until needed.

FINISH MAKING THE ICE CREAM

Transfer the semifrozen orange custard ice cream to a plastic container. Immediately fold in the chocolate chips and peanuts. Add the caramel sauce, using a large rubber spatula to give the mixture two folds. Add the chocolate bonbon sauce, once again using a large rubber spatula, and give the mixture 5 to 6 folds. Securely cover the container and place it in the freezer for several hours before serving. Serve within 3 days.

LATE HARVEST SORBET

YIELDS 1 ¾ QUARTS

INGREDIENTS

1 750ml bottle late harvest Riesling wine (3 ¼ cups)
1 cup granulated sugar
½ cup fresh orange juice
¼ cup honey
¼ cup fresh lemon juice
1 quart red seedless grapes, stemmed and washed

EQUIPMENT

Measuring cup, 3-quart saucepan, whisk, 3-quart stainless steel bowl, 5-quart stainless steel bowl, instant-read test thermometer, immersion blender, ice cream freezer, 2-quart plastic container with lid

PREPARE THE SORBET

Heat the late harvest Riesling wine, sugar, orange juice, honey, and lemon juice in a 3-quart saucepan over medium high heat. When hot, stir to dissolve the sugar. Bring to a boil. Add the grapes (they go in whole) and bring to a boil. Allow to boil for 15 minutes (this will yield 6 cups of slightly thickened late harvest grape syrup mixture).

Cool the mixture in an ice-water bath to a temperature of 40 to 45 degrees Fahrenheit, about 15 minutes. When the late harvest grape syrup mixture is thoroughly chilled, puree the mixture using an immersion blender. (If you do not have an immersion blender, puree the mixture in a food processor fitted with a metal blade.)

Freeze the chilled late harvest grape syrup mixture in an ice cream freezer, following the manufacturer's instructions. Transfer the semifrozen Late Harvest Sorbet to a plastic container. Securely cover the container and place it in the freezer for several hours before serving. Serve within 3 days.

THE CHEF'S TOUCH

Grapes harvested late in the picking season have a high intensity of sugar that lends a lush honeylike flavor to late harvest wines. The German wine makers seem to have a deft touch with this style of wine. All of Germany's greatest wines are produced from the Riesling grape, and it is from this grape that prizes known by the designations Auslese, Beerenauslese, and Trockenbeerenauslese are crafted—sweet nectar, to be sure. You may select any of these wines for this sorbet, although I suggest the more reasonably priced (they are all pricey) Auslese (we used a 1992 Schitt Sohne Auslese). Of course, you may also use your favorite late harvest wine from the United States or France (let me know if you choose Chateau Yquem—I'll invite myself over).

Although all the wines mentioned above (including the wine required for the recipe) are vinified from white grapes, I use fresh red seedless grapes to give the sorbet its vibrant color. Purchase about 1 ½ pounds of red seedless grapes on the stem to yield the necessary 1 quart of stemmed grapes.

HOLIDAY SUNDAE—ON MONDAY

YIELDS 12 TO 16 SUNDAES

INGREDIENTS

HARVEST PUMPKIN ICE CREAM
(YIELDS 2 QUARTS)

2 cups heavy cream

1½ cups whole milk

1 cup granulated sugar

¼ teaspoon ground cinnamon

⅛ teaspoon ground cloves

⅛ teaspoon ground nutmeg

6 large egg yolks

1½ cups fresh pumpkin puree or 100% natural solid pack pumpkin

BITTERSWEET CHOCOLATE ICE CREAM
(YIELDS 1 QUART)

2 cups whole milk

6 ounces unsweetened chocolate, broken into ½-ounce pieces

4 ounces semisweet chocolate, broken into ½-ounce pieces

1 cup heavy cream

1 cup granulated sugar

6 large egg yolks

CARAMEL ICE CREAM
(YIELDS 1 ¾ QUARTS)

1½ cups granulated sugar

¼ teaspoon fresh lemon juice

2 cups heavy cream

2 cups whole milk

6 large egg yolks

GOLDEN SUGAR SHARDS

1 cup granulated sugar

¼ teaspoon fresh lemon juice

DOUBLE CHOCOLATE SAUCE

Double Chocolate Sauce (see page 130), warm

EQUIPMENT

Measuring cup, measuring spoons, 3-quart saucepan, whisk, electric mixer with paddle, rubber spatula, instant-read test thermometer, 3 3-quart stainless steel bowls, 5-quart stainless steel bowl, ice cream freezer, 3 2-quart plastic containers with lids, plastic wrap, nonstick baking sheet with sides

PREPARE THE HARVEST PUMPKIN ICE CREAM

Heat 2 cups heavy cream, 1½ cups milk, ½ cup sugar, ¼ teaspoon cinnamon, ⅛ teaspoon cloves, and ⅛ teaspoon nutmeg in a 3-quart saucepan over medium high heat. When hot, stir to dissolve the sugar. Bring to a boil.

While the cream is heating, place 6 egg yolks and the remaining ½ cup sugar in the bowl of an electric mixer fitted with a paddle. Beat the eggs on high for 2 to 2½ minutes. Scrape down the sides of the bowl, then beat on high until slightly thickened and lemon-colored, 2½ to 3 minutes. (At this point, the cream should be boiling. If not, adjust the mixer speed to low and continue to mix until the cream boils. If the eggs are not mixed until the point the boiling cream is added, they will develop undesirable lumps.)

Pour the boiling cream into the beaten egg yolks and whisk to combine. Return mixture to the saucepan and heat over medium high heat, stirring constantly. Bring to a temperature of 185 degrees Fahrenheit, about 1 minute. Remove from the heat and transfer to a 3-quart stainless steel bowl. Add 1½ cups pumpkin puree and stir to combine. Cool in an ice-water bath to a temperature of 40 to 45 degrees Fahrenheit, about 15 minutes.

When the mixture is cold, freeze in an ice cream freezer, following the manufacturer's instructions. Transfer the semifrozen ice cream to a plastic con-tainer. Securely cover the container, then place in the freezer for several hours before serving. Serve within 3 to 4 days.

PREPARE THE BITTERSWEET CHOCOLATE ICE CREAM

Heat 1 inch of water in the bottom half of a double boiler over medium heat. Place 1 cup milk, 6 ounces unsweetened chocolate, and 4 ounces semisweet chocolate in the top half of the double boiler; tightly cover the top with plastic wrap. Allow to heat for 8 to 10 minutes. Remove from the heat and stir until smooth. Keep at room temperature until needed.

Heat the remaining 1 cup milk, 1 cup heavy cream, and ½ cup sugar in a 3-quart saucepan over medium high heat. When hot, stir to dissolve the sugar. Bring to a boil.

While the cream is heating, place 6 egg yolks and the remaining ½ cup sugar in the bowl of an electric mixer fitted with a paddle. Beat the eggs on high for 2 to 2½ minutes. Scrape down the sides of the bowl, then beat on high until slightly thick-ened and lemon-colored, 2½ to 3 minutes. (At this point, the cream should be boiling. If not, adjust the mixer speed to low and continue to mix until the cream boils. If the eggs are not mixed until the point the boiling cream is added, they will develop undesirable lumps.)

Pour the boiling cream into the beaten egg yolks and whisk to combine. Return mixture to the saucepan and heat over medium high heat, stirring constantly. Bring to a temperature of 185 degrees Fahrenheit, about 1 minute. Remove from the heat and transfer to a 3-quart stainless steel bowl. Add the melted chocolate–and–milk mixture and stir to combine. Cool in an ice-water bath to a tempera-ture of 40 to 45 degrees Fahrenheit, about 30 min-utes (this mixture takes additional time to cool to the desired temperature because it is very dense).

When the mixture is cold, freeze in an ice cream freezer, following the manufacturer's instructions. Transfer the semifrozen ice cream to a plastic container. Securely cover the container and place it in the freezer for several hours before serving. Serve within 3 to 4 days.

PREPARE THE CARAMEL ICE CREAM

Place 1 cup sugar and ¼ teaspoon lemon juice in a 3-quart saucepan. Stir with a whisk to combine (the sugar will resemble moist sand). Caramelize the sugar by heating for 4½ to 5 minutes over medium high heat, stirring constantly with a wire whisk to break up any lumps (the sugar will first turn clear as it liquefies, then light brown as it caramelizes).

Remove the saucepan from the heat. Immediately (and carefully) add ½ cup heavy cream and stir to combine (lots of steaming and bubbling will occur when you add the cream, so take care not to scald yourself). Transfer the caramel to a 5-quart stainless steel bowl and allow to cool to room temperature.

Heat the remaining 1½ cups heavy cream and 2 cups milk in a 3-quart saucepan over medium high heat. Bring to a boil.

While the cream is heating, place 6 egg yolks and the remaining ½ cup sugar in the bowl of an electric mixer fitted with a paddle. Beat the eggs on high for 2 to 2½ minutes. Scrape down the sides of the bowl, then beat on high until slightly thickened and lemon-colored, 2½ to 3 minutes. (At this point, the cream should be boiling. If not, adjust the mixer speed to low and continue to mix until the cream boils. If the eggs are not mixed until the point the boiling cream is added, they will develop undesirable lumps.)

Pour the boiling cream into the beaten egg yolks and whisk to combine. Return to the saucepan and heat over medium high heat, stirring constantly. Bring to a temperature of 185 degrees Fahrenheit, about 1 minute. Remove from the heat and immediately add to the prepared caramel, whisking to combine. Cool in an ice-water bath to a temperature of 40 to 45 degrees Fahrenheit, about 15 to 20 minutes.

THE CHEF'S TOUCH

On the evening of Monday, December 19, 1988, the Trellis presented the new winter menu with a special preview dinner. Besides offering a sampling of new menu items at such gala events, we always create a new, seasonally inspired dessert. For this preview, then–pastry chef John Twichell created this exceptional ice cream dessert.

I encourage you to take the time to use fresh pumpkin for this recipe. If fresh pumpkin meat is used (you may also use acorn squash as a substitute), you will need about 1¼ to 1½ pounds of peeled pumpkin meat to yield the required 1½ cups. Cut the pumpkin into ½-inch pieces and steam in a 3-quart uncovered saucepan with ½ cup water. Allow to cook for about 30 minutes, stirring occasionally to prevent sticking. Cool the cooked pumpkin to room temperature, then puree. Don't worry if you have a bit less than 1½ cups of puree; as little as 1 cup will work beautifully (although you will have just a bit less volume).

While preparing three ice creams for one dessert seems like a lot of work, it is well worth the effort. Since this recipe yields 12 to 16 sundaes, think about the great party you can throw. What's the best way to organize the making of this dessert? Suggestion 1: prepare one ice cream per day on three consecutive days, and serve the sundaes on the fourth day. Suggestion 2: prepare all the ice creams on the same day. First, prepare the pumpkin ice cream, and while it is freezing, prepare the ice cream mixtures for both the bittersweet chocolate and the caramel. After removing the remaining mixtures from the ice-water bath, cover them with plastic wrap and keep refrigerated until ready to freeze, one at a time, in the ice cream freezer.

The egg yolks and sugar for each recipe may be prepared using a hand-held electric mixer (mixing time may increase slightly) or by hand, using a wire whisk (mixing time may double). If either of these methods is used, be certain to continue whisking the yolks while waiting for the cream to come to a boil—otherwise you may end up with lumpy eggs and, consequently, lumpy ice cream.

When the mixture is cold, freeze in an ice cream freezer, following the manufacturer's instructions. Transfer the semifrozen ice cream to a plastic container. Securely cover the container, then place in the freezer for several hours before serving. Serve within 3 to 4 days.

PREPARE THE GOLDEN SUGAR SHARDS

Place 1 cup sugar and ¼ teaspoon lemon juice in a 3-quart saucepan. Stir with a whisk to combine (the sugar will resemble moist sand). Caramelize the sugar by heating for 4½ to 5 minutes over medium high heat, stirring constantly with a wire whisk to break up any lumps (the sugar will first turn clear as it liquefies, then light brown as it caramelizes). Pour the caramelized sugar onto a nonstick baking sheet and place in the freezer to harden, about 10 to 15 minutes. Turn the baking sheet over and drop the hardened golden sugar onto a clean, dry, hard surface (a large cutting board will work) to break the sugar into irregular shaped shards. Store the golden sugar shards in an airtight plastic container in the freezer until ready to use. (The shards will keep for several weeks if the container is tightly sealed.)

ASSEMBLE THIS KILLER SUNDAE

Place a large scoop of harvest pumpkin ice cream in the bottom of a large balloon wine glass. Next place a scoop (slightly smaller than the pumpkin ice cream) of caramel ice cream on top of the pumpkin ice cream. Now place a scoop (about half the amount of the pumpkin ice cream) of bittersweet chocolate ice cream on top of the caramel ice cream. Repeat for as many sundaes as desired. Sauce each sundae with 4 tablespoons of warm Double Chocolate Sauce and garnish with golden sugar shards. Serve immediately.

ROSE'S LEMON LUSCIOUS ICE CREAM

YIELDS 2 QUARTS

INGREDIENTS

2 cups granulated sugar

½ cup water

1 tablespoon minced lemon zest

3 cups heavy cream

1 cup whole milk

4 tablespoons unsalted butter

8 large egg yolks

1 cup fresh lemon juice

EQUIPMENT

Measuring cup, measuring spoons, 3-quart saucepan, whisk, electric mixer with paddle, rubber spatula, instant-read test thermometer, 3-quart stainless steel bowl, small bowl, 5-quart stainless steel bowl, ice cream freezer, 2-quart plastic container with lid

PREPARE THE ICE CREAM

Heat ½ cup granulated sugar, ½ cup water, and the minced lemon zest in a 1½-quart saucepan over medium high heat. When hot, stir to dissolve the sugar. Bring to a boil, then allow to boil for 5 minutes until slightly thickened (this should yield ½ cup syrup). Remove from the heat and cool to room temperature.

While the syrup is cooling, heat the heavy cream, milk, 1 cup sugar, and the butter in a 3-quart saucepan over medium high heat. When hot, stir to dissolve the sugar. Bring to a boil.

While the cream is heating, place the egg yolks and the remaining ½ cup sugar in a 5-quart stainless steel bowl. Use a hand-held whisk to whisk the egg yolks until slightly thickened and lemon-colored, about 6 to 8 minutes (less time if using an electric hand-held mixer). (At this point the cream should be boiling. If not, continue to slowly whisk the eggs until the cream boils. If the eggs are not mixed until the point when the boiling cream is added, they will develop undesirable lumps.)

Pour the boiling cream into the beaten egg yolks and whisk to combine. Return to the saucepan and heat over medium high heat, stirring constantly. Bring to a temperature of 185 degrees Fahrenheit, about 2 minutes. Remove from the heat and transfer to a 3-quart stainless steel bowl. Cool in an ice-water bath to a temperature of 40 to 45 degrees Fahrenheit, about 15 minutes.

When the mixture is cold, add the cooled lemon syrup and the fresh lemon juice and stir to combine. Freeze in an ice cream freezer, following the manufacturer's instructions. Transfer the semifrozen ice cream to a plastic container. Securely cover the container, then place in the freezer for several hours before serving. Serve within 3 to 4 days.

THE CHEF'S TOUCH

When Rose Beranbaum came to Williamsburg to promote her newly released cookbook Rose's Melting Pot *in March 1994, a book-signing was held at the Rizzoli bookstore next door to the Trellis. The following night, the Trellis celebrated the new spring menu with a preview dinner that concluded with the light and refreshing Rose's Lemon Luscious Ice Cream. Although we paired Rose's ice cream with delicate almond cookies, you may enjoy it with the Lemon and Fresh Berry "Shortcake" (see page 54).*

For 1 cup fresh lemon juice, squeeze 8 medium lemons (each lemon should weigh in at 3 ounces). But before you squeeze, I recommend using the palm of your hand to firmly press down on each lemon, one at a time, and roll it back and forth on a countertop for a few seconds. This loosens the pulp and makes the juice flow more freely. Having performed this maneuver with all 8 lemons, cut each one in half and squeeze the juice out of each half using a strainer to capture the seeds.

SWEET DREAMS ICE CREAM SANDWICHES

YIELDS 24 MINI SANDWICHES

INGREDIENTS

COGNAC ICE CREAM

1 cup cognac

2 cups heavy cream

1½ cups whole milk

1 cup granulated sugar

6 large egg yolks

¼ cup B & B (Benedictine and Brandy)

COCOA COOKIES

1½ cups cake flour

4 tablespoons unsweetened cocoa

¾ teaspoon baking powder

¼ teaspoon salt

½ pound unsalted butter

¾ cup granulated sugar

4 large eggs

1 teaspoon pure vanilla extract

CHOCOLATE MINT NIGHTCAPS

6 ounces semisweet chocolate, broken into
   ½-ounce pieces

¾ cup heavy cream

1 tablespoon chopped fresh mint

EQUIPMENT

Measuring cup, measuring spoons, cook's knife, cutting board, 1½-quart saucepan, 3-quart saucepan, whisk, electric mixer with paddle, rubber spatula, instant-read test thermometer, 2 3-quart stainless steel bowls, 5-quart stainless steel bowl, ice cream freezer, 2-quart plastic container with lid, sifter, wax paper, 4 9- by 13-inch baking sheets, parchment paper, large flat plastic container with lid, medium gauge strainer, #40 (¾-ounce) ice cream scoop, pastry bag, medium star or plain tip

PREPARE THE COGNAC ICE CREAM

Heat the cognac in a 1½-quart saucepan over medium high heat. Bring to a boil. Allow to boil for 4 minutes (this will yield ½ cup reduced cognac and a marvelous aroma). Remove from the heat and cool to room temperature.

Heat 2 cups heavy cream, the milk, and ½ cup granulated sugar in a 3-quart saucepan over medium high heat. When hot, stir to dissolve the sugar. Bring to a boil.

While the cream is heating, place 6 egg yolks and ½ cup sugar in the bowl of an electric mixer fitted with a paddle. Beat the eggs on high for 2 to 2½ minutes. Scrape down the sides of the bowl, then beat on high until slightly thickened and lemon-colored, 2½ to 3 minutes. (At this point, the cream should be boiling. If not, adjust the mixer speed to low and continue to mix until the cream boils. If the eggs are not mixed until the point when the boiling cream is added, they will develop undesirable lumps.)

Pour the boiling cream into the beaten egg yolks and whisk to combine. Return to the saucepan and heat over medium high heat, stirring constantly. Bring to a temperature of 185 degrees

Fahrenheit, about 1 minute. Remove from the heat and transfer to a 3-quart stainless steel bowl. Cool in an ice-water bath to a temperature of 40 to 45 degrees Fahrenheit, about 15 minutes.When the mixture is cold, add the cognac and the B & B and stir to combine. Freeze in an ice cream freezer, following the manufacturer's instructions. Transfer the semifrozen ice cream to a plastic container. Securely cover the container, then place in the freezer for several hours before assembling the ice cream sandwiches.

PREPARE THE COCOA COOKIES

While the ice cream is freezing, preheat the oven to 300 degrees Fahrenheit.

Sift together the flour, cocoa, baking powder, and salt onto the wax paper. Set aside.

Line 4 baking sheets with parchment paper.

Place the butter and ¾ cup granulated sugar in the bowl of an electric mixer fitted with a paddle. Beat on medium for 2 minutes. Scrape down the sides of the bowl and beat on high for an additional minute, until light in color. Scrape down the bowl. While beating on medium, add 4 eggs, one at a time, stopping to scrape down the bowl after incorporating each addition. Add the vanilla extract and beat on medium for 30 seconds. Add the sifted dry ingredients and mix on medium for 30 seconds. Remove the bowl from the mixer. Use a rubber spatula to finish mixing the batter until it is smooth and thoroughly combined.

Portion 12 cookies per parchment-covered baking sheet by dropping 1 heaping teaspoon of batter per cookie onto each of the 4 baking sheets. Place the cookies on the top and center shelves of the preheated oven and bake for 7 to 8 minutes, rotating the sheets from top to center about halfway through the baking time. Remove the cookies from the oven and allow to cool for a few minutes on the baking sheets. When cool, remove from the baking sheets and store in an airtight container in the freezer until ready to use.

The ice cream sandwiches may be assembled when the cognac ice cream is firm enough to scoop (this could take from 3 to 24 hours depending on the efficiency of your freezer—and how crowded it may be).

PREPARE THE CHOCOLATE MINT NIGHTCAPS

Place the chocolate pieces in a stainless steel bowl. Heat ¾ cup heavy cream and the chopped mint in a 1½-quart saucepan over medium high heat. Bring to a boil. Remove from the heat and pour through a medium gauge strainer into the bowl of chocolate pieces (discard the mint). Stir with a whisk until smooth. Transfer the chocolate mixture onto a baking sheet, using a rubber spatula to spread the chocolate to the edges. Place the baking sheet in the refrigerator for 30 minutes. While the chocolate mint mixture is cooling, assemble the ice cream sandwiches.

ASSEMBLE THE SWEET DREAMS ICE CREAM SANDWICHES

Place 12 cookies upside down on a baking sheet lined with parchment paper. Portion a heaping scoop of Cognac Ice Cream onto each of the cookies. Place a cookie, top side up, on each portion. Gently press the cookie into place. Place the sandwich in the freezer. Repeat this procedure with the remaining cookies. Hold the sandwiches in the freezer until the chocolate mint mixture has been refrigerated for 30 minutes.

Remove the chocolate mint mixture from the refrigerator. Transfer the mixture to a pastry bag fitted with a medium star or plain tip (depending on what form you prefer for the nightcap). Pipe a nightcap-shaped portion of chocolate (about a teaspoon) onto the center of each cookie (accomplish this effect by piping a small circle of chocolate, spiraling upward, and then pulling away from the circle, allowing a strip of chocolate to taper to a point towards the edge of the cookie). Serve immediately with your favorite postprandial (a complementary choice would be the same cognac used in the ice cream).

THE CHEF'S TOUCH
Rather than sing a lullaby to your darling, proffer a sweet dream or two—nocturnal bliss is guaranteed.

The cognac is reduced by half its volume during the 4 minutes of boiling, resulting in an evaporation of much of the alcohol. The evaporation of the alcohol is necessary; failure to do so would prevent the ice cream from freezing to the desired firmness.

A combination of a sweet aromatic liqueur and brandy, B & B is widely available.

The egg yolks and sugar may be prepared using a hand-held electric mixer (mixing time may increase slightly) or by hand, using a wire whisk (mixing time may double). If either of these methods is used, be certain to continue whisking the egg yolks while waiting for the cream to come to a boil—otherwise you may end up with lumpy eggs.

The ice cream sandwiches may be enjoyed immediately after assembling, as described in the recipe, or they may be kept frozen for a day or two. If your intention is to keep them frozen for up to two days, do not top the sandwiches with the nightcaps (this may be done just before serving). I suggest individually wrapping the sandwiches with plastic wrap and storing them in an airtight plastic container in the freezer.

For a more prosaic presentation, you may want to omit the nightcap and simply dust the frozen sandwiches with unsweetened cocoa just before serving. Just 1 tablespoon of cocoa will take care of all 24 "sweet dreams."

LONG ISLAND ICED TEA SORBET

YIELDS 1 ½ QUARTS

INGREDIENTS

1 ½ cups granulated sugar

1 cup dark rum

1 cup tequila

½ cup fresh lemon juice

¼ cup Rose's Lime Juice

1 teaspoon minced fresh lemon zest

1 teaspoon minced fresh lime zest

12 ounces cola

1 ½ cups water

¼ cup coffee liqueur

EQUIPMENT

Measuring cup, vegetable peeler, cook's knife, cutting board, measuring spoons, 3-quart saucepan, whisk, 3-quart stainless steel bowl, 5-quart stainless steel bowl, instant-read test thermometer, ice cream freezer, 2-quart plastic container with lid

PREPARE THE SORBET

Heat the sugar, dark rum, tequila, lemon juice, lime juice, lemon zest, and lime zest in a 3-quart saucepan over medium high heat. When hot, stir to dissolve the sugar. Bring to a boil. Allow to boil for 13 minutes. (This will yield 2 ¼ cups of slightly syrupy, intoxicatingly aromatic, caramel-colored, "spiked" tea.)

Cool the mixture in an ice-water bath to a temperature of 40 to 45 degrees, about 15 minutes. When the mixture is thoroughly chilled, stir in the cola, water, and coffee liqueur.

Freeze the Long Island iced tea mixture in an ice cream freezer, following the manufacturer's instructions. Transfer the semifrozen sorbet to a plastic container. Securely cover the container, then place in the freezer for several hours before serving. Serve within 24 hours.

DOUBLE CAPPUCCINO ICE CREAM

YIELDS 1 ½ QUARTS

INGREDIENTS

2½ cups heavy cream
1 cup whole milk
¾ cup granulated sugar
5 large egg yolks
4 tablespoons espresso powder
⅛ teaspoon ground cinnamon
½ cup hot brewed coffee

EQUIPMENT

Measuring cup, measuring spoons, 3-quart saucepan, whisk, electric mixer with paddle, rubber spatula, instant-read test thermometer, 3-quart stainless steel bowl, small bowl, 5-quart stainless steel bowl, ice cream freezer, 2-quart plastic container with lid

PREPARE THE ICE CREAM

Heat the heavy cream, milk, and half the amount of sugar in a 3-quart saucepan over medium high heat. When hot, stir to dissolve the sugar. Bring to a boil.

While the cream is heating, place the egg yolks and the remaining sugar in the bowl of an electric mixer fitted with a paddle. Beat the eggs on high for 2 to 2½ minutes. Scrape down the bowl, then beat on high until slightly thickened and lemon-colored, 2½ to 3 minutes. (At this point, the cream should be boiling. If not, adjust the mixer speed to low and continue to mix until the cream boils. If the eggs are not mixed until the point when the boiling cream is added, they will develop undesirable lumps.)

Pour the boiling cream into the beaten egg yolks and whisk to combine. Return to the saucepan and heat over medium high heat, stirring constantly. Bring to a temperature of 185 degrees Fahrenheit, about 1 minute. Remove from the heat and transfer to a 3-quart stainless steel bowl. Place the espresso powder and the ground cinnamon in a separate small bowl. Pour in the hot brewed coffee and stir to dissolve the espresso powder. Pour the coffee and espresso mixture into the cream and egg yolk mixture. Cool in an ice-water bath to a temperature of 40 to 45 degrees Fahrenheit, about 15 minutes.

Freeze the mixture in an ice cream freezer, following the manufacturer's instructions. Transfer the semifrozen ice cream to a plastic container. Securely cover, then place in the freezer for several hours before serving. Serve within 5 days.

THE CHEF'S TOUCH

Sitting in an outdoor cafe slowly sipping a cappuccino may be the way to go on a cool autumn day, but when the temperature sky-rockets, it's a large bowl of ice cream for me.

For an Italianate flair, fold about 8 to 10 Sambuca Almond Biscotti (see page 132)— chopped into ½-inch pieces—into the semi-frozen ice cream just before placing it in the freezer to harden.

The egg yolks and sugar may be prepared using a hand-held electric mixer (mixing time may increase slightly) or by hand, using a wire whisk (mixing time may double). If either of these methods is used, be certain to continue whisking the yolks while waiting for the cream to come to a boil—otherwise you may end up with lumpy eggs.

JONNY'S HARD CIDER ICE CREAM

YIELDS 2 QUARTS

INGREDIENTS

1 quart apple cider
1 cup bourbon
2 3-inch cinnamon sticks
12 whole cloves
1 cup tightly packed light brown sugar
2 cups heavy cream
1 cup whole milk
1 cup granulated sugar
6 large egg yolks

EQUIPMENT

Measuring cup, 3-quart saucepan, whisk, 2 3-quart stainless steel bowls, 5-quart stainless steel bowl, plastic wrap, electric mixer with paddle, rubber spatula, instant-read test thermometer, ice cream freezer, 2-quart plastic container with lid

PREPARE THE ICE CREAM

Heat the apple cider, bourbon, cinnamon sticks, and whole cloves in a 3-quart saucepan over medium high heat. Bring to a boil, then lower the heat to allow the mixture to simmer for 45 minutes (this should yield 2¼ to 2½ cups). Remove from the heat. Immediately add the brown sugar, stirring with a whisk to dissolve. Cool the mixture in an ice-water bath. When cool, cover with plastic wrap and refrigerate until needed.

Heat the heavy cream, milk, and ½ cup sugar in a 3-quart saucepan over medium high heat. When hot, stir to dissolve the sugar. Bring to a boil.

While the cream is heating, place the egg yolks and the remaining ½ cup sugar in the bowl of an electric mixer fitted with a paddle. Beat the eggs on high for 2 to 2½ minutes. Scrape down the sides of the bowl, then beat on high until slightly thickened and lemon-colored, 2½ to 3 minutes. (At this point, the cream should be boiling. If not, adjust the mixer speed to low and continue to mix until the cream boils. If the eggs are not mixed until the point when the boiling cream is added, they will develop undesirable lumps.)

Pour the boiling cream into the beaten egg yolks and whisk to combine. Return to the saucepan and heat over medium high heat, stirring constantly. Bring to a temperature of 185 degrees Fahrenheit, about 1 minute. Remove from the heat and transfer to a 3-quart stainless steel bowl. Cool in an ice-water bath to a temperature of 40 to 45 degrees Fahrenheit, about 15 minutes.

When the mixture is cold, combine with the chilled cider mixture and freeze in an ice cream freezer, following the manufacturer's instructions. Transfer the semifrozen ice cream to a plastic container. Securely cover the container, then place in the freezer for 24 hours before serving. Serve within 3 to 4 days.

THE CHEF'S TOUCH

You do not have to be a moonshiner to concoct (or enjoy) this delectation. Corn whiskey makes an interesting substitute for bourbon, as does apple brandy or calvados. French apple brandy blends well with the apple cider, as does grain alcohol (ouch) or rum. In fact, you can substitute almost anything you have a taste for—or should I say, have had a taste of. Seriously, though, most of the alcohol will evaporate during the simmering process, leaving the taste but not the punch. So, unless you become pixilated at the very thought of this type of concoction, do not fret about this dessert's intoxicating effect.

Select a good cider for this recipe. At the Trellis, we prefer an unfiltered freshly squeezed apple cider. Although quite cloudy, it has a very pleasant flavor without any of the cloying sweetness found in many commercial brands. Seek out a small regional producer in your area (thank goodness for the resurgence in small producers pressing high-quality sweet and fermented ciders).

The egg yolks and sugar may be prepared using a hand-held electric mixer (mixing time may increase slightly) or by hand, using a wire whisk (mixing time may double). If either of these methods is used, be certain to continue whisking the yolks while waiting for the cream to come to a boil—otherwise you may end up with lumpy eggs.

BLACKBERRY CHOCOLATE PRALINE ICE CREAM

YIELDS 1 $^3/_4$ QUARTS

INGREDIENTS

CHOCOLATE PRALINE

1 cup toasted pecans
1 cup granulated sugar
¼ teaspoon fresh lemon juice
1 ounce unsweetened chocolate, chopped into ¼-inch pieces

BLACKBERRY ICE CREAM

1 pint fresh blackberries, rinsed
¾ cup plus 2 tablespoons granulated sugar
1 teaspoon fresh lemon juice
1½ cups heavy cream
1 cup half-and-half
5 large egg yolks
½ cup cultured nonfat buttermilk

EQUIPMENT

Measuring cup, measuring spoons, baking sheet with sides, colander, pie tin, 3-quart saucepan, whisk, serrated slicer, cutting board, 2-quart plastic container with lid, 1½-quart saucepan, metal spoon, medium gauge strainer, rubber spatula, 3-quart stainless steel bowl, 5-quart stainless steel bowl, plastic wrap, electric mixer with paddle, instant-read test thermometer, ice cream freezer

MAKE THE CHOCOLATE PRALINE

Place the toasted pecans into a pie tin, spreading them to the inside edges. Set aside.

Combine 1 cup sugar and ¼ teaspoon lemon juice in a 3-quart saucepan. Stir with a whisk to combine (the sugar will resemble moist sand). Caramelize the sugar by heating for 4½ to 5 minutes over medium high heat, stirring constantly with a wire whisk to break up any lumps (the sugar will first turn clear as it liquefies, then light brown as it caramelizes). Remove the saucepan from the heat, add 1 ounce chopped chocolate, and stir to dissolve. Immediately and carefully pour the caramelized mixture over the pecans, covering all the nuts. Place the pie tin in the freezer to harden the praline, about 15 minutes.

Remove the praline from the freezer. Use a serrated slicer to cut the praline into ⅛-inch pieces. This should yield 2 cups chopped praline. Keep the praline in a tightly sealed plastic container in the freezer until needed.

PREPARE THE BLACKBERRY ICE CREAM

Heat the blackberries, 2 tablespoons sugar, and 1 teaspoon lemon juice in a 1½-quart saucepan over medium heat. As the mixture gets hot, the sugar will dissolve and the berries will liquefy and begin to boil, after about 5 minutes. Allow the mixture to boil until it becomes very thick, stirring occasionally, about 15 more minutes. Remove from the heat and strain through a strainer into a 2-quart bowl, using a rubber spatula to press down on the seeds and pulp (discard the seeds and pulp). This should yield about ½ cup blackberry puree. Cool the puree in an ice-water bath, about 10 minutes. When the puree is cold, cover with plastic wrap and refrigerate until needed.

Heat the heavy cream, half-and-half, and ¼ cup sugar in a 3-quart saucepan over medium high heat. When hot, stir to dissolve the sugar. Bring to a boil.

While the cream is heating, place the egg yolks and the remaining ½ cup sugar in the bowl of an electric mixer fitted with a paddle. Beat the eggs on high for 2 to 2½ minutes. Scrape down the sides of the bowl, then beat on high until slightly thickened and lemon-colored, 2½ to 3 minutes. (At this point, the cream should be boiling. If not, adjust the mixer speed to low and continue to mix until the cream boils. If the eggs are not mixed until the point when the boiling cream is added, they will develop undesirable lumps.)

Pour the boiling cream into the beaten egg yolks and whisk to combine. Return to the saucepan and heat over medium high heat, stirring constantly. Bring to a temperature of 185 degrees Fahrenheit, about 1 minute. Remove from the heat and transfer to a 3-quart stainless steel bowl. Cool in an ice-water bath to a temperature of 40 to 45 degrees Fahrenheit, about 15 minutes.

When the mixture is cold, stir in the buttermilk and freeze in an ice cream freezer, following the manufacturer's instructions. Transfer the semi-frozen ice cream to a plastic container. Use a rubber spatula to first fold in the chocolate praline, and then the blackberry puree. (Do not overmix—the idea is to contrast fanciful swirls of the puree with a homogeneously colored base). Securely cover the container, then place in the freezer for several hours before serving. Serve within 3 days.

THE CHEF'S TOUCH

In the hilly farm country north of Eau Claire, Wisconsin, stands of thorny blackberry bushes yield remarkably sweet and juicy (but diminutive) berries that can turn a picker's hands purple for three days. That's according to my assistant Jon Pierre Peavey, who is wont to rhapsodize about the bounties of his home state. As a young lad he spent many a pleasurable late summer day, pails tied to his waist, picking and eating the tiny berries that are known in those parts as black caps. He also assisted his mother in preparing creamy fresh blackberry ice cream. In this recipe Jon Pierre has elevated Mrs. Peavey's creation into the realm of indulgence with the addition of the chocolate praline.

Blackberries, which are plentiful during the summer, are available year-round if you are willing to pay the price for South American or New Zealand fruit.

Rinse the berries before using by placing them in a colander and spraying with lukewarm water. Drain the berries on paper towels to remove excess moisture.

Enhance the flavor of the pecans and reduce moisture by toasting them on a baking sheet in a 325 degree Fahrenheit oven for 10 to 12 minutes.

This prodigious batch of chocolate praline provides a generous amount of delicious crunch in every mouthful of this ice cream. If you prefer a less crunchy ice cream, simply divide the praline recipe in half. Of course, you can always prepare

the praline recipe as listed, and use half the amount of chopped praline, saving the remainder to sprinkle over your favorite ice cream or to eat alone (the praline will keep indefinitely in a tightly sealed plastic container in your freezer).

The egg yolks and sugar may be prepared using a hand-held electric mixer (mixing time may increase slightly) or by hand, using a wire whisk (mixing time may double). If either of these methods is used, be certain to continue whisking the yolks while waiting for the cream to come to a boil—otherwise you may end up with lumpy eggs.

For the final touch, garnish each portion of ice cream with fresh blackberries. Or, you can double the recipe for the blackberry puree and drizzle the extra puree over the ice cream.

VERMONT MAPLE SYRUP AND TOASTED WALNUT ICE CREAM

YIELDS 2 QUARTS

INGREDIENTS

MAPLE GLAZED WALNUTS

½ cup Vermont pure maple syrup

1½ cups toasted walnut halves

VERMONT MAPLE SYRUP ICE CREAM

2 cups heavy cream

1 cup half-and-half

1 cup Vermont pure maple syrup

5 large egg yolks

¼ cup granulated sugar

EQUIPMENT

Measuring cup, 1½-quart saucepan, metal spoon, pie tin, 2-quart plastic container with lid, 3-quart saucepan, whisk, electric mixer with paddle, rubber spatula, instant-read test thermometer, 3-quart stainless steel bowl, 5-quart stainless steel bowl, ice cream freezer

GLAZE THE WALNUTS

Heat ½ cup maple syrup in a 1½-quart saucepan over medium high heat. When the syrup begins to boil, reduce the heat to medium and allow the syrup to continue to boil and thicken for 10 minutes, stirring occasionally. Remove the very hot syrup from the heat. Immediately add 1½ cups toasted walnuts. Use a metal spoon to stir the walnuts into the hot syrup. Transfer the glazed walnuts to a pie tin and place in the freezer to harden.

Remove the walnuts from the freezer. Use your hands to separate the walnuts and break into pieces no larger than the original size of the individual walnut halves. Keep the glazed walnuts in a tightly sealed plastic container in the freezer until needed.

PREPARE THE VERMONT MAPLE SYRUP ICE CREAM

Heat the heavy cream, half-and-half, and maple syrup in a 3-quart saucepan over medium high heat. When hot, stir to dissolve the sugar. Bring to a boil.

While the cream is heating, place the egg yolks and sugar in the bowl of an electric mixer fitted with a paddle. Beat the eggs on high for 2 to 2½ minutes. Scrape down the sides of the bowl, then beat on high until slightly thickened and lemon-colored, 2½ to 3 minutes. (At this point, the cream should be boiling. If not, adjust the mixer speed to low and continue to mix until the cream boils. If the eggs are not mixed until the point the boiling cream is added, they will develop undesirable lumps.)

Pour the boiling cream into the beaten egg yolks and whisk to combine. Return to the saucepan and heat over medium high heat, stirring constantly. Bring to a temperature of 185 degrees Fahrenheit, about 1 minute. Remove from the heat and transfer to a 3-quart stainless steel bowl. Cool in an ice-water bath to a temperature of 40 to 45 degrees Fahrenheit, about 15 minutes.

When the mixture is cold, freeze in an ice cream freezer, following the manufacturer's instructions. Transfer the semifrozen ice cream to a plastic container. Use a rubber spatula to fold in the glazed walnuts. Securely cover the container, then place in the freezer for several hours before serving. Serve within 5 days.

> **THE CHEF'S TOUCH**
> *I have many delicious memories of licking Vermont maple syrup from my fingers as a youngster growing up in New England. Select your favorite pure maple syrup for this recipe. Be sure it is pure. I strongly recommend you do not use maple-flavored syrup or pancake syrup (the former is primarily corn syrup with a modicum of maple syrup and the latter is corn syrup with artificial flavoring).*
>
> *Boiling the syrup for 10 minutes before adding the walnuts is quite important—less time and the walnuts will be a sticky mass.*
>
> *For optimum flavor, toast the walnuts on a baking sheet in a 325 degree Fahrenheit oven for 12 to 14 minutes. Allow the nuts to cool thoroughly before you add them to the glaze.*
>
> *The glazed walnuts will keep indefinitely in a tightly sealed plastic container in the freezer.*
>
> *The egg yolks and sugar may be prepared using a hand-held electric mixer (mixing time may increase slightly) or by hand, using a wire whisk (mixing time may double). If either of these methods is used, be certain to continue whisking the yolks while waiting for the cream to come to a boil—otherwise you may end up with lumpy eggs.*

STRAWBERRY AND BANANA YIN YANG SORBET

YIELDS 2 QUARTS

INGREDIENTS

2 pints strawberries, stemmed

2 pounds medium-size bananas, peeled

1 medium-size lemon

2 cups water

1½ cups granulated sugar

4 tablespoons dark rum

EQUIPMENT

Measuring cup, measuring spoons, paring knife, colander, cook's knife, cutting board, 2 3-quart stainless steel bowls, vegetable peeler, 3-quart saucepan, small strainer, whisk, immersion blender, instant-read test thermometer, ice cream freezer, rubber spatula, 2-quart plastic container with lid

PREPARE THE SORBET

Place the strawberries in a colander and spray with lukewarm water. Drain the berries on paper towels to remove excess moisture. Slice the strawberries into ¼-inch-thick sections. Place the sliced berries in a 3-quart stainless steel bowl and set aside until needed.

Slice the bananas into ¼-inch-thick slices. Place the banana slices in a separate 3-quart stainless steel bowl and set aside while preparing the sugar syrup.

Peel the colored skin from the lemon using a vegetable peeler, being careful to remove only the colored skin and not the bitter white pith that lies beneath the skin. Use a sharp cook's knife to finely mince all the peeled lemon skin. Transfer the minced lemon zest to a 3-quart saucepan. Cut the peeled lemon in half. Squeeze the juice from the 2 lemon halves into the saucepan, using a small strainer to capture the seeds. Add the 2 cups water and the granulated sugar to the saucepan and bring the mixture to a boil over medium high heat (stir to dissolve the sugar). Allow the lemon sugar mixture to boil for 10 minutes (this should yield 2 cups syrup). Remove from the heat, add the rum, and stir to combine.

Pour 1 cup of hot syrup over the strawberries and the remaining cup over the bananas. Stir the fruit with a rubber spatula. Allow the fruit to steep in the syrup for 40 minutes, stirring occasionally. Use an immersion blender to puree each bowl of fruit. (If you do not have an immersion blender, the fruit may be pureed in a food processor with a metal blade. If using a food processor, puree the bananas first. Remove the bananas from the bowl of the processor, then without cleaning the blender, puree the strawberries. Return the pureed fruit to the separate bowls.) Cool the bowl of banana puree in an ice-water bath to a temperature of 40 to 45 degrees, about 15 minutes.

Freeze the banana puree in an ice cream freezer, following the manufacturer's instructions. While the banana sorbet is freezing, cool the strawberry puree in an ice-water bath to a temperature of 40 to 45 degrees. Transfer the semifrozen banana sorbet to a plastic container. Securely cover the container, then place in the freezer while freezing the strawberry puree. Freeze the strawberry puree in an ice cream freezer, following the manufacturer's instructions. Transfer the semifrozen strawberry sorbet to the container of banana sorbet. Use a rubber spatula to swirl the strawberry puree (the yin) into the banana sorbet (the yang). Securely cover the container, then place in the freezer for several hours before serving. Serve within 3 days.

THE CHEF'S TOUCH

The immersion blender (also called a hand blender—not to be confused with a hand mixer) is a great tool. Electrically powered and economically priced, the blender can easily puree cooked or partially cooked fruit and vegetables, as well as many soups. And the best part is that it is easy to clean.

After peeling, 2 pounds of medium-size bananas should yield about 22 ounces of fruit. Select ripe bananas that are uniformly yellow in color. Avoid bananas whose skin has green streaks (underripe) or lots of brown patches (overripe).

ESPRESSO WITH A TWIST ICE CREAM

YIELDS 1¾ QUARTS

INGREDIENTS

1 medium-size lemon
2 cups granulated sugar
1 cup water
2 cups whole milk
1 cup heavy cream
¼ cup freshly ground espresso beans
2 large eggs
2 large egg yolks

EQUIPMENT

Measuring cup, coffee grinder, vegetable peeler, cook's knife, cutting board, 1½-quart saucepan, small strainer, 2-quart stainless steel bowl, 5-quart stainless steel bowl, plastic wrap, 3-quart saucepan, whisk, cheesecloth, 3-quart stainless steel bowl, electric mixer with paddle, rubber spatula, instant-read test thermometer, ice cream freezer, 2-quart plastic container with lid

PREPARE THE ICE CREAM

Peel the colored skin from a whole lemon using a vegetable peeler. Remove the skin in long 1-inch wide strips, being careful to remove only the colored skin and not the bitter white pith that lies beneath the skin. Use a very sharp cook's knife to cut the peeled skin widthwise into very thin strips. Place the lemon strips in a 1½-quart saucepan. Cut the peeled lemon in half. Squeeze the juice from the 2 lemon halves into the saucepan, using a small strainer to capture the seeds. Add 1 cup sugar and 1 cup water to the saucepan and bring the mixture to a boil over medium high heat (stir to dissolve the sugar). Allow the lemon sugar mixture to boil for 5 minutes (this should yield slightly more than 1¼ cups syrup). Remove from the heat and cool in an ice-water bath. When cool, cover with plastic wrap and keep refrigerated until needed.

Heat the milk, heavy cream, and ground espresso beans in a 3-quart saucepan over medium high heat. Bring the mixture to a boil, stirring frequently with a whisk. Remove from the heat and strain, through several folds of cheesecloth, into a 3-quart stainless steel bowl (this should yield 2¾ cups espresso-flavored milk-and-cream mixture). Thoroughly wash and dry the saucepan. Return the mixture to the saucepan along with ½ cup sugar. Bring to a boil over medium high heat. (It should only take 2 minutes for the mixture to boil, so keep a close eye on the saucepan to make sure that the mixture does not boil over the sides of the pan.) Remove the saucepan from the heat and set aside while whisking the egg yolks.

Immediately place the eggs, egg yolks, and the remaining ½ cup sugar in the bowl of an electric mixer fitted with a paddle. Beat the eggs on high for 2 to 2½ minutes. Scrape down the sides of the bowl, then beat on high until slightly thickened and lemon-colored, 2½ to 3 minutes.

Pour the very hot cream into the beaten eggs and whisk to combine. Return to the saucepan and heat over medium high heat, stirring constantly. Bring to a temperature of 185 degrees Fahrenheit, about 1½ minutes. Remove from the heat and transfer to a 3-quart stainless steel bowl. Cool in an ice-water bath to a temperature of 40 to 45 degrees Fahrenheit, about 15 minutes.

When the mixture is cold, stir in the lemon sugar syrup. Freeze the mixture in an ice cream freezer, following the manufacturer's instructions. Transfer the semifrozen ice cream to a plastic container. Securely cover the container, then place in the freezer for several hours before serving. Serve within 3 to 4 days.

THE CHEF'S TOUCH

My culinary peregrinations have found me enjoying espresso all over the world. I admit to being a purist, as I take my espresso without the addition of sugar, and I most certainly eschew the sometime offered twist of lemon. So why do I now offer this smooth and intensely flavored frozen concoction with the aforementioned lemon twist? The answer is in the first spoonful.

For the record, ¼ cup of whole espresso beans will yield ¼ cup ground espresso. The weight of ¼ cup whole beans is ½ ounce.

Before cutting the whole lemon in half, use the palm of your hand to firmly press down on the lemon and roll it back and forth on a countertop. This will break up the membrane inside the lemon so that the juice will come flowing out when the halves are squeezed.

The whole eggs, yolks, and sugar may be prepared using a hand-held electric mixer (mixing time may increase slightly) or by hand, using a wire whisk (mixing time may double).

"WHAT A CHUNK OF CHOCOLATE" ICE CREAM TERRINE

SERVES 8 TO 10

INGREDIENTS

DARK CHOCOLATE NUT BARK

8 ounces semisweet chocolate, broken into ½-ounce pieces

½ cup toasted unsalted peanuts

½ cup raisins

WHITE CHOCOLATE ICE CREAM

8 ounces white chocolate, broken into ½-ounce pieces

2 cups half-and-half

1 cup whole milk

1 cup granulated sugar

5 large egg yolks

RED RASPBERRY SAUCE

Red Raspberry Sauce (see page 130)

EQUIPMENT

Measuring cup, baking sheet with sides, double boiler, plastic wrap, rubber spatula, cutting board, cook's knife, 2-quart plastic container with lid, 3-quart saucepan, whisk, electric mixer with paddle, instant-read test thermometer, 3-quart stainless steel bowl, 5-quart stainless steel bowl, ice cream freezer, 9- by 5- by 3-inch loaf pan, parchment paper, aluminum foil, serrated slicer

PREPARE THE DARK CHOCOLATE NUT BARK

Heat 1 inch of water in the bottom half of a double boiler over medium heat. Place the semisweet chocolate in the top half of the double boiler. Tightly cover the top with plastic wrap. Heat for 8 to 10 minutes. Remove from the heat and stir until smooth. Add the peanuts and raisins and combine thoroughly. Pour the dark chocolate nut bark out onto a baking sheet. Use a rubber spatula to spread the nut bark out to a thickness of ½ inch (the nut bark should cover an 8- by 10-inch rectangular area). Place in the freezer for 15 minutes or in the refrigerator for 40 minutes, until cold and solidified. Transfer the nut bark from the baking sheet to a cutting board. Chop the nut bark into ¼-inch pieces (this should yield 2¾ cups of nut bark). Keep the nut bark in a tightly sealed plastic container in the freezer until needed.

PREPARE THE WHITE CHOCOLATE ICE CREAM

Heat 1 inch of water in the bottom half of a double boiler over medium heat. Place the white chocolate and ½ cup half-and-half in the top half of the double boiler. Tightly cover the top with plastic wrap. Allow to heat for 7 to 8 minutes. Remove from the heat and stir until smooth. Keep at room temperature until ready to use.

Heat remaining 1½ cups half-and-half, the milk, and ½ cup sugar in a 3-quart saucepan over medium high heat. When hot, stir to dissolve the sugar. Bring to a boil.

While the cream is heating, place the egg yolks and the remaining ½ cup sugar in the bowl of an electric mixer fitted with a paddle. Beat the eggs on high for 2 to 2½ minutes. Scrape down the sides of the bowl, then beat on high until slightly thickened and lemon-colored, 2½ to 3 minutes. (At this point, the cream should be boiling. If not, adjust the mixer speed to low and continue to mix until the cream boils. If the eggs are not mixed until the point the boiling cream is added, they will develop undesirable lumps.)

Pour the boiling cream into the beaten egg yolks and whisk to combine. Return to the saucepan and heat over medium high heat, stirring constantly. Bring to a temperature of 185 degrees Fahrenheit, about 1 minute. Remove from the heat and transfer to a 3-quart stainless steel bowl. Add the melted white chocolate and half-and-half mixture and stir to combine. Cool in an ice-water bath to a temperature of 40 to 45 degrees Fahrenheit, about 20 minutes.

When the mixture is cold, freeze in an ice cream freezer, following the manufacturer's instructions. While the ice cream is freezing, line the bottom and 2 narrow sides of a loaf pan with a single strip of parchment paper 4 inches wide and 18 inches long. Set aside until needed.

Transfer the semifrozen white chocolate ice cream to a 3-quart stainless steel bowl. Use a rubber spatula to fold the chopped nut bark into the ice cream. Now transfer the ice cream into the loaf pan, spreading evenly. Cover the loaf pan with aluminum foil and freeze the ice cream terrine for 24 hours. Serve within 3 to 4 days.

TO SERVE

Remove the frozen terrine from the loaf pan. Take off the aluminum foil. Briefly (that is, for a few seconds) dip the loaf pan in a sink containing 1 inch of very hot water. Unmold the terrine by inverting it onto a baking sheet lined with parchment paper; discard the used parchment paper. Then return the terrine to the freezer for 5 to 10 minutes.

This is the fun part: splatter 1 to 2 tablespoons of Red Raspberry Sauce onto each of 8 to 10 10- to 12-inch plates. Slice the ends from the terrine (go ahead and indulge yourself), and cut the terrine in 8 to 10 portions. Place a slice of terrine in the center of each sauced plate and serve immediately.

CHAPTER FOUR

NOSTALGIC INDULGENCES

"Cooking is like love, it should be entered into with abandon or not at all."
—Harriet Van Horne

MRS. D'S CHOCOLATE CARAMELS

VIRGINIA'S PRECIOUS FRUIT CAKE

WHISKEY SOAKED RAISIN BREAD PUDDING WITH JACK'S HONEY RAISIN SAUCE

"24" CARROT CAKE

TOASTED BRANDY AND SPICE POUND CAKE

DAN'S BLUEBERRY JELLY ROLL

AUNTIE EM'S ANGEL FOOD CAKE

CONNIE'S STICKY BUNS

MRS. D'S CHOCOLATE CARAMELS

YIELDS 50 CARAMELS

INGREDIENTS

1 teaspoon unsalted butter, melted

2 cups heavy cream

1 cup granulated sugar

1 cup light corn syrup

6 ounces unsweetened chocolate, chopped into ¼-inch pieces

1 teaspoon pure vanilla extract

2 cups toasted walnut pieces

EQUIPMENT

Measuring cup, measuring spoons, small nonstick pan, cook's knife, cutting board, 10- by 15-inch baking sheet with sides, aluminum foil, pastry brush, 3-quart saucepan, whisk, rubber spatula, serrated slicer

MAKE THE INCREDIBLE CARAMELS

Line a baking sheet with aluminum foil. Lightly coat the foil with melted butter and set aside.

Heat the cream, sugar, corn syrup, and chopped chocolate in a 3-quart saucepan over medium heat. When hot, stir to dissolve the sugar and chocolate. Bring the mixture to a boil (about 20 minutes), then adjust heat to low and simmer slowly for 40 minutes, stirring frequently, until quite thick. Remove from the heat. Add the vanilla extract and stir to combine. Add the chopped walnuts and stir with a rubber spatula to combine. Pour the mixture onto the aluminum foil–lined baking sheet, using a rubber spatula to spread the mixture to the edges. Allow the mixture to stand at room temper-ature for 15 minutes, then refrigerate for 2 hours before cutting.

Turn the caramel out onto a cutting board. Use a serrated slicer to make 9 cuts across the width of the sheet of caramel at 1½-inch intervals. Then make 4 cuts across the length of the sheet at 2-inch intervals. Individually wrap each caramel in plastic wrap or aluminum foil, and store in the refrigerator until ready to devour.

THE CHEF'S TOUCH

This recipe may upset consummate candy makers. For starters, it's so simple. Further-more, I don't tell you at what temperature to cook the caramel, only for how long. Well, folks, this is my mom's recipe and she has been making it for all of my fifty years, so I will refer you to Mrs. D, if you feel like com-plaining. I do believe, though, that once these caramels are made, only kudos and proposals will be going her way (she is young and sin-gle, after all).

Toast the walnut pieces on a baking sheet in a 325 degree Fahrenheit oven for 12 to 14 minutes. Allow the nuts to cool thoroughly before adding to the recipe.

For professional-looking caramels, heat the blade of the slicer under hot running water, then wipe the blade dry before making each cut across the caramel sheet. The caramels will have a clean, precise look.

For long-term storage, the individually wrapped caramels may be placed in a tightly sealed plastic container in the freezer. They will keep beautifully for several months that way. The one caveat with freezing: be certain to thaw the caramels before biting into them—a frozen caramel will keep your jaw tied up for more time than you might like.

VIRGINIA'S PRECIOUS FRUIT CAKE

SERVES 16 TO 24

INGREDIENTS

1 pound candied cherries
4 cups all purpose flour
1 pound unsalted butter, cut into 16 1-ounce pieces
2½ cups granulated sugar
6 large eggs
2 teaspoons minced lemon zest
1 teaspoon pure vanilla extract
½ teaspoon salt
4 cups toasted pecan halves

EQUIPMENT

Measuring cup, cook's knife, cutting board, vegetable peeler, measuring spoons, 2 baking sheets, 3-quart stainless steel bowl, electric mixer with paddle, rubber spatula, 10-inch nonstick tube pan, wooden skewer, serrated slicer

PREPARE THE FRUIT CAKE

Preheat the oven to 275 degrees Fahrenheit.

Place the candied cherries in a 3-quart stainless steel bowl. Sprinkle ¼ cup flour over the cherries, then gently toss the cherries to coat lightly.

Place the butter and sugar in the bowl of an electric mixer fitted with a paddle. Beat on medium for 3 minutes. Scrape down the sides of the bowl. Increase the speed to high and beat for 4 more minutes, then once again scrape down the sides of the bowl. Add the eggs, one at a time, beating on high for 1 minute and scraping down the bowl after each addition. Add the lemon zest and the vanilla extract and beat on high for 1 minute. Operate the mixer on low while gradually adding the remaining flour and the salt. Allow to mix until combined, about 30 seconds. Scrape down the sides of the bowl. Add the cherries and 3 cups pecans and mix on low for 15 seconds. Remove the bowl from the mixer and use a rubber spatula to finish mixing the batter, until thoroughly combined.

Immediately transfer the fruit cake batter to the tube pan, then individually place the remaining 1 cup of pecan halves, smooth side down, onto the top of the batter using *all* of the remaining pecans (gently press down on each pecan to set it ever so slightly into the batter). Bake on the center rack of the preheated oven until a wooden skewer inserted in the center of the cake comes out clean, about 2½ hours. Remove the cake from the oven and allow to cool in the pan for 1 hour at room temperature. Unmold the cake from the pan. Allow the cake to cool at room temperature for 1 additional hour before slicing.

TO SERVE

Use a serrated slicer to cut the fruit cake into 1- to 1½-inch thick slices, depending on the desired number of servings. Serve immediately.

THE CHEF'S TOUCH

Virginia Warren is not the stereotypical mother-in-law, and her fruit cake is not the ubiquitous dark, liquor-soaked version that has the life expectancy of a sequoia. Virginia's cake is as delicious as she is beautiful in both appearance and temperament. I am a lucky guy to have such a super mother-in-law, and now we are all fortunate that she has shared her recipe with us.

Candied cherries (also called glace cherries) are available in most major supermarkets or specialty gourmet stores. Be prepared for a bit of wallet shock as they are expensive. We tried substituting dried cherries, but they draw too much moisture from the cake (even when hydrated).

You may use fresh cherries for this cake if you can overcome preconceived notions about serving fruit cake only during the holidays. Select fresh sweet cherries, which are usually available from late spring through early August. Replace the designated amount of candied cherries with 1½ pounds fresh cherries (as purchased), pitted and split in half. Do not toss them in flour. Add the fresh cherries to the batter as specified for the candied cherries, and complete the cake as described.

The candied cherries are lightly coated with flour to help prevent them from sinking in the batter while the cake is baking.

Virginia serves a homemade vanilla bean ice cream to accompany her delightful fruit cake. Perhaps I can encourage a bit of decadence here and suggest Cognac Ice Cream (see page 74), or if you are saving your calories for a second piece of cake (as I often am), a glass of cherry kijafa wine would make a magnificent accompaniment.

WHISKEY SOAKED RAISIN BREAD PUDDING

WITH JACK'S HONEY RAISIN SAUCE

SERVES 10

INGREDIENTS

WHISKEY SOAKED RAISINS

1½ cups raisins

½ cup sour mash whiskey

BUTTERY BUN DOUGH

Buttery Bun Dough (see page 102)

2 teaspoons unsalted butter, melted

CUSTARD

1 cup granulated sugar

4 large eggs

2 cups half-and-half

½ teaspoon pure vanilla extract

1 teaspoon ground cinnamon

2 cups toasted walnuts, chopped into ¼-inch pieces

JACK'S HONEY RAISIN SAUCE

2 cups raisins

1 cup sour mash whiskey

½ cup honey

EQUIPMENT

Measuring cup, measuring spoons, small nonstick sauté pan, baking sheet, plastic container with lid, plastic wrap, 100% cotton towel, pie tin, pastry brush, 9- by 5- by 3-inch loaf pan, small bowl, whisk, serrated slicer, cutting board, parchment paper, 5-quart stainless steel bowl, instant-read test thermometer, 1½-quart saucepan, double boiler, paring knife

SOAK THE RAISINS IN WHISKEY

Combine 1½ cups raisins and ½ cup whiskey in a plastic container with a tight-fitting lid. Allow to stand at room temperature for 6 hours or overnight.

MAKE THE BUTTERY BUN DOUGH

Preheat the oven to 325 degrees Fahrenheit.

Prepare the Buttery Bun Dough. Remove the bowl with the prepared dough from the mixer. Cover the dough with plastic wrap and refrigerate for 1 hour. Remove the bowl from the refrigerator. Discard the plastic wrap and cover the bowl of dough with a cotton towel, then place in a warm location and allow the dough to rise until it has doubled in volume, about 1 hour. Punch down the dough to its original size, transfer the dough to a pie tin, tightly cover with plastic wrap, and place in the freezer for 15 minutes.

Lightly coat the insides of a 9- by 5- by 3-inch loaf pan with 1 teaspoon melted butter. Set aside.

Remove the dough from the freezer. Use your hands to flatten the dough into an 8- by 10-inch rectangle on a clean, dry, lightly floured work surface, using the remaining ¼ cup flour (from the Buttery Bun Dough recipe) as necessary. Starting from the narrow end, roll the dough in a tight spiral to form it into an 8-inch-long loaf. Place the loaf into the buttered loaf pan. Whisk the remaining egg and milk (from the Buttery Bun Dough recipe), then gently and lightly brush the top of the dough with this egg wash.

Bake on the center rack of the preheated oven for 40 minutes. Remove from the oven and allow the baked loaf to cool in the pan for 15 minutes before removing. Remove the baked loaf from the pan and allow to cool to room temperature before cutting. Using a serrated slicer, first cut the loaf into 1-inch-thick slices; then cut the slices into 1-inch cubes (don't trim off the crust). Cover with plastic wrap and refrigerate until needed.

Lightly coat the insides of a clean 9- by 5- by 3-inch loaf pan with the remaining teaspoon melted butter. Line the bottom and long sides (not the narrow ends) of the loaf pan with an 8-inch-wide by 12-inch-long strip of parchment paper. Set aside.

PREPARE THE CUSTARD

Combine the granulated sugar and eggs in a 5-quart stainless steel bowl and whisk lightly to combine. Add the half-and-half, vanilla, and cinnamon and whisk to combine. Set aside.

ASSEMBLE AND BAKE THE BREAD PUDDING

Preheat the oven to 300 degrees Fahrenheit.

Add the whiskey soaked raisins to the custard and stir to combine. Now add the cubed loaf and the toasted walnut pieces. Use your hands to gently but thoroughly toss the ingredients together. Transfer the bread pudding mixture to the loaf pan, a handful at a time, gently pressing the bread pieces into the corners of the pan. Pour any custard remaining in the bowl over the ingredients in the loaf pan.

Bake the bread pudding on the center rack of the preheated oven for 1 hour and 30 minutes, or until the internal temperature of the pudding reaches 140 degrees Fahrenheit. Remove the baked bread pudding from the oven and keep in the pan for 1 hour before slicing and serving.

WHILE THE PUDDING BAKES, PREPARE JACK'S HONEY RAISIN SAUCE

Heat 2 cups raisins and 1 cup whiskey in a 1½-quart saucepan over medium heat. Bring the mixture to a boil, then adjust the heat and allow to simmer slowly for 20 minutes. Remove the saucepan from the heat. Add the honey and stir to incorporate. Hold the sauce warm in a double boiler until needed. You may also cool the sauce in an ice-water bath to a temperature of 40 to 45 degrees Fahrenheit. When cold, transfer to a plastic container, securely cover, and refrigerate until needed. Jack's Honey Raisin Sauce may be kept refrigerated for several days (the sauce will get sweeter by the day). Heat the sauce before serving—actually, it is also delicious cold or at room temperature, especially on a scoop or two of White Chocolate Ice Cream (see page 86).

TO SERVE

Remove the bread pudding from the loaf pan by using a thin-bladed paring knife to loosen the ends of the pudding away from the narrow ends of the pan, then grasp the parchment paper and lift the pudding out of the pan. Discard the parchment paper. Use a serrated slicer to cut the warm bread pudding into 10 ¾-inch-thick slices.

Serve each slice of bread pudding with 2 tablespoons of warm Jack's Honey Raisin Sauce.

THE CHEF'S TOUCH

"Not lumpy, gummy glop again!" That was an oft-heard cry (especially from me) whenever bread pudding was proffered at boarding school many years ago. I confess to hating this stuff based merely on its appearance. However, my bread pudding epiphany came in April 1983 at the renowned Commander's Palace in New Orleans, where I attended a symposium on American cuisine. The black tie dinner at Commander's was the most eagerly anticipated dining experience of the symposium, and as usual the proprietors of Commander's, Ella and Dick Brennan, did not disappoint. Although the entire meal was phenomenal, it was the bread pudding soufflé that I most keenly remember. The sensuous blend of texture, the rich flavor... my perception was changed for good. Back home, I quickly encouraged the pastry chef at the Trellis to develop our own version of a sublime bread pudding to serve at one of our seasonal preview dinners. The results may change your perception of bread pudding as well.

Although our bread pudding is not a soufflé, its extraordinary lightness comes from the Buttery Bun Dough (which is very similar to brioche). Don't even consider preparing this recipe if you are thinking about using a store-bought bread.

For improved flavor and texture, toast the walnuts on a baking sheet in a 325 degree Fahrenheit oven for 12 to 14 minutes.

Traditional bread puddings (the gloppy ones) are often served with heavy cream poured straight from the carton. In this transcendental version, however, I suggest either unsweetened whipped cream or White Chocolate Ice Cream (guaranteed to suppress those boarding school memories).

"24" CARROT CAKE

SERVES 10 TO 12

INGREDIENTS

CARROT CAKE

½ pound plus 1 tablespoon unsalted butter
(1 tablespoon melted)

1½ cups grated carrot

1 cup diced fresh pineapple

½ cup finely chopped dried apricots

½ cup golden raisins

½ cup orange juice

½ cup finely chopped toasted hazelnuts

3 cups all purpose flour

2 teaspoons baking soda

1 teaspoon ground cinnamon

½ teaspoon salt

2 cups granulated sugar

3 large eggs

CREAM CHEESE ICING

1½ pounds cream cheese, softened

4 tablespoons orange liqueur

1 teaspoon pure vanilla extract

½ cup confectioners' sugar

½ cup finely chopped dried apricots

½ cup finely chopped toasted hazelnuts

CARROT TOP GARNISH

1 cup grated carrot

EQUIPMENT

Measuring spoons, small nonstick sauté pan, vegetable peeler, hand grater, measuring cup, cook's knife, cutting board, baking sheet, pastry brush, 2 9- by 2-inch round cake pans, parchment paper, 3-quart stainless steel bowl, plastic wrap, sifter, wax paper, electric mixer with paddle, rubber spatula, toothpick, 2 cardboard cake circles, cake spatula, serrated slicer

PREPARE THE CARROT CAKE

Preheat the oven to 325 degrees Fahrenheit.

Lightly coat the insides of 2 9- by 2-inch cake pans with melted butter. Line each pan with parchment paper, then lightly coat the parchment paper with more melted butter. Set aside.

Combine together in a 3-quart stainless steel bowl 1½ cups grated carrot, diced pineapple, ½ cup finely chopped apricots, raisins, orange juice, and ½ cup finely chopped hazelnuts. Tightly cover the top with plastic wrap and set aside at room temperature until needed.

Combine together in a sifter the flour, baking soda, ground cinnamon, and salt. Sift onto wax paper and set aside.

Place the remaining butter and the granulated sugar in the bowl of an electric mixer fitted with a paddle. Beat on medium for 3 minutes. Scrape down the sides of the bowl. Increase the speed to high and beat for 3 additional minutes. Scrape down the sides of the bowl.

Add the eggs, one at a time, beating on high for 1 minute and scraping down the sides of the bowl after each addition. Operate the mixer on low while gradually adding the sifted dry ingredients. Allow to mix for 30 seconds. Add the fruit-and-nut mixture and mix on low for 20 seconds. Remove the bowl from the mixer and use a rubber spatula to finish mixing the batter, until thoroughly combined.

Immediately divide the carrot cake batter between the prepared pans, spreading evenly. Bake on the center rack in the preheated oven until a toothpick inserted in the center of the cake comes out clean, about 50 minutes. Remove the cakes from the oven and cool in the pans for 20 minutes at room temperature. Invert the cakes onto cake circles. Carefully remove the parchment paper. Allow the cakes to continue to cool at room temperature for 1 hour. While the cakes are cooling, move on to the next step.

MAKE THE CREAM CHEESE ICING

Place the softened cream cheese in the bowl of an electric mixer fitted with a paddle. Beat on low for 1 minute. Scrape down the sides of the bowl and the paddle. Increase the speed to medium and beat for 3 additional minutes. Scrape down the sides of the bowl. Add the orange liqueur and vanilla extract and beat on medium for 30 seconds (if you enjoy the fragrance of a tropical paradise that rises from the mixing bowl, wait until you taste the icing). Add the confectioners' sugar and mix on low for 30 seconds. Scrape down the sides of the bowl. Now beat on high until the icing is light and smooth, about 3 minutes. Remove the bowl from the mixer. Transfer 1 cup of the icing to a small bowl, then add ½ cup diced apricots and ½ cup chopped hazelnuts to this icing and use a rubber spatula to thoroughly combine. Set both icings aside at room temperature until ready to ice the cake (remember, the cakes need to be out of the pan and at room temperature for 1 hour before being iced).

ASSEMBLE THE CAKE

Place the apricot and hazelnut cream cheese icing onto one of the inverted cake layers. Use a cake spatula to spread the icing evenly to the edges. Place the other inverted cake layer on top of the iced layer and press gently into place. Use a cake spatula to spread the plain cream cheese icing evenly over the top and sides of the cake. Refrigerate the cake for 1 hour before serving.

TO SERVE

Cut the carrot cake with a serrated slicer, heating the blade of the slicer under hot running water and wiping the blade dry before making each slice. Equally divide 1 cup of grated carrots onto the tops of the cake slices. Serve immediately.

THE CHEF'S TOUCH

My assistant Jon Pierre Peavey developed a similar version of this cake for his sister Melanie's wedding several years ago. Jon named it "24" Carrot Cake because of its golden interior. For the nuptial celebration, Melanie had requested a dense and moist cake, but did not want a dark interior (something about her lighthearted personality suggested this) or an overly spiced flavor that would overwhelm the champagne bubbles. No need to wait for a wedding to feel blissful, though—this cake will ring your chimes any day of the year.

A word about carrots: select small to medium carrots (they tend to be sweeter). You'll need about ³/₄ pound of carrots, as purchased, to yield the 2¹/₂ cups of grated carrot for this recipe. When choosing the carrots, pass over those that are cracked and have a withered appearance.

The carrots may be grated several hours before being used. Refrigerate the grated carrots in a stainless steel bowl, tightly covered with plastic wrap (do not store grated carrots in water as this will diminish their flavor).

You may substitute dark raisins for the golden. The golden raisins, however, contribute to the sunny blond interior of the cake, and tend to be moister and plumper than the dark variety.

Deciding the best beverage to enjoy with carrot cake causes me no vexation. A vivacious Iron Horse Vineyards sparkling wine would be marvelous.

TOASTED BRANDY AND SPICE POUND CAKE

SERVES 24

INGREDIENTS

5 cups cake flour

½ teaspoon baking soda

½ teaspoon ground mace

½ teaspoon salt

1 pound unsalted butter

3 cups granulated sugar

5 large eggs

2 tablespoons brandy

1 cup whole milk

EQUIPMENT

Measuring cup, measuring spoons, sifter, wax paper, electric mixer with paddle, rubber spatula, 10-inch nonstick tube pan, wooden skewer, serrated slicer, cutting board, 2 baking sheets

PREPARE THE POUND CAKE

Preheat the oven to 325 degrees Fahrenheit.

Combine together in a sifter the cake flour, baking soda, mace, and salt. Sift onto wax paper and set aside.

Place the butter and the sugar in the bowl of an electric mixer fitted with a paddle. Mix on low for 2 minutes. Scrape down the sides of the bowl. Increase the speed to medium and beat for 3 minutes. Scrape down the sides of the bowl again, then beat on medium for an additional 3 minutes. Scrape down the sides of the bowl, then beat on high for 3 minutes. Scrape down the sides of the bowl. Add the eggs, one at a time, beating on medium for 1 minute and scraping down the bowl after each addition. Continue to beat on medium for an additional 4 minutes. Scrape down the sides of the bowl. Add the brandy and beat on medium for 2 minutes. Operate the mixer on low while adding a third of the sifted dry ingredients and ½ cup milk; allow to mix for 30 seconds.

Add another third of the sifted dry ingredients and the remaining milk and mix for another 30 seconds. Add the remaining dry ingredients and mix for an additional 30 seconds before removing the bowl from the mixer. Use a rubber spatula to finish mixing the batter until it is smooth and thoroughly combined.

Immediately transfer the pound cake batter into the tube pan and bake on the center rack of the preheated oven for about 1 hour and 35 minutes to 1 hour and 40 minutes, until a wooden skewer inserted in the center of the cake comes out clean. Remove the cake from the oven and allow to cool in the pan for 15 to 20 minutes. Unmold the cake from the pan. Allow the cake to cool at room temperature for 1 hour before slicing.

TO SERVE

Preheat the oven on the broil setting.

Use a serrated slicer to cut the pound cake into 24 1-inch-thick slices (measured from the outside edge of the cake). Divide the pound cake slices onto 2 baking sheets. Place in the preheated oven and toast the slices for about 1 minute on each side, until golden brown and warm throughout. Remove from the oven and serve immediately, one slice per portion.

THE CHEF'S TOUCH

Probably not too many cupboards in America have a recipe file without a recipe for pound cake. Its simplicity and infallibility no doubt contribute to this cake's popularity.

Pound cake garnered its name from an "original" recipe reputed to have a pound of each of the primary ingredients (if you count flour, butter, sugar, and eggs you end up with a 4-pound cake). There seems to be no shortage of variations on a theme for pound cake. Although this recipe doesn't add up poundwise, it surpasses most with its light texture and iconoclastic flavors of mace and brandy.

One of the secrets to baking a moist pound cake is to use a nonstick tube pan versus a loaf pan. It was tradition in my wife Connie's family that a pound cake had to be baked in one of those pans "with the holes in them," according to Connie's cousin Letha. As Connie's mother, Virginia, sagely surmised, "It seems to me that a pound cake baked in a loaf pan either is too gooey in the center or too dry if cooked through." We experimented, and Virginia is right.

The substantial amount of batter for this cake fills the tube pan to near capacity. The baked result of this extravagance is a high, crested golden brown crust that lifts itself away from the pan with little regard to previously established pound cake behavior.

Although the pound cake is delicious at room temperature, toasting the slices enhances both the flavor and the texture. For added pleasure I recommend serving the toasted slices of pound cake with White Chocolate Ice Cream (see page 86) and fresh berries (see what is available at the market).

If the pound cake is not to be polished off the day it is baked, cover with plastic wrap (after it has cooled) and keep at air-conditioned room temperature for two to three days.

A cold glass of milk is a perfect accompaniment for this nostalgic pound cake, but with a Dessert To Die For, why be prosaic? Try a glass of glistening golden sauternes.

DAN'S BLUEBERRY JELLY ROLL

SERVES 8

INGREDIENTS

BLUEBERRY JELLY ROLL FILLING

1 pint fresh blueberries, rinsed and stemmed

¾ cup granulated sugar

1 teaspoon fresh lemon juice

½ pint red raspberries

REALLY MOIST JELLY ROLL SPONGE CAKE

¼ pound plus 1 tablespoon unsalted butter (1 tablespoon melted)

1 cup granulated sugar

5 large eggs

1 teaspoon pure vanilla extract

½ teaspoon almond extract

1 cup cake flour, sifted

½ teaspoon salt

2 tablespoons confectioners' sugar

BITTER ALMOND BUTTERCREAM

2 cups sliced almonds

¾ pound unsalted butter, softened

3 large egg whites

¾ cup granulated sugar

½ teaspoon pure vanilla extract

½ teaspoon almond extract

2 tablespoons unsweetened cocoa

FRESH BLUEBERRY SAUCE

1 pint fresh blueberries, rinsed and stemmed

¼ cup granulated sugar

EQUIPMENT

Measuring cup, measuring spoons, sifter, wax paper, 3-quart saucepan, whisk, 3-quart stainless steel bowl, 5-quart stainless steel bowl, instant-read test thermometer, plastic wrap, 10½- by 15½-inch jelly roll pan, pastry brush, parchment paper, electric mixer with paddle and balloon whip, rubber spatula, sharp paring knife, cake spatula, 2 baking sheets, double boiler, medium gauge strainer, serrated slicer

PREPARE THE BLUEBERRY JELLY ROLL FILLING

Heat 1 pint blueberries, ¾ cup granulated sugar, and the lemon juice in a 3-quart saucepan over medium heat. As the mixture heats, the sugar will dissolve and the blueberries will liquefy and begin to boil, after about 7 minutes. Allow the mixture to boil until it becomes very thick, stirring frequently, about 20 more minutes. Remove the mixture from the heat, add the raspberries, and cool in an ice-water bath to a temperature of 40 to 45 degrees Fahrenheit, about 20 minutes. Cover the jelly roll filling with plastic wrap and set aside at room temperature until needed.

MAKE THE REALLY MOIST JELLY ROLL SPONGE CAKE

Preheat the oven to 325 degrees Fahrenheit.

Lightly but thoroughly coat the bottom and sides of the jelly roll pan with melted butter. Line the pan with parchment paper, then lightly coat the parchment paper with more melted butter. Set aside.

Place remaining ¼ pound butter and 1 cup granulated sugar in the bowl of an electric mixer fitted with a paddle. Beat on medium for 2 minutes. Scrape down the sides of the bowl, then beat on high for 3 minutes. Scrape down the sides of the bowl. Add 5 eggs, one at a time, beating on medium for 1 minute and scraping down the sides of the bowl after each addition. Add 1 teaspoon vanilla extract and ½ teaspoon almond extract and beat on high for 1 additional minute. Gradually add the sifted flour and the salt and mix on low for 40 seconds. Remove the bowl from the mixer and use a rubber spatula to finish mixing the batter, until smooth and thoroughly combined.

Pour the cake batter into the prepared jelly roll pan, spreading evenly to the edges. Place the pan on the center rack of the preheated oven and bake for 14 to 15 minutes, until the edges of the cake start to brown and pull away from the sides of the pan. Remove the cake from the oven.

Sift the confectioners' sugar over a large (approximately 18- by 22-inch) sheet of parchment paper. Invert the still very warm cake onto the paper (first use a sharp knife to loosen the cake from the pan). Remove the parchment paper from the baked, inverted side of the cake. Using a cake spatula, spread the filling over the inverted cake. Spread evenly to the edges. Starting with the long side nearest you, roll the cake away from you using the parchment paper to help lift the cake over onto itself. Continue to roll the cake to the opposite end, making a tight roll. Now wrap the parchment paper around the jelly roll. Place on a baking sheet and refrigerate for 1 hour, until firm.

PREPARE THE BITTER ALMOND BUTTERCREAM

Preheat the oven to 325 degrees Fahrenheit.

Toast the sliced almonds on a baking sheet in the preheated oven for 25 minutes, until uniformly dark brown (but not burnt). Remove from the oven and allow to cool to room temperature. Set the nuts aside until needed.

Place ¾ pound butter in the bowl of an electric mixer fitted with a paddle. Beat the butter on low for 2 minutes, then on medium for 3 minutes. Scrape down the sides of the bowl. Beat on high until light and fluffy, about 3 minutes. Transfer the butter to a 5-quart stainless steel bowl and set aside until needed.

Heat 1 inch of water in the bottom half of a double boiler over medium heat. Place the egg whites and ¾ cup sugar in the top half of the double boiler. Gently whisk the egg whites as they heat, until they reach a temperature of 120 degrees Fahrenheit, about 2 minutes. Transfer the heated egg whites to the clean bowl of an electric mixer fitted with a balloon whip. Whisk on high until stiff peaks form, about 4 minutes. Add ½ teaspoon vanilla extract and ½ teaspoon almond extract and whisk on high for 30 seconds. Remove the bowl from the mixer. Sift the cocoa onto the whipped egg white mixture. Use a rubber spatula to fold the

cocoa into the egg whites. Gently but thoroughly fold the egg white–and–cocoa mixture into the butter. Set aside for a few moments.

ASSEMBLE DAN'S BLUEBERRY JELLY ROLL

Remove the jelly roll from the refrigerator. Unwrap the jelly roll and discard the parchment paper. Carefully place the jelly roll, seam side down, onto a clean baking sheet or a large platter. Using a cake spatula, evenly spread the bitter almond buttercream over the top and sides, but not the ends (and not the seam side bottom), of the jelly roll. Now gently and evenly press the toasted almonds into the buttercream on the top and sides of the jelly roll. Refrigerate for at least 1 hour before serving.

MAKE THE FRESH BLUEBERRY SAUCE

Heat 1 pint blueberries and ¼ cup sugar in a 3-quart saucepan over medium heat. As the mixture heats, the sugar will dissolve and the blueber-

ries will liquefy and begin to boil, after about 5 minutes. Remove the mixture from the heat and strain through a medium gauge strainer into a small stainless steel bowl. Use a rubber spatula to press the berries through the strainer, releasing as much berry juice as possible. Discard the pulp from the strainer.

Cool in an ice-water bath to a temperature of 40 to 45 degrees Fahrenheit, about 15 to 20 minutes. The sauce may be used immediately or transferred to a plastic container (securely covered) and kept refrigerated for 4 to 5 days.

TO SERVE

Use a serrated slicer to trim a ¼-inch-thick slice from each end of the jelly roll. Cut the jelly roll into 8 1¼-inch slices. Heat the blade of the serrated slicer under hot running water and wipe the blade dry before cutting each slice.

Drizzle 2 tablespoons of blueberry sauce onto each serving plate. Stand a slice of jelly roll in the center of each plate and serve immediately.

AUNTIE EM'S ANGEL FOOD CAKE

YIELDS 6 MINI CAKES

INGREDIENTS

MINI ANGEL FOOD CAKES
10 large egg whites
1 teaspoon cream of tartar
¼ teaspoon salt
1 cup granulated sugar
3 tablespoons minced orange zest
1 tablespoon orange liqueur
1 cup cake flour, sifted

CARAMEL PINEAPPLE SAUCE
¾ cup heavy cream
1¼ cups granulated sugar
½ teaspoon fresh lemon juice
1 large pineapple (about 3½ pounds), peeled, core
    removed, and cut into ¼-inch pieces

WARM STRAWBERRIES
2 tablespoons unsalted butter
2 tablespoons granulated sugar
2 pints strawberries, stemmed and sliced
    ¼ inch thick

DOUBLE CHOCOLATE SAUCE
½ recipe of Double Chocolate Sauce
    (see page 130), warm

EQUIPMENT

Measuring spoons, measuring cup, vegetable peeler,
cook's knife, cutting board, sifter, wax paper,
electric mixer with balloon whip, rubber spatula,
1 unit of 6 individual nonstick mini angel food cake
pans, 2 coffee cups, small plastic knife, 1½-quart
saucepan, 3-quart saucepan, whisk, 3-quart stainless
steel bowl, 5-quart stainless steel bowl, instant-read
test thermometer, large nonstick sauté pan

PREPARE THE MINI ANGEL FOOD CAKES

Preheat the oven to 350 degrees Fahrenheit.

Place the egg whites, cream of tartar, and salt in the bowl of an electric mixer fitted with a balloon whip. Whisk on medium for 1 minute until foamy. Increase speed to high and whisk for 2 more minutes, until soft peaks form. Gradually add 1 cup of sugar while whisking on high until stiff but not dry, about 4 minutes. Add the orange zest and orange liqueur and whisk on high for an additional 20 seconds (gradually move the speed to high to prevent spewing the orange liqueur from the bowl). Remove the bowl from the mixer. Using a rubber spatula, fold in the cake flour, combining thoroughly.

Use a tablespoon to evenly divide the angel food cake batter into each individual mini angel food cake pan (about 8 heaping tablespoons per mini pan), filling them to just below the rim of each pan. Use the back of the spoon to smooth the top of the batter in each mini pan. Place the unit of 6 mini pans on the center rack of the preheated oven. Bake for 30 minutes, until golden brown and the tops are dry to the touch.

Remove from the oven and invert over 2 coffee cups (the inverted cakes should be suspended high enough so that they do not touch the surface below). Allow to cool for 30 minutes at room temperature. To remove the cakes, use a small plastic knife to "cut" around the edges of each cake to loosen it from the sides and center tubes of the mini pan; then gently twist each cake to free it from the pan without tearing the delicate outer crust. Set the cakes aside at room temperature until needed.

MAKE THE CARAMEL PINEAPPLE SAUCE

Heat the heavy cream in a 1½-quart saucepan over low heat.

While the cream is heating, place 1¼ cups sugar and the lemon juice in a 3-quart saucepan. Stir with a whisk to combine (the sugar will resemble moist sand). Caramelize the sugar by heating for 7 minutes over medium high heat, stirring constantly with a wire whisk to break up any lumps (the sugar will first turn clear as it liquefies, then light brown as it caramelizes).

Slowly and carefully add the hot cream, whisking briskly to combine. Immediately add the pineapple pieces and stir to combine. Adjust the heat as necessary to allow the sauce to simmer for 20 minutes, stirring frequently, until the sauce becomes slightly thickened. Remove from the heat and transfer to a stainless steel bowl, then cool in an ice-water bath to a temperature of 40 to 45 degrees Fahrenheit. The cooled caramel pineapple sauce may be held at room temperature while preparing the warm strawberries, or cover with plastic wrap and refrigerate for up to 3 to 4 days.

TO SERVE

Heat the butter and 2 tablespoons sugar in a large nonstick saute pan over medium high heat, constantly stirring to dissolve the sugar. When the mixture begins to bubble, add the strawberries and heat until warmed through, about 2 minutes (use a rubber spatula to gently stir the strawberries while heating). Remove the pan from the heat.

Portion 3 to 4 heaping tablespoons of caramel pineapple sauce onto each dessert plate. Place a mini angel food cake in the center of each plate. Spoon 2 to 3 tablespoons of warm Double Chocolate Sauce onto the top and sides of each cake, allowing some of the sauce to spill into the center of the cake. Portion 3 tablespoons of warm strawberries directly on top of the caramel pineapple sauce and around each cake. Serve immediately.

THE CHEF'S TOUCH

These mini cakes are elevated above the commonplace with a zestful orange infusion and the company of Caramel Pineapple Sauce, warm strawberries, and decadent Double Chocolate Sauce.

Legend has it that thrifty Pennsylvania Dutch cooks developed angel food as a way to use the surfeit of egg whites that remained after producing the yolk-rich noodles they favored. Although it is nice to know the genesis, don't wait until you make noodles to prepare these cakes. A few yolks are a worthy sacrifice for the small indulgence of supernal angel food.

Do use freshly separated egg whites for the preparation of these cakes. Some cooks are fond of saving egg whites in the freezer or refrigerator for long periods of time. Don't do it, or your angel will not be as heavenly.

One medium orange should yield the necessary zest for this recipe.

Once cooled, the mini cakes may be covered with plastic wrap and kept at air-conditioned room temperature for two or three days.

Given Auntie Em's predilection for stepping out in borrowed red 4-inch high heels, her preference for a refreshing glass of orange juice as an accompaniment to her angel food may seem mundane. Knowing her as I do, however, I wouldn't be surprised to find her juice laced with vodka.

CONNIE'S STICKY BUNS

YIELDS 6 BUNS

INGREDIENTS

BUTTERY BUN DOUGH

2 tablespoons granulated sugar

½ cup warm water

2 tablespoons active dry yeast

5 large eggs

4¼ cups all purpose flour

1 teaspoon salt

16 tablespoons unsalted butter, softened

1 tablespoon whole milk

CINNAMON WALNUT FILLING

1 cup chopped toasted walnuts

1 cup tightly packed light brown sugar

1 teaspoon ground cinnamon

STICKY GLAZE

¼ pound unsalted butter, softened

¼ cup pure maple syrup

½ cup tightly packed dark brown sugar

1 cup chopped toasted walnuts

EQUIPMENT

Measuring spoons, measuring cup, baking sheet, cook's knife, cutting board, electric mixer with paddle and dough hook, whisk, plastic wrap, 2 small stainless steel bowls, rubber spatula, 6 8-ounce ovenproof soufflé cups, pastry brush, serrated slicer, 100% cotton towel, wooden skewer

PREPARE THE BUTTERY BUN DOUGH

Preheat the oven to 325 degrees Fahrenheit.

In the bowl of an electric mixer, dissolve the granulated sugar in the warm water. Add the yeast and stir gently to dissolve. Allow the mixture to stand and foam for 3 minutes.

Attach the mixing bowl to the electric mixer fitted with a paddle. Add 4 eggs on top of the yeast mixture, then add 4 cups flour, and finally add the salt. Combine on low speed for 1 minute. Remove the paddle and replace it with the dough hook. Mix on medium low until the dough forms a smooth ball, about 3 minutes. Adjust the mixer speed to medium, and add 16 tablespoons butter, one tablespoon at a time, being certain each tablespoon is thoroughly incorporated (this takes about 1 minute for each) before adding the next tablespoon. (If the dough creeps to the top of the dough hook, which often happens to me, stop the mixer and pull the dough off the hook and back into the bowl.) Continue to add the butter until all 16 tablespoons have been thoroughly incorporated into the dough.

Remove the bowl from the mixer and take out the dough hook. Cover the bowl with plastic wrap and refrigerate for 1 hour.

MAKE THE CINNAMON WALNUT FILLING

Place 1 cup chopped walnuts, the light brown sugar, and the cinnamon in a small bowl. Use a rubber spatula and stir the mixture until thoroughly combined. Set aside at room temperature until needed.

MAKE THE STICKY GLAZE

Place ¼ pound butter in the bowl of an electric mixer fitted with a paddle. Beat on high for 2 minutes. Scrape down the sides of the bowl. Add the maple syrup and dark brown sugar and beat on medium for 1 minute, until thoroughly combined.

Generously coat the insides of each of the 6 ovenproof soufflé cups with 3 level tablespoons of glaze. Evenly divide 1 cup chopped walnuts into the soufflé cups, sprinkling the nuts onto the bottom of each cup. Place the prepared cups onto a baking sheet and set aside until needed.

ASSEMBLE AND BAKE THE STICKY BUNS

Make an egg wash by whisking together the remaining egg and the tablespoon of milk from the Buttery Bun Dough recipe.

Transfer the dough (after it has been refrigerated for 1 hour) to a clean, dry, lightly floured work surface, using the remaining flour as necessary. Use your hands to flatten the dough into a 10- by 14-inch rectangle, then gently and lightly brush the entire surface of the dough with the egg wash (there will be some leftover wash). Evenly sprinkle the cinnamon walnut filling over the egg-washed surface of the dough, leaving a 1-inch wide border along the 14-inch edge nearest you. Now roll the dough, from the other 14-inch edge, toward you (creating a spiral of dough around the filling).

Use a serrated slicer to cut the rolled dough into 6 ¾-inch pieces (although the dough was only 14 inches long, it stretches out and gets longer—about 16 inches—when rolled). Place the pieces, cut side up, in the prepared soufflé cups. Use your fingers to gently press down on the dough to eliminate any large gaps between the dough and the inside surface of the cup.

Cover with a cotton towel and allow to rise in a warm location for 30 minutes, until the dough reaches about 1 inch above the top edge of the soufflé cups. Place the baking sheet with the soufflé cups in the preheated oven and bake for 35 minutes, until golden brown and a wooden skewer inserted in the center comes out clean. Remove the buns from the oven and allow them to stay in the soufflé cups for 10 to 15 minutes before unmolding.

TO SERVE

If serving warm from the oven, invert the sticky buns from the soufflé cups onto individual serving plates. Use a rubber spatula to spread the glaze remaining in the soufflé cups onto the tops of the buns. Serve immediately. The buns may be kept at room temperature for several hours, then reheated in a 300 degree Fahrenheit oven for several minutes, until warm throughout. For reheating, place the buns on a parchment paper–covered baking sheet.

THE CHEF'S TOUCH

I consider this recipe to be the most decadent of our nostalgic indulgences, especially when the buns are served warm from the oven with the Vermont Maple Syrup and Toasted Walnut Ice Cream (see page 82).

Before chopping, toast the walnuts on a baking sheet in a 325 degree Fahrenheit oven for 12 to 14 minutes. (Cool the nuts thoroughly before chopping).

Leave the sticky buns in the soufflé cups for 10 to 15 minutes after baking in order to set the glaze on the buns; if the buns are removed from the cups too soon, the glaze will dribble off the buns in thin rivulets.

My wife, Connie, recommends enjoying a cold glass of skim milk with the sticky buns (lest the sticky buns lead to mighty buns).

CHAPTER FIVE

DROP-DEAD DELECTATIONS

"Nothing succeeds like excess."

—OSCAR WILDE

AUTUMNAL PASTICHE

CHERRY BOMB WITH CHERRIES AND BERRIES

WILD ORCHID

CHOCOLATE MADONNA

CHOCOLATE EXQUISITE PAIN

CHOCOLATE RESURRECTION

PILLARS OF CHOCOLATE WITH COCOA THUNDERHEADS

TERCENTENARY EXTRAVAGANZA

AUTUMNAL PASTICHE

SERVES 8

INGREDIENTS

AUTUMNAL GARNISH

½ cup dried currants

½ cup port wine

½ cup toasted hazelnuts, halved (see page 22 for tips on toasting hazelnuts)

AUTUMN LEAF COOKIES

½ pound unsalted butter

1 cup granulated sugar

¼ teaspoon salt

6 large egg whites

½ teaspoon pure vanilla extract

2 cups all purpose flour

2 tablespoons tightly packed dark brown sugar

2 tablespoons warm water

WARM CINNAMON ANGLAISE

1 cup half-and-half

½ cup heavy cream

2 large egg yolks

3 tablespoons granulated sugar

1 teaspoon cornstarch

½ teaspoon ground cinnamon

LATE HARVEST SORBET

Late Harvest Sorbet (see page 68)

EQUIPMENT

Measuring cup, 2 10- by 15-inch baking sheets with sides, paring knife, cutting board, measuring spoons, plastic container with lid, oak or maple leaf (leaf should be no larger than 4½ by 6½ inches), lightweight cardboard, pencil, X-Acto knife, electric mixer with paddle, rubber spatula, 1-quart stainless steel bowl, parchment paper, cake spatula, large flat plastic container with lid, 1½-quart saucepan, whisk, 2 3-quart stainless steel bowls, instant-read test thermometer, ice cream scoop

SOAK THE CURRANTS

Combine the currants and port wine in a plastic container with a tight-fitting lid. Allow to stand at room temperature for several hours or overnight.

PREPARE THE AUTUMN LEAF COOKIES

Preheat the oven to 300 degrees Fahrenheit.

Pick out a suitably shaped leaf, then make a template: using a pencil, trace an outline of the leaf onto a 5- by 7-inch piece of lightweight cardboard; then cut along the outline of the leaf using a sharp X-Acto knife (remove the leaf-shaped cutout). The outer piece of cardboard with the leaf-shaped hole is the template.

To make the cookie batter, place the butter, 1 cup sugar, and the salt in the bowl of an electric mixer fitted with a paddle. Beat on low for 1 minute, then on medium for 1 minute. Scrape down the sides of the bowl and beat on high for 1 additional minute. Once again, scrape down the sides of the bowl.

Add the egg whites, one at a time, beating on high for 1 minute and scraping down the bowl after each addition. Add the vanilla extract and beat on medium for 30 seconds. Add the flour and beat on low for 15 seconds, then on medium for 10 seconds. Remove the bowl from the mixer and use a rubber spatula to finish mixing the batter, until smooth and thoroughly combined.

Transfer ½ cup of the autumn leaf cookie batter to a 1-quart bowl. Add the dark brown sugar and warm water. Use a rubber spatula to stir gently, until thoroughly combined. Form a pastry cone with parchment paper. Transfer the mixture to the pastry cone. Cut off a ⅛-inch tip from the cone. (This mixture will be used to create the "veins" in the leaves.)

Line 2 10- by 15-inch baking sheets with parchment paper.

Place the template on the parchment paper so that it touches one of the inside corners of the baking sheet. Place 1 level tablespoon of the plain cookie batter in the center of the leaf outline. Use a cake spatula to smear a thin coating of batter to completely cover the inside of the template (carefully scrape away any excess batter on the surface of the template).

Carefully lift the template away from the leaf-shaped batter. Repeat this procedure to form 3 more leaves, one at a time, in the 3 remaining corners of the baking sheet. Then repeat to form 4 more leaves on the second baking sheet. Pipe out "veins" onto each leaf-shaped batter using the pastry bag filled with the darkened batter. Bake both sheets on the center rack in the preheated oven for 6 to 8 minutes, until golden brown.

While the leaf cookies are baking, cut 10 more pieces of parchment paper to fit the insides of the baking sheets.

Remove the cookies from the oven. Work quickly, using a cake spatula to lift the baked cookies off the parchment paper, resting each cookie against the outside edge of a dinner plate so that it bends in a naturalistic way as it cools. (This must be done quickly—otherwise the leaves will harden before they are shaped.)

Prepare the remaining leaves using the same procedure used with the first batch, baking 8 cookies at a time on 2 baking sheets (line the baking sheets with unused parchment paper for each batch of cookies).

Once all the leaf cookies have been baked and cooled, they may be stored in a tightly sealed plastic container at room temperature until needed (they will stay crisp for several days in a tightly sealed container at air-conditioned room temperature).

PREPARE THE WARM CINNAMON ANGLAISE

Heat the half-and-half and heavy cream in a 1½-quart saucepan over medium high heat. Bring to a boil.

While the cream is heating, whisk the egg yolks, 3 tablespoons sugar, cornstarch, and cinnamon in a 3-quart stainless steel bowl for 4 minutes, until slightly thickened and lemon-colored. Pour the boiling cream into this mixture and stir gently to combine. Return to the saucepan and heat over medium heat, stirring constantly, until the cream reaches a temperature of 180 degrees Fahrenheit, 1 to 1½ minutes. Remove from the heat and transfer to a stainless steel bowl.

The anglaise may be used immediately or cooled in an ice-water bath to a temperature of 40 degrees Fahrenheit, about 15 minutes. Transfer the cooled anglaise to a tightly sealed plastic container. Refrigerate until ready to use, for up to 3 days. To use, heat the anglaise in a double boiler over medium heat.

ARRANGE THE AUTUMNAL PASTICHE

Place 4 to 5 leaf cookies in the center of each plate. Place 3 small scoops of Late Harvest Sorbet in the center of each grouping of leaf cookies. Drizzle 3 tablespoons of warm cinnamon anglaise over the sorbet. Sprinkle the port-soaked currants and the toasted hazelnuts over the sorbet on each plate and serve immediately.

Using a pencil, trace an outline of the leaf onto a 5- by 7-inch piece of lightweight cardboard.

Cut along the outline of the leaf, using a sharp X-Acto knife.

The completed template.

Use a cake spatula to smear a thin coating of the batter to completely cover the inside of the template.

Carefully lift the template away from the leaf-shaped batter.

Transfer the darkened batter to the pastry cone.

Pipe out veins onto the leaf-shaped batter using the pastry bag filled with the darkened batter.

Working quickly, use a cake spatula to lift the baked cookies off the parchment paper, resting each cookie against the outside edge of a dinner plate so that the cookie bends in a naturalistic way as it cools.

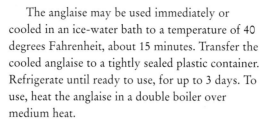

THE CHEF'S TOUCH

This extraordinary dessert was served for a special dinner party at my home a few years ago. The Autumnal Pastiche was presented as part of a seasonal menu that included a parsnip soup with Comice pear puree, salad of local greens with wild mushroom crisps, and loin of rabbit and tenderloin of moulard duck with julienne of pumpkin and tiny green beans.

To achieve the smooth batter needed to create the velvety texture for the autumn leaf cookies, be sure to follow the recipe closely. The best results come from using a table-model electric mixer.

Be certain to use warm (100 to 110 degrees Fahrenheit), not hot, water to dilute the brown sugar—otherwise the batter for the "veins" may break (the butter will separate from the batter).

The number of cookies produced will depend on the thickness of the cardboard used for the template. Consequently, as many as 52 cookies (using lightweight cardboard) or as few as 40 cookies (using a heavier-weight cardboard) may be produced. Either way there will be enough to provide the 4 to 5 recommended cookies per serving.

I doubt that your guests will protest if a glass of late harvest wine is proffered with the Autumnal Pastiche. I would suggest the same wine used to prepare the sorbet.

CHERRY BOMB WITH CHERRIES AND BERRIES

SERVES 6

INGREDIENTS

BURNT ORANGE SNAP FIRECRACKERS

Burnt Orange Snaps (see page 136), uncooked

WHITE CHOCOLATE MOUSSE

4 ounces white chocolate, broken into
    ½-ounce pieces

2 cups heavy cream

CHERRIES AND BERRIES

2 pints fresh strawberries, stemmed

1 pint fresh blueberries, rinsed and stemmed

4 tablespoons granulated sugar

1 tablespoon fresh lemon juice

1 pound fresh cherries, pitted and cut in half
    (save 6 whole cherries with stems for the
    firecracker fuses)

2 tablespoons orange liqueur

EQUIPMENT

Vegetable peeler, cook's knife, cutting board, measuring cup, measuring spoons, paring knife, electric mixer with paddle and balloon whip, rubber spatula, 2 baking sheets, parchment paper, cake spatula, 7- to 8-inch by 1½- to 2-inch wooden dowel, double boiler, plastic wrap, 2 3-quart stainless steel bowls, stiff wire whisk, food processor with metal blade, pastry bag, medium straight tip, oval soup spoon

PREPARE THE BURNT ORANGE SNAP FIRECRACKERS

Make the Burnt Orange Snap batter.

Preheat the oven to 350 degrees Fahrenheit.

Line 2 baking sheets with parchment paper.

Portion 1 heaping tablespoon of the batter in the center of both parchment paper–lined baking sheets (do not spread the batter—it will spread in the oven). Bake on the center rack of the preheated oven for 11 to 12 minutes, until uniformly golden brown in the center and dark brown around the edges. Remove both baking sheets from the oven. Set one baking sheet aside. Immediately remove the parchment paper with the Burnt Orange Snap from the other baking sheet. Invert the snap (parchment paper side up) onto a clean flat surface. Peel the parchment paper from the snap using a cake spatula to press down one edge of the snap while peeling away the paper. Avoid tearing the snap.

Lay a 7- to 8-inch long by 1½- to 2-inch diameter dowel (or similarly shaped object, such as a section of PVC pipe purchased at the hardware store) centered horizontally at the edge of the snap. Roll the snap around the dowel to form a tubular-shaped firecracker (this must be done quickly or the snap will harden and break when rolled around the dowel). Once the snap has been completely rolled, push the dowel through the snap to remove. Repeat this procedure with the remaining snap. (If the snap becomes too hard and brittle to roll, pop it in the oven for 30 to 45 seconds). Set the firecrackers aside to cool.

Bake the remaining 4 firecrackers, two at a time, following the same procedure used with the first 2 (use new parchment paper for each). Allow the rolled firecrackers to thoroughly cool before using.

MAKE THE WHITE CHOCOLATE MOUSSE

Heat 1 inch of water in the bottom half of a double boiler over medium heat. Place the white chocolate in the top half of the double boiler. Tightly cover the top with plastic wrap and allow to heat for 6 to 7 minutes. Remove from the heat and stir until smooth. Transfer the melted white chocolate to a 3-quart stainless steel bowl. Set aside at room temperature until needed.

Place the heavy cream in the well-chilled bowl of an electric mixer fitted with a well-chilled balloon whip. Mix on high until stiff, about 30 seconds. Remove the bowl from the mixer. Transfer one third of the whipped cream to the bowl of white chocolate. Use a stiff hand-held wire whisk to vigorously whisk the cream and chocolate together. Add the remaining whipped cream to the combined chocolate and cream, and use a rubber spatula to fold together until smooth. Cover the bowl with plastic wrap and refrigerate for at least 30 minutes before assembling the dessert.

PREPARE THE CHERRIES AND BERRIES

First place 1 pint whole strawberries, ½ cup blueberries, granulated sugar, and lemon juice in the bowl of a food processor fitted with a metal blade. Process the berries until liquefied, about 30 seconds (this should yield 1¾ cups of berry puree). Transfer the puree to a stainless steel bowl, cover with plastic wrap, and refrigerate until needed.

Cut the remaining strawberries into quartered sections. Place the quartered strawberries, the remaining blueberries, and the cherry halves in a 3-quart stainless steel bowl. Sprinkle the orange liqueur over the berries. Toss gently to combine. Cover with plastic wrap and refrigerate until needed.

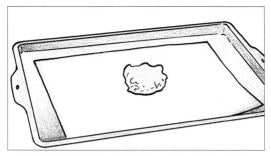

Portion 1 heaping tablespoon of the batter in the center of the parchment paper–lined baking sheet.

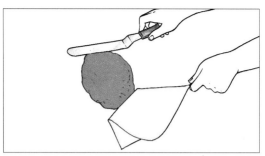

Peel the parchment paper from the snap, using a cake spatula to press down one edge of the snap while peeling.

TO SERVE

Splatter 2 to 3 heaping tablespoons of berry puree onto each 10- to 12-inch diameter plate (if splattering a plate with puree seems a bit odd, see the chef's touch for the "What a Chunk of Chocolate" Ice Cream Terrine on page 87). Alternately, you can simply ladle the puree onto the base of each plate.

Fill a pastry bag fitted with a medium straight tip with half the mousse. Pipe a small mound of mousse onto the center of each plate, evenly dividing the mousse between the 6 plates. Stand a firecracker on its end in the center of each mound of mousse. Use an oval soup spoon to fill each firecracker with about 3 tablespoons of the flavored cherries-and-berries mixture, leaving about ½ inch of space from the top. Fill the pastry bag with the remaining white chocolate mousse, then top the fruit in each firecracker with an equal amount of the mousse. Place a whole cherry with stem (the fuse) on top of the mousse on each firecracker. Sprinkle the remaining cherries and berries (about 3 tablespoons per plate) around the base of each firecracker. Serve immediately.

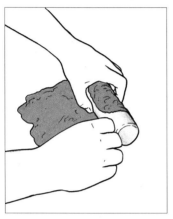

Roll the snap around the dowel to form a firecracker shape.

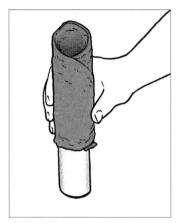

Once the snap has been completely rolled, push the dowel through the snap to remove.

Pipe a small mound of mousse onto the center of each plate, evenly dividing the mousse among the six plates.

Use an oval soup spoon to fill each firecracker with about 3 tablespoons of the flavored cherries-and-berries mixture, leaving about ½ inch of space from the top.

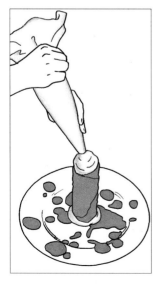

Fill the pastry bag with the remaining mousse, then top the fruit in each firecracker with an equal amount of the mousse.

For several years, former Colonial Williamsburg Foundation senior vice president Duncan Cocke celebrated Bastille Day with a soirée conviviale at the Trellis. The finale to each of those special dinners was always a red, white, and blue dessert. The Cherry Bomb with Cherries and Berries is my favorite of the bunch (in fact, I liked it so much that the following year we used it as our special Fourth of July dessert at the Trellis).

I recommend baking the Burnt Orange Snap firecrackers on sturdy baking sheets. Flimsy baking sheets will buckle and cause the batter to run awry.

The tricky part about making the fire-crackers is the shaping of the snap to form a firecracker while it is hot. As previously mentioned, if the baked batter cools, the snaps will become hard and brittle and indeed snap into pieces. Therefore you may want to bake only one snap at a time. As you get the knack of it, you may be able to bake all the snaps at once (as we at the Trellis do, using several pairs of hands).

The snaps are brittle and susceptible to humidity. Store them in a tightly sealed plastic container in an air-conditioned room for up to three or four days.

The snap batter may be prepared using a hand-held electric mixer; however, the preparation time may increase slightly.

The white chocolate mousse may be prepared using a hand-held electric mixer (mixing time may increase slightly) or by hand, using a wire whisk (mixing time may double or triple depending on the strength of your wrist).

A snifter of Grand Marnier would be an excellent accompaniment to celebrate this dessert.

WILD ORCHID

SERVES 8

INGREDIENTS

MACADAMIA NUT PETALS

½ pound unsalted butter

½ cup granulated sugar

½ cup light corn syrup

1 teaspoon pure vanilla extract

1 cup toasted macadamia nuts, finely chopped

1¼ cups all purpose flour

COCONUT CREAM

1 pound cream cheese, softened

8 ounces fresh coconut, finely chopped

¼ cup coconut liquid

6 tablespoons confectioners' sugar

MANGO PUREE

2 ripe medium mangos, pitted, peeled, and
    cut into large chunks

½ cup granulated sugar

½ cup water

2 tablespoons fresh lemon juice

½ cup fresh orange juice

2 tablespoons dark rum

GARNISH

4 whole kiwi, peeled, halved lengthwise, and
    cut into 24 ¼-inch slices

8 whole strawberries, stemmed and quartered

1 cup toasted macadamia nuts, quartered

EQUIPMENT

Measuring cup, measuring spoons, 2 9- by 13-inch
baking sheets, food processor with metal blade,
cook's knife, cutting board, parchment paper,
electric mixer with paddle, rubber spatula, cake
spatula, 2 8- to 10-inch long by 1¾-inch in
diameter wooden dowels, flat plastic container with
lid, 2-quart stainless steel bowl, plastic wrap,
3-quart saucepan, 3-quart stainless steel bowl,
5-quart stainless steel bowl, instant-read test
thermometer, pastry bag, medium straight tip

PREPARE THE MACADAMIA NUT PETALS

Preheat the oven to 325 degrees Fahrenheit.

Line 2 baking sheets with parchment paper.

Place the butter, ½ cup sugar, and the corn syrup in the bowl of an electric mixer fitted with a paddle. Beat on medium for 2 minutes. Scrape down the sides of the bowl. Beat on medium for an additional 2 minutes. Scrape down the sides of the bowl. Add the vanilla extract and beat on high for 30 seconds. Add the chopped macadamia nuts and beat on high for 30 seconds. Once more, scrape down the sides of the bowl. Add the flour and beat on low for 30 seconds. Remove the bowl from the mixer and use a rubber spatula to finish mixing the batter, until it is smooth and thoroughly combined.

Portion 4 level *tablespoons* of batter, evenly spaced, onto each of the 2 parchment paper–lined baking sheets (no need to spread the batter—it will

do so on its own). Bake both sheets on the center rack of the preheated oven for 12 minutes, until the petals are golden brown around the edges. Remove both baking sheets from the oven. Use a cake spatula to immediately remove the petals, one at a time, from the baking sheets and drape each over one of the wooden dowels (if the petals are so delicate they tear, wait a few seconds before removing them from the parchment paper). Allow the petals to cool on the dowels, about 2 to 3 minutes. Set the petals aside until needed.

Prepare 2 more batches of petals following the same procedure used with the first batch, making 8 petals at a time on 2 baking sheets until 24 petals have been baked. (Line the baking sheets with unused parchment paper for each batch of petals you make.)

Next, prepare smaller petals. Portion 6 level *teaspoons* of batter, evenly spaced, onto each of

2 parchment paper–lined baking sheets. Bake both sheets on the center rack of the preheated oven for 7 to 8 minutes, until the petals are golden brown around the edges. Remove both baking sheets from the oven. Immediately use a cake spatula to remove the petals, one at a time, from the baking sheets, draping each over the wooden dowel.

Allow the petals to cool on the dowels, about 2 to 3 minutes. Set the petals aside until needed.

Prepare 1 more batch of small petals following the same procedure used with the first batch, baking 12 petals on 2 baking sheets. (Line the baking sheets with unused parchment paper for the last batch of petals.)

Once all the petals have been baked and cooled, they may be stored in a tightly sealed plastic container at air-conditioned room temperature. They will stay crisp for several days.

MAKE THE COCONUT CREAM

Place the softened cream cheese, chopped coconut, and coconut liquid in the bowl of an electric mixer fitted with a paddle. Beat on medium for 3 minutes. Scrape down the sides of the bowl. Add the confectioners' sugar and beat on low for 1 minute. Scrape down the sides of the bowl. Beat on medium for an additional 2 minutes, until smooth. Remove the bowl from the mixer. Transfer the coconut cream to a stainless steel bowl. Cover with plastic wrap and refrigerate for 1 hour before using.

PREPARE THE MANGO PUREE

Heat the mango chunks, ½ cup sugar, water, and lemon juice in a 3-quart saucepan over medium high heat. When hot, stir to dissolve sugar. Bring to a boil, then adjust heat and allow the mixture to simmer for 15 minutes, until thick. Remove the mixture from the heat. Cool in an ice-water bath to a temperature of 40 to 45 degrees Fahrenheit, about 20 minutes.

Transfer the cold mango mixture to the bowl of a food processor fitted with a metal blade. Add the orange juice and rum and process until smooth, about 1 minute (this should yield about 1¾ cups puree). Transfer the puree to a stainless steel bowl, cover with plastic wrap, and refrigerate until needed.

ASSEMBLE THE WILD ORCHIDS

Portion 2 to 3 tablespoons mango puree onto each dessert plate.

Fill a pastry bag, fitted with a medium straight tip, with the coconut cream.

Arrange 3 of the larger petals, like a propeller, in the center of each plate (the curved edges of the petals should be facing up). Place a slice of kiwi fruit onto the sauce in between the petals (3 slices of kiwi per plate). Pipe approximately 1½ tablespoons of coconut cream in the center of the petals. Then pipe approximately 1½ tablespoons of coconut cream into each open petal (the coconut cream is very rich and the recipe yield is very exact, so make sure to use the amount suggested).

Arrange 3 small petals around the mound of coconut cream in the center of each plate. The curved edges of the petals should be facing toward the center. Arrange 4 strawberry quarters around the inside of the small petals on each plate. Finish each wild orchid by sprinkling a few quartered macadamia nuts over each. Serve immediately.

Using a cake spatula, immediately remove the petals, one at a time, from the baking sheet.

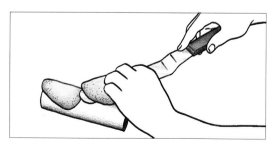

Drape each petal over a wooden dowel and allow to cool, about 2 to 3 minutes.

CHOCOLATE MADONNA

SERVES 6

INGREDIENTS

CHOCOLATE BUSTIERS

½ cup tightly packed light brown sugar

¼ pound unsalted butter

¼ cup dark corn syrup

8 ounces semisweet chocolate, broken into ½-ounce pieces

⅔ cup cake flour

4 ounces white chocolate, broken into ½-ounce pieces

RED RASPBERRY MOUNDS

1 pint fresh red raspberries

¼ cup granulated sugar

2 tablespoons raspberry liqueur

3 cups heavy cream

RED RASPBERRY SAUCE

Red Raspberry Sauce (see page 130)

EQUIPMENT

Measuring cup, measuring spoons, 3-quart saucepan, whisk, rubber spatula, 3 10- by 15-inch baking sheets with sides, parchment paper, 2 large (6½ to 6¾ inches in length) cone-shaped cream horn molds, double boiler, plastic wrap, cooling rack, oval soup spoon, electric mixer with balloon whip, 3-quart stainless steel bowl

PREPARE THE CHOCOLATE BUSTIERS

Preheat the oven to 325 degrees Fahrenheit.

Heat the light brown sugar, butter, and dark corn syrup in a 3-quart saucepan over medium heat. Bring to a boil, stirring frequently with a whisk. Remove the pan from the heat and add 1 ½-ounce piece of semisweet chocolate. Stir with a rubber spatula until the chocolate has melted and blended into the mixture. Add the flour and stir the mixture for several minutes, until the batter is thoroughly combined.

Line 2 baking sheets with parchment paper.

Portion 1 slightly heaping tablespoon (about 1 ounce) of batter in the center of each of the parchment paper–lined baking sheets (do not spread the batter—it will spread in the oven).

Bake in the center of the preheated oven for 7 to 8 minutes, until evenly browned. Remove both baking sheets from the oven. Set 1 baking sheet aside in a warm place (on top of the stove). Immediately remove the parchment paper with the baked batter from the other baking sheet. Invert the now flat (but soon to be voluptuous) baked bustier batter (parchment paper side up) onto a clean flat surface. Peel the parchment paper from the baked batter (this will be quite easy, as the ample butter in the batter will prevent it from sticking to the paper). Place a cream horn mold on its side directly onto the edge of the baked batter at the narrowest point. Roll the baked batter around the mold to form a pointed cone (this must be done quickly or the baked batter will harden and break while being rolled around the metal mold). Allow the cone to cool to room temperature before removing the mold. Repeat this procedure with the remaining portion of baked batter (if the batter has become hard and brittle, pop it in the oven for 30 to 45 seconds—this will make the batter pliable again).

Bake the remaining 10 cones, 2 at a time, following the same procedure used with the first 2 (use new parchment for each). Allow the cones to thoroughly cool before proceeding.

ADORN THE CONES WITH CHOCOLATE

Heat 1 inch of water in the bottom half of a double boiler over medium heat. Place the remaining semisweet chocolate in the top half. Tightly cover the top with plastic wrap. Allow to heat for 8 to 9 minutes. Remove from the heat and stir until smooth.

Place a cooling rack on a baking sheet with sides. Put 1 cone seam side down on the cooling rack. Using an oval soup spoon, drizzle thin and separate parallel lines (think stripes) of chocolate across the width of the cone, starting at the tip and working toward the open end.

Move the decorated cone, seam side down, onto a baking sheet lined with parchment paper. Repeat this procedure with the remaining cones. Use two baking sheets so that the decorated cones are not touching each other. When all the cones have received their dark chocolate stripes, place them in the refrigerator while preparing the white chocolate.

Heat 1 inch of water in the bottom half of a double boiler over medium heat. Place the white chocolate in the top half of the double boiler. Tightly cover the top with plastic wrap. Heat for 4 minutes. Remove from the heat and stir until smooth. Remove the cones from the refrigerator. Repeat the decorating procedure used with the dark chocolate, making the white chocolate lines parallel to the dark (this will create a zebra stripe effect). Refrigerate the cones until needed.

PREPARE THE RED RASPBERRY MOUNDS

Place ½ pint of raspberries, the granulated sugar, and the raspberry liqueur in the well-chilled bowl of an electric mixer fitted with a well-chilled balloon whip. Whisk on low for 30 seconds. Add the heavy cream and whisk on high until stiff, about 1 minute. Remove 12 whole red raspberries from the remaining ½ pint of raspberries, and refrigerate until needed (as garnish). Fold the remaining whole berries into the whipped cream. Refrigerate until needed.

ASSEMBLE THE MADONNA

Spoon 3 to 4 tablespoons of Red Raspberry Sauce onto each of 6 dessert plates. Form 2 red raspberry mounds in the center of each plate, 1 heaping tablespoon of the red raspberry cream mixture per mound. Spoon 2 tablespoons of the cream mixture into a cone. Place the cone into a mound of cream, tip side up. Repeat with the remaining 11 cones, placing each cone into its own mound of cream. Crown the tip of each cone with a whole red raspberry. Serve immediately.

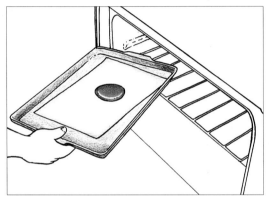

Bake in the center of the preheated oven (the batter will spread as it heats).

Set one baking sheet aside in a warm place (such as on top of the stove).

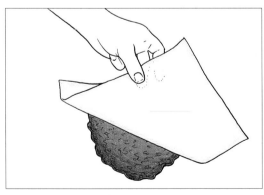

Invert the baked batter onto a clean, dry surface and immediately remove the parchment paper from the baked batter.

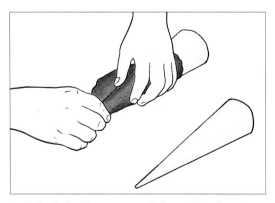

Roll the baked batter around the mold to form a pointed cone.

CHOCOLATE EXQUISITE PAIN

SERVES 10

INGREDIENTS

CHOCOLATE TART SHELL DOUGH

1¼ cups all purpose flour

1 tablespoon granulated sugar

¼ teaspoon unsweetened cocoa

¼ teaspoon salt

4 tablespoons chilled unsalted butter, cut into 1-tablespoon pieces

6 tablespoons ice water

INTRIGUING INTERIOR

6 ounces semisweet chocolate, broken into ½-ounce pieces

¼ pound unsalted butter

3 large eggs

½ cup granulated sugar

½ teaspoon salt

½ teaspoon pure vanilla extract

GLAZE

½ cup heavy cream

2 tablespoons unsalted butter

4 ounces semisweet chocolate, broken into ½-ounce pieces

SHARDS

8 ounces semisweet chocolate, chopped into ¼-inch pieces

BITTER MOUSSE

4 ounces semisweet chocolate, broken into ½-ounce pieces

4 ounces unsweetened chocolate, broken into ½-ounce pieces

1½ cups heavy cream

2 tablespoons creme de cacao

2 large egg whites

EQUIPMENT

Measuring cup, measuring spoons, electric mixer with paddle and balloon whip, plastic wrap, parchment paper, rolling pin, 10- by 15-inch baking sheet, 9½- by ¾-inch false-bottom tart pan, cook's knife, double boiler, rubber spatula, toothpick, 1½-quart saucepan, 2 3-quart stainless steel bowls, instant-read test thermometer, cake spatula, cutting board, whisk, serrated slicer

PREPARE THE CHOCOLATE TART SHELL DOUGH

Place 1 cup flour, 1 tablespoon sugar, cocoa, and ¼ teaspoon salt in the bowl of an electric mixer fitted with a paddle. Mix on low for 15 seconds to combine the ingredients. Add 4 tablespoons chilled butter and mix on low for 2 minutes, until the butter is "cut into" the flour and the mixture develops a coarse, mealy texture. Add the ice water and continue to mix on low until the dough comes together, about 30 seconds. Remove the dough from the mixer and form it into a smooth round ball. Wrap in plastic wrap and refrigerate for at least 1 hour.

After the tart shell dough has relaxed in the refrigerator for 1 hour, transfer it to a clean, dry, lightly floured sheet of parchment paper (wax paper will work). Roll the dough (using the remaining ¼ cup flour as necessary to prevent the dough from sticking) into a circle about 12 inches in diameter and ⅛ inch thick. Place the rolled dough (leave it on the parchment paper) on a baking sheet (the baking sheet is for convenience and keeps the dough flat) and refrigerate for 10 to 15 minutes. Remove the parchment paper with the dough from the baking sheet. Invert the rolled dough into the tart pan. Carefully remove the parchment paper and gently press the dough around the bottom and sides of the pan. Cut away the excess dough, leaving it flush with the top edge of the pan. Refrigerate until needed, at least 30 minutes.

CREATE THE INTRIGUING INTERIOR

Preheat the oven to 325 degrees Fahrenheit.

Heat 1 inch of water in the bottom half of a double boiler over medium heat. Place 6 ounces semisweet chocolate and ¼ pound butter in the top half. Tightly cover the top with plastic wrap. Allow to heat for 8 to 10 minutes. Remove from the heat and stir until smooth. Set aside at room temperature until needed.

Place the eggs, ½ cup sugar, ½ teaspoon salt, and the vanilla extract in the bowl of an electric mixer fitted with a paddle. Beat on high for 10 minutes until thickened and velvety smooth. Add the melted chocolate mixture and beat on medium until combined, about 1 minute. Remove the bowl from the mixer and use a rubber spatula to finish mixing the batter until smooth and thoroughly combined.

Remove the tart shell from the refrigerator. Pour the batter into the tart shell. Place the tart on a baking sheet and bake on the center rack of the preheated oven until a toothpick inserted in the center comes out clean, about 23 to 25 minutes. Remove the tart from the oven and allow to cool to room temperature for 30 minutes. Cover the tart with plastic wrap and refrigerate for 30 minutes.

MAKE THE GLAZE

Heat ½ cup heavy cream and 2 tablespoons butter in a 1½-quart saucepan over medium high heat. Bring to a boil. Place 4 ounces semisweet chocolate in a 3-quart stainless steel bowl and pour the boiling cream over the chocolate. Allow to stand for 5 minutes, then stir until smooth.

Remove the tart from the refrigerator and remove the plastic wrap. Pour the glaze onto the top of the baked filling (the filling will flow towards the edges on its own). Place the tart, uncovered, in the freezer for 30 minutes, or refrigerate for at least 1 hour to set the glaze (once the glaze is firm the tart should be kept refrigerated while preparing the shards and the mousse).

PREPARE THE SHARDS

Line a 10- by 15-inch baking sheet with a sheet of parchment paper.

Heat 1 inch of water in the bottom half of a double boiler over medium heat. Place 8 ounces semisweet chocolate in the top half. Heat the chocolate uncovered, while stirring constantly until it has melted, about 3 minutes. Transfer the melted chocolate to a stainless steel bowl and continue to stir until the temperature of the chocolate is reduced to 90 degrees Fahrenheit.

Pour the chocolate onto the parchment paper–lined baking sheet. Use a cake spatula to spread the chocolate evenly over the surface of the parchment paper to within ¼ inch of the edges. Place the baking sheet in the refrigerator until the chocolate has hardened, about 10 minutes. Remove the hardened chocolate from the refrigerator. Invert the chocolate (parchment paper side up) onto a cutting board. Remove the parchment paper from the chocolate. Use a cook's knife to cut the chocolate rectangle in half lengthwise. Cut each half, widthwise, into thin, uneven strips (shards) about ⅛ to ¼ inch wide (this should be done quickly—otherwise, the chocolate may soften, especially if the ambient room temperature is above 78 degrees Fahrenheit).

Transfer the shards to a baking sheet, then tightly wrap the baking sheet with plastic wrap. Place in the freezer until ready to use.

PREPARE THE BITTER MOUSSE

Heat 1 inch of water in the bottom half of a double boiler over medium heat. Place 4 ounces semisweet chocolate and 4 ounces unsweetened chocolate in the top half. Tightly cover the top with plastic wrap. Allow to heat for 8 to 10 minutes. Remove from the heat and stir until smooth. Set aside until needed.

Place 1½ cups heavy cream and the creme de cacao in the well-chilled bowl of an electric mixer fitted with a well-chilled balloon whip. Whisk on high until stiff peaks form, about 1 minute. Set aside for a few moments.

Whisk the egg whites in a 3-quart stainless steel bowl until stiff peaks form, about 2 minutes. Use a rubber spatula to fold one half of the whisked egg whites into the melted chocolate. Then place the whipped cream and the remaining egg whites on top of the mixture and use a rubber spatula to fold together until smooth and completely combined.

Remove the tart from the refrigerator. Transfer all the mousse onto the glazed tart. Use a cake spatula to spread the mousse over the surface of the tart to the edges, creating a dome-shaped layer of mousse. Refrigerate for 30 minutes before cutting and serving.

TO SERVE

Heat the blade of the slicer under hot running water and wipe the blade dry before cutting each slice. Place a piece of tart in the center of each serving plate. For the coup de grace, sprinkle an equal amount of chocolate shards onto the mousse layer of each tart. Serve immediately.

THE CHEF'S TOUCH

This remarkable creation is from the Marquis de Sade school of desserts. Here, chocolate is taken to the limits of indulgence.

To spread out the preparation of Chocolate Exquisite Pain, the chocolate tart shell dough can be prepared in advance and kept frozen in the tart pan several days or even a couple of weeks before being baked (completely thaw the dough by refrigeration before baking).

The chocolate shards may be kept frozen for several days before using.

After assembly, you may keep the dessert refrigerated (minus the shards—keep them in the freezer) for a couple of days before serving.

Depending on your threshold for "pain," this dessert can be cut into as many as twenty slices. However, if you find the chocolate elements—dense, moist, rich, textural, voluptuous—as compelling as I do, you may opt for fewer but more intense slashes.

For chocolate-induced delirium, I suggest accompanying Chocolate Exquisite Pain with a glass of your favorite cocoa-flavored liqueur.

CHOCOLATE RESURRECTION

SERVES 4

INGREDIENTS

GOLDEN CHALICES

1 teaspoon vegetable oil

1 cup granulated sugar

⅛ teaspoon fresh lemon juice

RESURRECTION CAKES

½ pound plus 2 tablespoons unsalted butter
   (2 tablespoons melted)

6 ounces semisweet chocolate, broken into
   ½-ounce pieces

3 large eggs

3 large egg yolks

⅓ cup granulated sugar

1 teaspoon pure vanilla extract

⅓ cup all purpose flour

¼ teaspoon salt

ESPRESSO KAHLUA CREAM

Espresso Kahlua Cream (see page 131), warm

RED RASPBERRY OFFERING

1 pint fresh red raspberries

EQUIPMENT

Measuring spoons, measuring cup, small nonstick pan, pastry brush, 4 4½-inch diameter and 1-inch deep round, solid-bottomed, plain-sided tartelette molds, 3-quart saucepan, whisk, parchment paper, oval soup spoon, flat plastic container with lid, 4 8- to 9-ounce ovenproof soufflé cups or ramekins, double boiler, plastic wrap, rubber spatula, electric mixer with paddle, baking sheet

MAKE THE GOLDEN CHALICES

Lightly coat the insides of the tartelette molds with vegetable oil.

Place 1 cup sugar and the lemon juice in a 3-quart saucepan. Stir with a whisk to combine (the sugar will resemble moist sand). Caramelize the sugar by heating for 4½ minutes over medium high heat, stirring constantly with a wire whisk to break up any lumps (the sugar will first turn clear as it liquefies, then light brown as it caramelizes). Remove the saucepan from the heat. Allow the caramelized sugar to stand at room temperature for about 1 minute. Place the tartelette molds 2 to 3 inches apart on a large piece of parchment paper. Dip an oval soup spoon into the caramelized sugar and drizzle the hot sugar in a thin stream onto the inside of a tartelette mold creating a spiderweblike pattern. Use 5 to 6 spoonfuls of caramelized sugar to create a golden chalice. Repeat this procedure with the 3 remaining tartelette molds. Allow the caramelized sugar to harden in the molds. Use your fingers to break away any sugar that has hardened onto the top edge of the tartelette mold.

Remove the chalices from the tartelette molds, 1 at a time, by holding a mold in one hand and turning the chalice out into the other hand. The chalices are delicate, so handle them gently. After removing all the chalices from the molds, store them in a tightly sealed plastic container at air-conditioned room temperature.

PREPARE THE RESURRECTION CAKES

Preheat the oven to 400 degrees Fahrenheit.

Lightly coat the inside of each soufflé cup with melted butter.

Heat 1 inch of water in the bottom half of a double boiler over medium heat. Place the remaining butter and the chocolate in the top half of the double boiler. Tightly cover the top with plastic wrap. Allow to heat for 8 to 10 minutes. Remove from the heat and stir until smooth. Set aside at room temperature until needed.

Place the eggs, egg yolks, and ⅓ cup sugar in the bowl of an electric mixer fitted with a paddle. Beat on high until slightly thickened, about 4 minutes. Scrape down the sides of the bowl. Add the vanilla and beat on high for 30 seconds. Add the melted chocolate and butter, and beat on medium for 30 seconds. Add the flour and salt and beat on medium for 30 seconds. Remove the bowl from the electric mixer and use a rubber spatula to finish mixing the batter, until smooth and thoroughly combined.

Evenly divide the resurrection batter into the prepared soufflé cups. Place the soufflé cups on a baking sheet on the center rack of the preheated oven and bake for 14 to 15 minutes. Remove from the oven and allow the resurrection cakes to stay at room temperature in the soufflé cups for 3 to 4 minutes (at this point the cakes will be cool enough to handle—any longer and they will continue to cook, which would eliminate the delectable liquid center).

TO SERVE

Invert the cakes onto a clean sheet of parchment paper (if the cakes do not release from the cups, use a thin bladed paring knife to cut around the outside edges of the cakes).

Use a spatula to place a still-warm inverted resurrection cake in the center of each plate. Spoon 3 to 4 tablespoons of Espresso Kahlua Cream directly over each cake, allowing the sauce to flow over the cakes onto the plates. Crown each cake with a golden chalice. Equally divide the red raspberries into the chalices. Serve immediately.

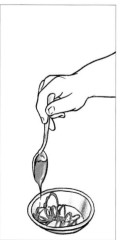

Create a spiderweblike pattern with the hot sugar: dip an oval spoon into the caramelized sugar and drizzle in a thin stream onto the inside of a tartelette mold.

Use 5 to 6 spoonfuls of caramelized sugar to create a Golden Chalice.

PILLARS OF CHOCOLATE WITH COCOA THUNDERHEADS

SERVES 8

INGREDIENTS

DOUBLE CAPPUCCINO ICE CREAM

Double Cappuccino Ice Cream (see page 77)

CHOCOLATE CAKE

½ pound plus 2 tablespoons unsalted butter
   (2 tablespoons melted)

8 ounces semisweet chocolate, broken into
   ½-ounce pieces

6 large egg yolks

¾ cup granulated sugar

10 large egg whites

GANACHE

1½ cups heavy cream

1 tablespoon granulated sugar

1 tablespoon unsalted butter

16 ounces semisweet chocolate, broken into
   ½-ounce pieces

3 cups toasted sliced almonds

COCOA THUNDERHEADS

3 cups heavy cream

⅓ cup granulated sugar

2 tablespoons unsweetened cocoa

EQUIPMENT

Measuring cup, measuring spoon, baking sheet, small nonstick pan, pastry brush, 3 10- by 15-inch baking sheets with sides, parchment paper, double boiler, plastic wrap, whisk, electric mixer with paddle and balloon whip, rubber spatula, 5-quart stainless steel bowl, paring knife, 3-quart stainless steel bowl, food processor with metal blade, 1-quart stainless steel bowl, cake spatula, cutting board, serrated knife, serrated slicer, cooling rack

PREPARE THE DOUBLE CAPPUCCINO ICE CREAM

Make the ice cream, then place in the freezer for at least 2 hours before assembling the pillars.

PREPARE THE CHOCOLATE CAKE

Preheat the oven to 325 degrees Fahrenheit.

Lightly coat the bottoms and sides of 2 10- by 15-inch baking sheets with melted butter. Line each sheet with parchment paper, then lightly coat the parchment with more melted butter. Set aside.

Heat 1 inch of water in the bottom half of a double boiler over medium heat. Place the remaining ½ pound butter and 8 ounces semisweet chocolate in the top half of the double boiler. Tightly cover the top with plastic wrap. Allow to heat for 10 to 12 minutes. Remove from heat, stir until smooth, and set aside at room temperature until needed.

Place the egg yolks and ¾ cup sugar in the bowl of an electric mixer fitted with a paddle. Beat on high until slightly thickened and lemon-colored, about 4 minutes. Scrape down the sides of the bowl and beat on high for 2 additional minutes.

While the egg yolks are beating, whisk the egg whites in a 5-quart stainless steel bowl until stiff but not dry, about 5 to 6 minutes.

Using a rubber spatula, fold the melted chocolate mixture into the beaten egg yolk mixture. Add a quarter of the beaten egg whites and stir to incorporate, then gently fold in the remaining egg whites.

Divide the batter between the prepared baking sheets, spreading evenly. Bake on the center rack in the preheated oven until the tops of the cake are dry to the touch, about 12 minutes (when touched prior to that the cakes will leave you with sticky fingers). Remove the cakes from the oven and cool in the baking sheets for 5 minutes.

Invert the cakes onto 2 clean sheets of parchment paper cut to fit the insides of the baking sheets. (If the cakes adhere to the sides of the baking sheets, use a sharp paring knife and cut along the inside edges of the sheets to free the cakes.) Remove the parchment paper from the baked inverted side of each cake. Wash and dry the baking sheets. Slide the cake layers with the clean sheets of parchment paper on the bottom back into the baking sheets and place them in the freezer while preparing the ganache.

PREPARE THE GANACHE

Heat 1½ cups heavy cream, 1 tablespoon granulated sugar, and 1 tablespoon butter in a 3-quart saucepan over medium high heat. When hot, stir to dissolve the sugar. Bring to a boil. Place 16 ounces semisweet chocolate in a 3-quart stainless steel bowl. Pour the boiling cream over the chocolate and allow to stand for 5 minutes. Stir until smooth.

Process the almonds in the bowl of a food processor fitted with a metal blade until finely ground, about 20 seconds.

In a small bowl, combine one third of the ground almonds with 1 cup of chocolate ganache. Keep the chocolate almond ganache and the remaining plain chocolate ganache at room temperature until needed.

BEGIN ASSEMBLING THE PILLARS

Remove the cakes from the freezer. Evenly divide the chocolate almond ganache onto the cakes. Spread the ganache evenly to within an ⅛ inch of the edges of each cake. Return the cakes to the freezer for 30 minutes.

Remove 1 cake layer from the freezer. Transfer all of the ice cream onto the top of the cake layer. Use a cake spatula to evenly spread the ice cream to the edges of the cake. Remove the other cake layer from the freezer and invert it onto the ice cream, pressing gently with your hands to even the layer. Place in the freezer for 30 minutes.

Remove the cake from the freezer. Invert it onto a cutting board. Remove the parchment paper. Using a very sharp serrated knife, cut away the uneven edges of the cake so that it will measure 9 by 12 inches. Use a serrated slicer to cut the cake widthwise into 8 1½-inch-wide pillars. Place the pillars onto the baking sheet and return to the freezer for 30 minutes.

Place a cooling rack on a baking sheet with sides. Warm the chocolate ganache over hot water until it is smooth and flowing. Remove one of the cake pillars from the freezer and place lengthwise on the cooling rack. Spoon 2 tablespoons of ganache over the top of the pillar. Use a cake spatula to evenly spread the ganache over the top and sides of the pillar. Return the coated pillar to the freezer, placing it on the baking sheet, plain side down. Repeat the coating step with the remaining 7 pillars, coating them and returning them to the freezer 1 at a time. (To prevent the coated pillars from touching each other, place them on 2 baking sheets in the freezer.)

Spread the remaining ground almonds onto a clean baking sheet with sides. One at a time, roll the pillars in the ground almonds, coating them on all 4 long sides. Place the coated pillars on a clean baking sheet, cover with plastic wrap, and return to the freezer for at least 2 hours before serving the dessert.

PREPARE THE COCOA THUNDERHEADS

Place 3 cups heavy cream, ⅓ cup sugar, and the cocoa in the well-chilled bowl of an electric mixer fitted with a well-chilled balloon whip. Mix on high until stiff, about 1 minute.

TO SERVE

Spoon 3 tablespoons of billowy Cocoa Thunderheads onto each of the dessert plates. Remove the pillars from the freezer. Trim about ⅛ inch from each end to form a flat surface. Use a serrated slicer to cut each pillar in half diagonally (heat the blade of the slicer under hot running water and wipe the blade dry before making each slice). Stand 2 pillar halves, flat end down, into the Cocoa Thunderheads. Serve immediately.

Use a serrated slicer to cut each pillar in half diagonally.

Stand the pillar halves, flat end down, into the cocoa thunderheads.

TERCENTENARY EXTRAVAGANZA
SERVES 8

INGREDIENTS

WILLIAM'S GLORIFIED FRUIT
1 quart cold water

½ cup plus 1 tablespoon fresh lemon juice

2 Granny Smith apples

2 Red Delicious apples

2 pears

1 cup honey

1 cup port wine

½ cup dried currants

MARY'S HONEY VANILLA CAKES
6 ounces plus 1 tablespoon unsalted butter (1 tablespoon melted)

1½ cups all purpose flour

1 teaspoon baking soda

½ teaspoon salt

1 whole vanilla bean

½ cup heavy cream

½ cup honey

2 large eggs

1 cup toasted sliced almonds

THIRD CENTURY ALMOND MORTAR BOARDS
¼ pound unsalted butter

½ cup tightly packed light brown sugar

¼ teaspoon salt

2 large egg whites

¼ teaspoon almond extract

1 cup toasted sliced almonds, finely chopped

¾ cup all purpose flour

HONEY VANILLA CREAM
2 cups heavy cream

½ cup honey

1 teaspoon pure vanilla extract

EQUIPMENT

Measuring cup, measuring spoons, small nonstick pan, 2 9- by 13-inch baking sheets with sides, food processor with metal blade, 3-quart stainless steel bowl, paring knife, cook's knife, cutting board, 3-quart saucepan, whisk, colander, rubber spatula, plastic wrap, small bowl, 8 4½-inch-diameter and 1-inch-deep round, solid-bottomed, plain-sided tartelette molds, pastry brush, sifter, wax paper, 1½-quart saucepan, electric mixer with paddle and balloon whip, toothpick, parchment paper, cake spatula, pizza cutter, double boiler

PREPARE WILLIAM'S GLORIFIED FRUIT

In a 3-quart stainless steel bowl, acidulate the water with 1 tablespoon lemon juice.

Peel, core, quarter, and chop the apples and pears, one at a time, into ¼-inch pieces, placing the pieces in the acidulated water as each individual fruit is chopped (this will prevent the fruit from discoloring). Set aside at room temperature while preparing the honey and port syrup.

Heat 1 cup honey, the port wine, and the remaining lemon juice in a 3-quart saucepan over medium high heat. Bring the mixture to a boil, stirring frequently with a whisk to dissolve the honey, then adjust the heat to medium and continue to boil for 15 minutes. Remove the syrup from the heat.

Thoroughly drain the chopped fruit in a colander. Add the fruit to the hot syrup and stir with a rubber spatula to combine. Add the currants and stir to combine. Allow the fruit to steep in the syrup for 1 hour. Strain the syrup from the fruit into a 3-quart saucepan. Transfer the fruit to a 3-quart stainless steel bowl or other appropriately sized noncorrosive container, cover with plastic wrap, and refrigerate until needed. Heat the syrup to a boil over medium high heat, and boil for 15 minutes. Cool the syrup in an ice-water bath to a temperature of 40 to 45 degrees Fahrenheit, about 15 minutes. Refrigerate the syrup until needed.

PREPARE MARY'S HONEY VANILLA CAKES

Preheat the oven to 325 degrees Fahrenheit.

Lightly coat the insides of the tartelette molds with the melted butter.

Combine together in a sifter 1½ cups all purpose flour, baking soda, and ½ teaspoon salt. Sift onto wax paper and set aside.

Use a sharp paring knife to split the vanilla bean in half lengthwise. Heat ½ cup heavy cream and the split bean in a 1½-quart saucepan over medium high heat. Bring to a boil. Remove from the heat and allow to cool at room temperature for 30 minutes. Remove the vanilla bean halves from the cream. Using the back of a paring knife, scrape the tiny seeds from each bean half, then discard the halves. Place the seeds in the cream and whisk to disperse. Set aside until needed.

Place 6 ounces butter and ½ cup honey in the bowl of an electric mixer fitted with a paddle. Beat on medium for 2 minutes. Scrape down the sides of the bowl. Increase the speed to high and beat for an additional 2 minutes. Scrape down the sides of the bowl. Add 2 eggs, 1 at a time, beating on medium for 30 seconds and scraping down the bowl after each addition. Increase the speed to high and beat for 1 minute. Scrape down the sides of the bowl. Add the sifted dry ingredients and combine on low for 15 seconds. Add the vanilla-infused cream and beat on medium for 30 seconds. Remove the bowl from the mixer and use a rubber spatula to finish mixing the batter, until smooth and thoroughly combined (all of the mixing and scraping down creates a velvety smooth and ethereal batter).

Evenly divide the cake batter into the prepared tartelette molds (about 4 heaping tablespoons per mold). Sprinkle an equal amount of sliced almonds over the batter in each tartelette mold. Divide the molds onto 2 baking sheets and bake on the center rack of a preheated oven until a toothpick inserted in the center comes out clean, about 15 to 16 minutes. Remove the baked cakes from the oven and allow to cool in the molds at room temperature for

15 minutes. Remove the cakes from the molds, 1 at a time, by holding a mold in one hand and turning the cake upside down into the other hand. Place the cakes right side up on a large piece of parchment paper or wax paper. Set aside at room temperature until needed, or up to 2 hours. (For longer storage, thoroughly cooled and unmolded cakes may be placed in a tightly sealed plastic container and held at room temperature for two to three days.)

PREPARE THE THIRD CENTURY ALMOND MORTAR BOARDS

With a pencil, trace a 7- by 11-inch rectangle on each of 4 sheets of parchment paper (each one cut to fit a baking sheet).

Place ¼ pound unsalted butter, light brown sugar, and ¼ teaspoon salt in the bowl of an electric mixer fitted with a paddle. Beat on medium for 2 minutes. Scrape down the sides of the bowl. Add 2 egg whites, 1 at a time, while mixing on high for 10 seconds and scraping down the bowl after each addition. Add the almond extract and beat on high for 10 seconds. Add the chopped almonds and beat on high for 10 seconds. Scrape down the sides of the bowl. Add ¾ cup all purpose flour and combine on low for 15 seconds. Remove the bowl from the mixer and use a rubber spatula to finish mixing the batter until smooth and thoroughly combined.

Place a sheet of parchment paper with the trace mark down on each of 2 baking sheets. Place ½ cup of batter in the center of each rectangle. Use a cake spatula to smear a uniformly thin coating of batter to cover completely the inside of each rectangle. Bake both sheets on the center rack of the preheated oven for 6½ to 7 minutes, until most of the surface of the baked rectangle is a light golden brown. Remove both baking sheets from the oven. Set 1 baking sheet aside. Immediately remove the parchment paper with the baked rectangle from the other baking sheet onto a cutting board.

Use a pizza cutter to cut the rectangle into 6 square pieces (cut the rectangle in half lengthwise, then make 2 cuts across the width of the rectangle at 3¾- to 4-inch intervals). Repeat this procedure with the remaining rectangle (it is essential that the rectangles are cut within seconds of being removed from the oven—otherwise they will harden, become brittle, and break apart during the cutting). Bake the next 2 rectangles following the same procedure (use new parchment paper for each). Allow the almond mortar boards to cool for 30 minutes before using.

MAKE THE HONEY VANILLA CREAM

Place 2 cups heavy cream, ½ cup honey, and the vanilla extract in the well-chilled bowl of an electric mixer fitted with a well-chilled balloon whip. Whisk on medium for 15 seconds. Scrape down the sides and bottom of the bowl (this will release any honey that may be sticking to the bowl). Now whisk the cream on high until stiff, about 1 minute. Refrigerate the honey vanilla cream until needed.

TO SERVE

Heat 1 inch of water in the bottom half of a double boiler over medium heat. Place the glorified fruit in the top half. Heat until warm throughout, gently stirring with a rubber spatula for about 6 minutes.

Portion 4 tablespoons of the fruit onto each of the dessert plates, spreading the fruit evenly over the surface of the plates. Drizzle 2 level tablespoons of the syrup over the fruit on each plate. Place a honey vanilla cake on the fruit in the center of each plate. Portion 1 heaping tablespoon of honey vanilla cream onto each cake. Top each mound of cream with an almond mortar board. Continue alternating the honey vanilla cream and the almond mortar boards on each plate, finishing each extravaganza with a mortar board on top (3 mortar boards per extravaganza, one for every hundred years). For the final touch, drizzle ½ tablespoon of syrup onto each of the top mortar boards. Serve immediately.

Use a cake spatula to smear a uniformly thin coating of batter to completely cover the inside of the rectangle.

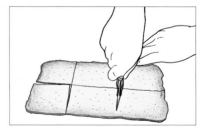

Use a pizza cutter to cut the rectangle into 6 square pieces.

CHAPTER SIX

SWEET NOTHINGS

"My tongue is smiling."

—ABIGAIL TRILLIN

DOUBLE CHOCOLATE SAUCE

RED RASPBERRY SAUCE

CHOCOLATE SOUR MASH SAUCE

ESPRESSO KAHLUA CREAM

SAMBUCA ALMOND BISCOTTI

CITRUS SHORTBREAD COOKIES

CHOCOLATE CINNAMON TIGER COOKIES

BURNT ORANGE SNAPS

CHOCOLATE VALENCIENNES

WHITE CHOCOLATE LULLABY

DOUBLE CHOCOLATE SAUCE

YIELDS 3 $\frac{1}{3}$ CUPS

INGREDIENTS

4 ounces semisweet chocolate, broken into
    $\frac{1}{2}$-ounce pieces
4 ounces unsweetened chocolate, broken into
    $\frac{1}{2}$-ounce pieces
2 cups heavy cream
$\frac{1}{2}$ cup granulated sugar
4 tablespoons unsweetened cocoa, sifted
2 tablespoons dark creme de cacao
1 teaspoon pure vanilla extract

EQUIPMENT

Measuring cup, measuring spoons, sifter, wax paper,
3-quart stainless steel bowl, 3-quart saucepan,
whisk, 5-quart stainless steel bowl, instant-read test
thermometer, plastic container with lid

MAKE THE DOUBLE CHOCOLATE SAUCE

Place both the semisweet and unsweetened chocolate in a 3-quart stainless steel bowl.

Heat the heavy cream and sugar in a 3-quart saucepan over medium high heat. When hot, stir to dissolve the sugar. Bring to a boil. Remove from the heat and add the sifted cocoa, whisking until smooth. Add the dark creme de cacao and the vanilla, stirring to incorporate. Pour the hot cream mixture over the chocolate and allow to stand for 5 minutes. Whisk vigorously until smooth.

Cool the Double Chocolate Sauce in an ice-water bath to a temperature of 40 to 45 degrees Fahrenheit, about 15 minutes. Transfer to a plastic container, securely cover, and refrigerate for up to 5 days. Before serving, warm the sauce in a double boiler. Serve warm or at room temperature.

> ### THE CHEF'S TOUCH
> *One could make a case for labeling this confection "quadruple chocolate" sauce instead of "double chocolate." Although the two primary ingredients are semisweet and unsweetened chocolate, the sauce also boasts additional chocolate in the form of cocoa and creme de cacao. But why nitpick—this doubly delicious sauce can be harmoniously paired with an infinite variety of desserts, not the least of which is For Chocolate Lovers Only (see page 21).*

RED RASPBERRY SAUCE

YIELDS 2 CUPS

INGREDIENTS

2 pints fresh red raspberries
2 tablespoons granulated sugar
1 teaspoon fresh lemon juice
2 tablespoons raspberry liqueur

EQUIPMENT

Measuring spoons, 3-quart saucepan, kitchen
spoon, medium gauge strainer, 3-quart stainless
steel bowl, plastic wrap

PREPARE THE RED RASPBERRY SAUCE

Heat 1 pint raspberries, the sugar, and lemon juice in a 3-quart saucepan over medium heat. As the mixture heats, the sugar will dissolve and the raspberries will liquefy. Bring to a boil, then adjust the heat and allow the mixture to simmer, stirring frequently, for 5 minutes. Remove the mixture from the heat and strain through a medium gauge strainer into a stainless steel bowl. Discard the seeds. Immediately add the remaining pint of raspberries and the raspberry liqueur and stir to combine.

Cool in an ice-water bath to a temperature of 40 to 45 degrees Fahrenheit, about 20 minutes. Cover with plastic wrap and keep refrigerated until needed, up to 3 days.

> ### THE CHEF'S TOUCH
> *Raspberries commonly come to market in $\frac{1}{2}$-pint units (1 cup). Consequently, you will need to purchase 4 individual half-pints to make this remarkably uncomplicated and delightful Red Raspberry Sauce.*
>
> *If the subtle flavor of the suggested amount of raspberry liqueur is too much of a palate teaser, consider doubling the quantity or adding a shooter of raspberry-flavored brandy (of course, you may also omit the spirits altogether).*

CHOCOLATE SOUR MASH SAUCE

YIELDS 3¼ CUPS

INGREDIENTS

6 ounces semisweet chocolate, broken into
  ½-ounce pieces

4 ounces unsweetened chocolate, broken into
  ½-ounce pieces

2 cups heavy cream

¾ cup granulated sugar

¼ teaspoon salt

½ cup sour mash whiskey

1 teaspoon pure vanilla extract

EQUIPMENT

Measuring cup, measuring spoons, 3-quart stainless steel bowl, 3-quart saucepan, whisk, 5-quart stainless steel bowl, instant-read test thermometer, plastic container with lid

PREPARE THE CHOCOLATE SOUR MASH SAUCE

Place both the semisweet chocolate and unsweetened chocolate in a 3-quart stainless steel bowl.

Heat the heavy cream, sugar, and salt in a 3-quart saucepan over medium high heat. When hot, stir to dissolve the sugar. Bring to a boil. Remove from the heat and immediately pour over the chocolate and allow to stand for 5 minutes. Add the sour mash whiskey and vanilla extract. Whisk vigorously until smooth.

Cool the Chocolate Sour Mash Sauce in an ice-water bath to a temperature of 40 to 45 degrees Fahrenheit, about 15 minutes. Transfer to a plastic container. Securely cover and refrigerate until ready to use. The sauce may be kept refrigerated for up to 3 days. Before serving, warm the sauce in a double boiler. Serve warm.

THE CHEF'S TOUCH

Obviously not for the abstemious, the Chocolate Sour Mash Sauce comes loaded with gratifying flavor. Designed to accompany the Chocolate Pecan Sour Mash Bash (see page 34), this consort to confectionery pleasure will have you dipping your beak to satisfaction, especially if you are wise enough to choose a designated driver.

This sauce should be heated in a double boiler before serving (when cool, it is too thick to pour).

ESPRESSO KAHLUA CREAM

YIELDS 1¾ CUPS

INGREDIENTS

2 cups heavy cream

¼ cup freshly ground espresso beans

¼ cup granulated sugar

¼ cup Kahlua

EQUIPMENT

Measuring cup, coffee grinder, 3-quart saucepan, whisk, 3-quart stainless steel bowl, medium gauge strainer, cheesecloth

MAKE THE ESPRESSO KAHLUA CREAM

Heat the heavy cream, ground espresso beans, and sugar in a 3-quart saucepan over medium high heat. Bring the mixture to a boil. Adjust the heat and allow to simmer for 20 minutes, stirring gently but frequently with a whisk (to prevent the cream from boiling over the sides of the saucepan), until the mixture becomes dark and slightly thickened. Remove from the heat and strain through several folds of cheesecloth into a stainless steel bowl. Add the Kahlua and stir to combine. Serve warm immediately or keep warm in a double boiler, over low heat, for up to 2 hours.

THE CHEF'S TOUCH

The viscosity of the Espresso Kahlua Cream will change dramatically if reheated (it will lose texture and become quite thin, albeit still delicious). For this reason, I recommend preparing the sauce as close to serving time as possible.

If Kahlua is not on your shelf, another coffee liqueur may be used.

SAMBUCA ALMOND BISCOTTI

YIELDS 2 DOZEN BISCOTTI

INGREDIENTS

2 cups whole almonds
2¼ cups all purpose flour
1½ teaspoons baking powder
½ teaspoon salt
¾ cup granulated sugar
¼ pound unsalted butter
2 large eggs
2 tablespoons Sambuca

EQUIPMENT

Measuring cup, measuring spoons, 2 baking sheets, cook's knife, cutting board, sifter, wax paper, electric mixer with paddle, rubber spatula, parchment paper, serrated slicer, cooling rack, plastic container with lid

MAKE THE BISCOTTI

Preheat the oven to 325 degrees Fahrenheit.

Toast the whole almonds on a baking sheet in the preheated oven until they turn from cinnamon-colored to chestnut-colored, about 15 minutes. Remove from the oven and allow to cool to room temperature. Use a cook's knife to cut the almonds in half widthwise. Set aside until needed.

Combine together in a sifter 2 cups flour, baking powder, and salt. Sift onto wax paper and set aside.

Place the sugar and butter in the bowl of an electric mixer fitted with a paddle. Beat on medium for 2 minutes. Use a rubber spatula to scrape down the sides of the bowl, then beat on medium for an additional 2 minutes. Scrape down the sides of the bowl, then beat on high for 2 minutes. Add the eggs, one at a time, while beating on medium for 1 minute, stopping to scrape down the bowl after incorporating each addition. Operate the mixer on low while gradually adding the sifted dry ingredients. Once all the dry ingredients have been incorporated, about 30 seconds, turn off the mixer and add the almond pieces and the Sambuca and mix on low for 20 seconds.

Remove the bowl from the mixer and use a rubber spatula to finish mixing the batter, until thoroughly combined.

Transfer the biscotti dough to a clean, dry, lightly floured work surface. Divide the dough into 2 equal portions, and shape each into a log 8 inches long, 2½ inches wide, and 1¼ inches high (using the remaining flour as necessary to prevent sticking). Carefully place the 2 logs, about 2 inches apart, onto a baking sheet that has been lined with parchment paper. Bake the biscotti logs on the center rack of the preheated oven for 35 minutes, until lightly browned and firm to the touch. Remove the logs from the oven and reduce the oven temperature to 275 degrees Fahrenheit. Allow the logs to cool for about 15 minutes at room temperature before handling. Place the biscotti logs onto a cutting board. Using a very sharp serrated slicer, trim the rounded ends from each log. Cut each biscotti log into ½-inch diagonal slices (12 slices per log). Divide the slices onto 2 baking sheets lined with parchment paper.

Bake the biscotti slices in the center of the preheated oven for 30 minutes, until crisp and evenly browned. Transfer the biscotti to a cooling rack to thoroughly cool before storing in a sealed plastic container.

THE CHEF'S TOUCH

At Ristorante Giannino in Milan, I modified the pleasurable ritual of dipping an almond biscotti into a glass of sweet wine. My palate was searching for a more intense postprandial than the requisite Vin Santo, so I requested a medium-size, bowl-shaped wine glass with a double measure of Sambuca. Una delizioza armonia di gusti!

If you are more temperate than I, enjoy the biscotti with a steaming cup of cappuccino.

Be certain to store the biscotti in a tightly sealed plastic container as soon as they have cooled to room temperature. They will stay crisp and delicious stored this way for several days.

For an extra measure of decadence, try drizzling both white and dark chocolate over the baked biscotti. This indulgence requires 1 ounce each of chopped semisweet chocolate and white chocolate. First heat 1 inch of water in the top half of a double boiler over medium heat. Melt the semisweet chocolate in the top half of the double boiler while stirring constantly with a rubber spatula. Immediately remove the melted chocolate and transfer it to a small bowl. Using a teaspoon, drizzle a thin stream of melted chocolate in diagonal zigzags across the width of the biscotti. Then do the same with the white chocolate. Store the chocolate-striped biscotti in a cool place.

CITRUS SHORTBREAD COOKIES

YIELDS 1 DOZEN COOKIES

INGREDIENTS

¼ pound unsalted butter

5 tablespoons granulated sugar

1 teaspoon minced lemon zest

1 teaspoon minced orange zest

1 teaspoon orange flavored liqueur

1 cup all purpose flour

¼ teaspoon salt

EQUIPMENT

Measuring cup, measuring spoons, vegetable peeler, cook's knife, cutting board, electric mixer with paddle, rubber spatula, plastic wrap, 2 9- by 13-inch nonstick baking sheets, plastic container with lid

THE CHEF'S TOUCH

This cookie was born from the search for an appropriate biscuit to use as a crust for our Lemon and Blueberry Cheesecake (see page 23). Not only does this recipe yield exactly the amount of cookie crumbs needed to prepare the cheesecake crust, it is also perfect for the crust for My Cherry Clafouti (see page 51). If you fall in love with these little beauties as I have and enjoy eating them au naturel, I suggest doubling the recipe.

Use a sharp vegetable peeler to zest the citrus fruit. Be careful to remove only the colored skin and not the bitter pith that lies directly beneath the skin. After removing the colored skin with a vegetable peeler, cut it into thin strips with a very sharp cook's knife. Mince the thin strips with the cook's knife.

For most people, a cool glass of lemonade would be the perfect accompaniment for the Citrus Shortbread Cookies. My preference after dinner, however, would be a more gratifying dry sherry or a madeira.

MAKE THE COOKIES

Preheat the oven to 325 degrees Fahrenheit.

Place the butter and sugar in the bowl of an electric mixer fitted with a paddle. Beat on medium for 2 minutes. Scrape down the sides of the bowl. Beat on high for 3 minutes, until the batter is light (but not fluffy). Add the minced lemon and orange zest and the orange-flavored liqueur. Beat on high for 30 seconds. Operate the mixer on low while gradually adding the flour and salt, and mix for 1 minute. Remove the bowl from the mixer and use a rubber spatula to finish mixing the dough, until thoroughly combined.

Wrap the dough in plastic wrap. Roll the dough on a flat surface to form a 6-inch-long and 1½-inch-in-diameter cylinder. Place the dough in the refrigerator for 1 hour and 30 minutes.

Remove the dough from the refrigerator and discard the plastic wrap. Cut the dough into 12 individual ½-inch-thick slices. Divide the slices onto 2 baking sheets. Place the baking sheets onto the center rack in the preheated oven and bake for 16 to 18 minutes, until lightly browned around the edges. Halfway through the baking time, rotate each baking sheet 180 degrees. Remove the cookies from the oven and cool to room temperature on the baking sheets, about 20 minutes. The cooled cookies may be stored in a tightly sealed plastic container for several days at room temperature, or for several weeks in the freezer.

CHOCOLATE CINNAMON TIGER COOKIES

YIELDS 1 DOZEN COOKIES

INGREDIENTS

CINNAMON STRIPES

1½ cups all purpose flour

½ teaspoon ground cinnamon

½ teaspoon baking soda

½ teaspoon salt

1 cup tightly packed light brown sugar

8 tablespoons unsalted butter

2 large eggs

½ teaspoon pure vanilla extract

1 cup chopped toasted pecans

CHOCOLATE STRIPES

5 ounces semisweet chocolate, broken into
   ½-ounce pieces

2 ounces unsweetened chocolate, broken into
   ½-ounce pieces

¾ cup all purpose flour

¼ cup unsweetened cocoa

½ teaspoon baking soda

½ teaspoon salt

¾ cup tightly packed light brown sugar

8 tablespoons unsalted butter

1 large egg

½ teaspoon pure vanilla extract

1 cup semisweet chocolate chips

EQUIPMENT

Measuring cup, measuring spoons, sifter, wax paper, electric mixer with paddle, rubber spatula, 3-quart stainless steel bowl, double boiler, plastic wrap, whisk, 3 nonstick baking sheets, flexible pancake turner, cooling rack, plastic container with lid

MAKE THE CINNAMON STRIPES DOUGH

Preheat the oven to 325 degrees Fahrenheit.

Sift together 1½ cups all purpose flour, cinnamon, ½ teaspoon baking soda, and ½ teaspoon salt onto wax paper. Set aside.

Place 1 cup light brown sugar and 8 tablespoons butter in the bowl of an electric mixer fitted with a paddle. Beat on medium for 1 minute. Scrape down the sides of the bowl and beat on high for an additional 30 seconds. Scrape down the bowl. Add 2 eggs, one at a time, while beating on medium, stopping to scrape down the sides of the bowl after incorporating each addition. Add ½ teaspoon vanilla extract and beat on medium for 30 seconds. Add the sifted dry ingredients and mix on low until the batter is thoroughly combined, about 30 seconds. Scrape down the bowl. Add the chopped pecans and mix on medium for 15 seconds. Remove the bowl from the mixer and use a rubber spatula to finish mixing the batter, until thoroughly combined. Transfer the Cinnamon Stripes cookie dough to a separate container and set aside.

MAKE THE CHOCOLATE STRIPES DOUGH

Heat 1 inch of water in the bottom half of a double boiler over medium heat. Place the semisweet and unsweetened chocolate in the top half of the double boiler. Tightly cover the top with plastic wrap and allow to heat for 7 to 8 minutes. Remove from the heat and stir until smooth. To keep out of trouble while the chocolate is heating, sift together ¾ cup all purpose flour, the cocoa, ½ teaspoon baking soda, and ½ teaspoon salt onto wax paper. Set sifted ingredients aside.

Place ¾ cup light brown sugar and 8 tablespoons butter in the bowl of an electric mixer fitted with a paddle. Beat on medium for 1 minute. Scrape down the sides of the bowl and beat on high for an additional 30 seconds. Scrape down the bowl. Add the egg and beat on medium until thoroughly incorporated, about 1 minute. Scrape down the bowl and continue to beat on medium for an additional 30 seconds. Add ½ teaspoon vanilla extract and beat on medium for 30 seconds. Add the melted chocolate and mix on low for 10 seconds. Add the sifted dry ingredients and the chocolate chips and mix on low for 30 seconds. Remove the bowl from the mixer and use a rubber spatula to finish mixing the batter, until thoroughly combined.

BAKE THE TIGER COOKIES

On each of 3 nonstick baking sheets, portion 4 cookies per sheet. For each cookie, drop 2 slightly heaping tablespoons of Chocolate Stripes dough directly on top of 2 slightly heaping tablespoons of Cinnamon Stripes dough. Place the baking sheets on the top and center racks of the preheated oven and bake for 20 to 24 minutes, rotating the sheets from top to center halfway through the baking time. Remove the cookies from the oven, then allow to cool for 5 to 6 minutes on the baking sheets. Transfer the cookies to a cooling rack and thoroughly cool before storing in a sealed plastic container.

CHOCOLATE VALENCIENNES

YIELDS ABOUT 3 ½ DOZEN COOKIES

INGREDIENTS

4 rounded tablespoons light brown sugar

¼ cup granulated sugar

¼ cup water

4 tablespoons unsalted butter

4 ounces semisweet chocolate, broken into
  ½-ounce pieces

½ cup cake flour, sifted

EQUIPMENT

Measuring cup, measuring spoons, sifter, wax paper, 3-quart saucepan, whisk, 3-quart stainless steel bowl, 2 10- by 15-inch nonstick baking sheets, metal spatula, paper towels

MAKE THE VALENCIENNES

Preheat the oven to 325 degrees Fahrenheit.

Heat the light brown sugar, granulated sugar, water, and butter in a 3-quart saucepan over medium high heat. When hot, stir to dissolve the sugar. Bring to a boil. Place the chocolate in a stainless steel bowl. Pour the boiling liquid over the chocolate and allow to stand for 5 minutes. Stir until smooth. Add the sifted cake flour and stir until smooth.

Portion 6 cookies per nonstick baking sheet by dropping 1 teaspoon of batter per cookie onto each of the 2 baking sheets. Since the batter spreads quite a bit during baking, portion only 6 cookies per baking sheet. Bake the cookies, one baking sheet at a time, on the center rack of the preheated oven (have the second baking sheet with the 6 teaspoons of batter ready to place in the oven as soon as the first batch is removed). Bake for 6½ to 7½ minutes. Remove the cookies from the oven and allow to cool until crisp, about 3 minutes. Transfer the crisp cookies to paper towels to cool completely. Continue this procedure until all the cookies have been baked. Serve immediately or store the cookies in a tightly sealed plastic container at room temperature for up to 3 days.

THE CHEF'S TOUCH

Former pastry chef Andrew O'Connell developed this lacelike chocolate cookie for a luncheon the Trellis prepared for 350 members of the American Institute of Wine and Food in Santa Barbara, January 1985. The cookies accompanied a white grape and currant sorbet that Andrew made in Williamsburg and transported in dry ice to the luncheon site at the Biltmore Hotel. After Andrew baked more than five hundred cookies in the Biltmore's pastry shop, a housekeeper remarked that the cookies reminded her of Valenciennes (a type of lace). I wasted no time in appropriating the name for our cookie.

If nonstick baking sheets are not available, line your baking sheets with parchment paper or aluminum foil (both will work well). Do not under any circumstances butter or grease the baking sheets. There is an ample amount of butter in the recipe; any additional butter will make the cookies greasy and unpleasant to handle.

Room temperature will vary from kitchen to kitchen. If your kitchen is cool, you can keep the cookie batter warm during the baking process by placing the bowl of batter over a 3-quart saucepan containing 1 inch of heated (not boiling) water. Try to keep the batter at a temperature of 110 to 120 degrees Fahrenheit (an instant-read test thermometer comes in handy) so that it has a smooth, but not watery, consistency. (You may also place the bowl of batter on top of your warm oven with similar results.)

I suggest that you avoid distractions during the baking of the valenciennes since they are gossamer thin and will quickly overbake.

Chocolate Valenciennes can be an elegant finale to an evening of dining, especially if they are enjoyed with a steaming cup of your favorite tea.

WHITE CHOCOLATE LULLABY

SERVES 2

INGREDIENTS

3 cups White Chocolate Ice Cream (see page 86)
½ cup brandy
¼ cup dark creme de cacao
¼ cup Frangelico
¼ teaspoon unsweetened cocoa

EQUIPMENT

Measuring cup, measuring spoons, blender

MAKE THE WHITE CHOCOLATE LULLABIES

First place the White Chocolate Ice Cream in the blender. Add the brandy, dark creme de cacao, and Frangelico. Blend until smooth. Pour the blended drink into 10-ounce glasses and garnish with cocoa. Enjoy, and sweet dreams!

THE CHEF'S TOUCH

The name for this delightful frozen concoction was inspired by "Golden Slumbers," from the Beatles' Abbey Road *album (Apple Records).*

To make four lullaby drinks at once, double the ingredients and use a food processor fitted with a metal blade. Process all the ingredients until smooth. (Incidentally, the recipe for the White Chocolate Ice Cream makes 6 cups of ice cream—exactly what you need for four drinks.)

If time does not permit the preparation of the White Chocolate Ice Cream ("pretty darling, do not cry"), purchase top-quality vanilla ice cream and use that instead.

TECHNIQUES AND EQUIPMENT

In this section, I want to give you the tricks of the trade that will bring kudos to you, the dessert maker.

You will notice that each recipe in *Desserts To Die For* has a section called "The Chef's Touch," where you will find anecdotes and helpful information regarding techniques, equipment, handling, and storage for that particular confection. Then why do you need an additional section dealing with more information? My feeling is that a dessert maker can never be overly informed, and the more you know about chilling, melting, slicing, sifting, and whipping, the more luscious your desserts will be.

The following information is pertinent for creating all desserts, especially *Desserts To Die For*.

TECHNIQUES

CHILLING OUT

Be sure to follow instructions about refrigerating or freezing a cake or dessert component for a specific period of time. In most instances, the chilling firms the dessert to the consistency needed for successful assembly. If the time specified is cut short, the results could be a very messy—although perhaps still delicious—dessert.

It is important to note that the designated length of time for "chilling out" is planned for spaces that are not unusually crowded. If you need to lean an armoire against your refrigerator door to keep it closed, the airflow inside the refrigerator will be restricted and it will take much longer for the dessert to cool or freeze properly.

COOLING IN AN ICE-WATER BATH

The fastest and most effective way to cool sauces and other liquids is to place the container holding the food in another, larger container that is partially filled with ice and water. Stir the food frequently to cool it as quickly as possible. A large container or cooking pan can be cooled in a kitchen sink partially filled with water and ice.

The purpose of quickly chilling foods is to inhibit bacteria. Consequently, these foods are less likely to spoil as quickly as foods that were incorrectly handled.

CARAMELIZING SUGAR

Caramelizing sugar is like spinning flax into gold.

Turning a saucepan of granulated sugar into a smooth and lustrous liquid requires some attention. The best advice when caramelizing sugar is to concentrate on that task, and don't get involved with anything but the constant stirring of the sugar as it turns to liquid. As the liquid sugar heats, it picks up color (and flavor) very quickly, so keep a watchful eye. Also, be quite careful in handling this molten sugar, as it is extremely hot and will cause a serious burn if it comes into contact with the skin.

CUTTING UP

I suggest using a 10- to 12-inch serrated slicer when cutting cakes and other solid desserts into portions. Always place the dessert to be cut on a solid surface, such as a clean cutting board. For professional-looking portions with clean lines and even cuts, heat the blade of the slicer under hot running water and wipe the blade dry before making each slice.

A word on "to die for" portion sizes: the recommended portions in each recipe create the most opulent and visually decadent desserts possible. For instance, most cakes serve 10 to 12 portions so that when cut, each slice will tower straight up, offering an orgy for the eye before the pleasure is consummated on the palate. Many more portions could potentially be cut from most cakes if you prefer a more discreet, but still delicious, confectionary rendezvous.

HANDLING EGGS

"Prudence" is the word that comes to mind when discussing how to handle eggs. Governmental agencies have made us aware of the unhealthy and often

serious results from consuming raw eggs. Obviously, the danger of salmonella is present in the handling of many foods derived from animals.

Many risks can be mitigated by proper handling, which in the case of eggs means that they should be refrigerated until utilized. I also don't believe in storing separated eggs for more than two or three days under refrigeration, and I advise against freezing separated eggs. If you have concerns regarding the use of raw or lightly cooked eggs, see the last page of every issue of *Chocolatier* magazine, which always contains some good instructions on this subject.

In several of the recipes in *Desserts To Die For*, egg yolks are combined with cream to make a custard. I emphasize the necessity of continuously whisking the egg yolks (to ensure a smooth custard) while waiting for the cream to boil. When the boiling cream is added to the eggs and returned to the heat, it is essential to bring the mixture to a temperature of 185 degrees Fahrenheit to cook the eggs and inhibit the growth of bacteria.

Also, immediately remove the custard from the heat source once it reaches 185 degrees Fahrenheit. Otherwise, the custard may separate.

Finally, cool the custard quickly in an ice-water bath to guard against the introduction of bacteria.

MELTING CHOCOLATE

Of all the recommended methods for melting chocolate (including using the microwave and such idiosyncratic ways as using a blow-dryer), I find that slowly heating chocolate in a double boiler is the most foolproof. Overheating chocolate will cause it to do some weird things, including something called seizing. Seizing occurs when melted chocolate stiffens and separates like spoiled cottage cheese (this sad situation can also occur if small amounts of liquid, such as water, inadvertently come into contact with melting or melted chocolate). Additionally, chocolate will scorch and have an unpleasant taste if heated too intensely over a direct heat source. Use a double boiler (see this page) and melt the chocolate slowly—the reward will be a glistening pool of ecstasy.

SIFTING DRY INGREDIENTS

Certain batters call for sifting the flour or the dry ingredients. Fundamentally, sifting serves to aerate the mixture, thereby promoting the incorporation of the dry ingredients into the liquids. Also, sifting eliminates any foreign objects or lumps from flour or other dry ingredients and evenly distributes dry leavening agents (such as baking soda) and seasonings (such as ground cinnamon). It is a good idea to sift the dry ingredients onto a large piece of wax paper or parchment paper (the paper facilitates carrying the sifted ingredients, and because it can be folded, it also makes adding the ingredients to a mixing bowl a cinch). Make certain the paper is large enough to hold all the ingredients once you pick it up. Once sifted, flour becomes quite light, so be careful to sneeze away from your sifted ingredients.

TOASTING NUTS

"Nuts," you say . . . peanuts, hazelnuts, almonds, walnuts, pecans, and even precious macadamia nuts. Twenty-three of the recipes in *Desserts To Die For* list one of these nuts as a crunchy component. In every recipe, I suggest toasting the nuts before adding them. Although most of the nuts you purchase have been roasted, additional toasting brings out the flavor. Furthermore, nuts can acquire moisture during the time they have been stored, so the suggested toasting will help to dissipate that moisture.

Nonsalted nuts are the preferred choice for baking.

HAZELNUTS

If you are unable to purchase skinned hazelnuts, you can skin them yourself. First, toast the nuts on a baking sheet at 325 degrees Fahrenheit for 18 to 20 minutes (be certain not to overtoast the nuts as they have a tendency to become bitter). Remove the toasted nuts from the oven and immediately cover with a damp 100% cotton kitchen towel. Invert another baking sheet over the first one to hold in the steam (this makes the nuts easier to skin). After 5 minutes, remove the skins from the nuts by placing them, a few at a time, inside a folded dry kitchen towel and rubbing vigorously. If skinned hazelnuts are purchased, toast at 325 degrees Fahrenheit for 10 to 12 minutes, then allow the nuts to cool before using.

WHIPPING HEAVY CREAM

The whipping cream we use at the Trellis is a fresh 40% butterfat content heavy cream. For several years, we had to make do with ultrapasteurized heavy cream. Ultrapasteurization is usually disdained by professional chefs because it neutralizes some of the flavor. Also, the butterfat content (that means flavor) is usually only 36% in ultrapasteurized cream. Be sure to check out the packaging when you next purchase heavy cream, and select fresh if available. One caveat: fresh cream has a significantly shorter refrigerated shelf life than the ultrapasteurized variety, so only purchase what you need for short-term use (no more than several days).

I always recommend whipping the cream with well-chilled equipment. Getting the equipment as cold as possible—in the freezer or with ice water (be certain to wipe dry before using)—will ensure that the cream whips quickly and voluminously.

EQUIPMENT

BAKING SHEETS AND CAKE PANS

I believe a cookbook author should use the same equipment typically found in the home kitchen. Accordingly, all of the baking sheets and cake pans used for testing *Desserts To Die For* were purchased either in a hardware store or at the supermarket. I suggest purchasing the best-quality, heaviest-gauge steel baking sheets and pans you can find. Purchase baking sheets with sides (sides give the pans extra rigidity, which hopefully will keep them from warping in the oven). If you don't mind the extra cost, you can purchase double gauge aluminum pans and sheets from a food service or bakery supplier; baking times will be a wee bit longer with this equipment, but you will have something to leave to your grandchildren.

COOLING RACK

Most baked items should be cooled to room temperature upon removal from the oven, before slicing or being used as a component in a dessert. In most situations, cooling is most efficient when the baked item is placed on a cooling rack, which increases the airflow around the item. The cooling times will fluctuate depending on the temperature in your kitchen (I estimated cooling times based on an air-conditioned room ranging from 68 to 78 degrees Fahrenheit).

If you don't have a cooling rack, you can always improvise by using anything that allows airflow under the pan or baking sheet, such as an extra oven rack. Whatever you use, be certain that it is stable.

DOUBLE BOILER

A double boiler is a double pot with a lower section that holds water and an upper section that holds the food to be heated.

I must confess I do not own a double boiler. For all these years I have always improvised, typically using a 3-quart stainless steel or heatproof glass-ceramic bowl placed over the top of a 3-quart saucepan. This set-up accomplishes all you need from a double boiler: the top pan does not come into contact with the water in the pan beneath; the item is heated or melted slowly; and the steam is prevented from coming into contact with the food being heated.

ELECTRIC MIXER

Although a quality table-model (stand-up) electric mixer is a substantial investment, it is essential for achieving professional results with many of the *Desserts To Die For*. Various recipes such as the Lemon and Fresh Berry "Shortcake" (see page 54) require lengthy mixing times, and others like the Buttery Bun Dough (see page 102) necessitate the incorporation of ingredients into a rather rigid mass. These tasks are difficult to do by hand or even by using a hand-held electric mixer. In every recipe using an electric mixer, I also list the proper attachment (balloon whip, paddle, or dough hook). The success of the recipe depends on using the proper attachment. So, if you want great desserts, bite the bullet and buy a stand-up mixer.

FOOD PROCESSOR

As much as I enjoy using a cook's knife to slice, dice, and chop, some of these tasks are best accomplished by using a food processor. Whenever noted in the equipment section of a recipe, the food processor will not only save you time but will also yield results superior to those achieved by hand. Nuts, for instance, can be chopped more finely and uniformly in the food processor than is possible otherwise. The downside to using the processor is the cleaning time; this is quite often the most dangerous time—especially when handling the very sharp metal blade.

ICE CREAM FREEZER

The only thing smoother than the delicious ice cream recipes in *Desserts To Die For* is making them in an electronically cooled countertop ice cream freezer. For testing in this book, we used the same machine I have used since 1987, a workhorse from the Simac Appliance Corporation that produces about 2 quarts of ice cream or sorbet per batch (look for the magnum model). Whichever manufacturer you select for a countertop ice cream freezer, I suggest selecting a machine with a removable bowl, which makes cleaning it easier.

Smaller machines that operate on elbow grease also create fine results (just don't buy any that make less than 1 quart). These hand-cranked machines are economical, simple to operate, and virtually never break down. All of our ice cream and sorbet recipes can be adjusted to suit whatever size machine you purchase (divide recipes in half or in fourths).

OVENS

While turning on your oven sounds simple enough, getting it to the correct temperature is quite another story. Fairly exact temperatures are essential for successful baking. Almost without exception, I have found ovens in home kitchens to be notoriously out of calibration no matter their vintage. Temperature variances of 25 to 75 degrees Fahrenheit are the norm.

So how then can you successfully bake? You need an accurate oven thermometer, available at a kitchen supply store. Put it in your oven and use it to set the oven temperature accurately.

How about preheating? Depending on oven capacity, the heat source, and the quality of the insulation, it takes from 20 to 45 minutes to preheat an oven to 300 or more degrees Fahrenheit (natural gas–powered ovens take less time to preheat than do electric ovens). Be sure the oven temperature reaches the desired setting before the item is placed in the oven. Incorrect oven temperature both affects the baking time and inhibits leavening.

PASTRY BAG

I have always enjoyed squeezing buttercream out of a pastry bag, a process that is called "piping." To pipe an exquisite row of buttercream stars or shells is indeed a pleasurable endeavor. Always choose a pastry bag suitably sized for the task, and be certain not to overfill the pastry bag or the contents of the bag will come oozing out of the top. Filling a pastry bag will be easier if you first fold down about one third of the bag, from the inside out, like a cuff. Then carefully fill the bag with buttercream, ganache, mousse, meringue, or whatever while holding the bag in one hand directly underneath the cuff. After the bag is filled (but not too full), unfold the cuff and twist it closed. Hold the bag with one hand placed over the twisted top and squeeze the bag firmly while using the other hand to guide the tip of the bag.

Check out your kitchen supply store for a selection of pastry bags. I prefer the plastic-lined cloth bags, and generally find an 18-inch bag the most useful.

Parchment paper can also be fashioned into a piping bag, especially for use with lighter icings and for fine decorating. First, roll a sheet of parchment into a cone. Clip the narrow end of the cone to make an opening that is the desired width of the piping. Fill and use the parchment cone as described for the pastry bag above.

RUBBER SPATULA

Just when you thought it was safe to pour the batter into the pan, I tell you to "finish mixing with a rubber spatula." Why have I spent the big dollars for a stand-up mixer only to have to resort to completing the task by hand? A rubber spatula makes it possible to thoroughly combine and remove all the batter from the sides of the bowl, as well as from the paddle, dough hook, or balloon whip.

WHISK

What comes in a variety of lengths as well as degrees of stiffness? Well, whisks, of course. These utensils are an essential item in any cook's equipment closet. Although I did not specify the type of whisk needed in each recipe, a general rule would be to select the stiffer whisks for sauces (the length should be determined by the volume of product in the saucepan) and the more flexible types for whisking meringue and whipping heavy cream.

STAINLESS STEEL BOWL

I have been a strong advocate for stainless steel bowls since I started writing cookbooks in 1987. I like these bowls because they are a worthy investment in equipment that will not break; they are noncorrosive (which is an important consideration when storing foods, especially those which are acidic); and they are easily cleaned, which helps keep "Uncle Sal" (salmonella) out of your food.

THERMOMETERS

OVEN THERMOMETER

Do not bake without an oven thermometer in your oven (as mentioned previously, many ovens are not calibrated properly). I suggest the mercury-filled tube thermometer over the spring-style. Remember to remove these thermometers from your oven if you are electronically cleaning since the high heat of the cleaning cycle will ruin the thermometers.

INSTANT-READ TEST THERMOMETER

For accurate temperature readings, select a high-quality thermometer with a range of 0 to 220 degrees Fahrenheit. Keep the packaging that describes how to recalibrate the thermometer. To minimize the need for recalibration, store the thermometer in a safe place (that is, not under all your kitchen spoons and whisks). And remember that this thermometer is not designed for oven use.

Sources

DRIED FRUIT

For quality dried cherries and cranberries:
AMERICAN SPOON FOODS
1668 Clarion Avenue
Petoskey, MI 49770-0566
Phone: 800-222-5886
Fax: 800-647-2512

ICE CREAM FREEZER

For information on the Italian-manufactured Simac
ice cream freezer, call the American distributor:
ELECTROCRAFT
250 Halsey Street
Newark, NJ 07102
Phone: 800-223-1898

CHOCOLATE, DRIED FRUIT, AND UNSALTED NUTS

For bulk chocolate and other baking needs:
TROPICAL FRUIT & NUT
P.O. Box 7507
Charlotte, NC 28241
Phone: 800-438-4470
Fax: 704-588-3092

VIRGINIA PEANUTS

For the most delicious unsalted and salted
peanuts imaginable:
PEANUT SHOP OF WILLIAMSBURG
P.O. Box G N
Williamsburg, VA 23187
Phone: 804-566-0930
Fax: 804-566-1605

COFFEE

For gourmet-blend coffee, including mocha java:
FIRST COLONY COFFEE & TEA COMPANY, INC.
P.O. Box 11005
Norfolk, VA 23517
Phone: 804-622-3658

PROFESSIONAL BAKING EQUIPMENT

For quality baking and pastry tools:
J.B. PRINCE COMPANY
29 West 38th Street
New York, NY 10018
Phone: 212-302-8611
Fax: 212-819-9147

Bibliography

Amendola, Joseph. *The Bakers Manual for Quantity Baking and Pastry Making.* New York: Aherns Publishing Company, Inc., 1960.

Baggett, Nancy. *The International Chocolate Cookbook.* New York: Stewart, Tabori & Chang, 1991.

Beranbaum, Rose Levy. *The Cake Bible.* New York: William Morrow and Company, Inc., 1988.

Braker, Flo. *The Simple Art of Perfect Baking.* New York: William Morrow and Company, Inc., 1985.

Brody, Lora. *Chocolate.* New York: Time-Life Books, 1993.

Chalmers, Irena. *The Great Food Almanac.* San Francisco: Collins Publishers, 1994.

Choate, Judith. *The Great American Pie Book.* New York: Simon & Schuster, 1992.

Desaulniers, Marcel. *Death by Chocolate.* New York: Rizzoli, 1992.

Etlinger, Steven, and Irena Chalmers. *The Kitchenware Book.* New York: Macmillan Publishing Company, 1993.

Glenn, Camille. *The Heritage of Southern Cooking.* New York: Workman Publishing, 1986.

Heatter, Maida. *Maida Heatter's Book of Great Desserts.* New York: Alfred A. Knopf, 1974.

Lipinski, Robert A., and Kathleen A. Lipinski. *The Complete Beverage Dictionary.* New York: Van Nostrand Reinhold, 1992.

Mariani, John F. *The Dictionary of American Food & Drink.* New Haven: Ticknor & Fields, 1983.

McGee, Harold. *On Food and Cooking.* New York: Charles Scribner's Sons, 1984.

Medrich, Alice. *Cocolat—Extraordinary Chocolate Desserts.* New York: Warner Books, 1990.

Scicolone, Michele. *La Dolce Vita.* New York: William Morrow and Company, Inc., 1993.

Stewart, Martha. *Pies & Tarts.* New York: Clarkson N. Potter, Inc., 1985.

Tyler-Herbst, Sharon. *Food Lover's Companion.* New York: Barron's, 1990.

Walters, Carol. *Great Cakes.* New York: Ballantine Books, 1991.

INDEX

METRIC CONVERSIONS

MEASURING SPOONS

U.S.	Metric	U.S.	Metric
¼ tsp	1 mL	¼ tbsp	5 mL
½ tsp	2 mL	½ tbsp	10 mL
¾ tsp	4 mL	¾ tbsp	15 mL
1 tsp	5 mL	1 tbsp	20 mL
1¼ tsp	6 mL	1¼ tbsp	25 mL
1½ tsp	7 mL	1½ tbsp	30 mL
1¾ tsp	9 mL	1¾ tbsp	35 mL
2 tsp	10 mL	2 tbsp	40 mL
2¼ tsp	11 mL	2¼ tbsp	45 mL
2½ tsp	12 mL	2½ tbsp	50 mL
2¾ tsp	14 mL	2¾ tbsp	55 mL
3 tsp	15 mL	3 tbsp	60 mL

MEASURING CUPS

U.S.	Metric
¼ cup	50 mL
⅓ cup	75 mL
½ cup	125 mL
1 cup	250 mL
1¼ cups	300 mL
1⅓ cups	325 mL
1½ cups	375 mL
2 cups	500 mL
2¼ cups	550 mL
2⅓ cups	575 mL
2½ cups	625 mL
3 cups	750 mL
3¼ cups	800 mL
3⅓ cups	825 mL
3½ cups	875 mL
4 cups	1 L
8 cups	2 L
16 cups	4 L
20 cups	8 L

MEASURING LIQUIDS

U.S.	Metric
½ oz	15 mL
1 oz	30 mL
1½ oz	45 mL
2 oz	60 mL
2½ oz	75 mL
3 oz	90 mL
3½ oz	105 mL
4 oz	125 mL
4½ oz	140 mL
5 oz	155 mL
5½ oz	170 mL
6 oz	185 mL
6½ oz	200 mL
7 oz	220 mL
7½ oz	235 mL
8 oz	250 mL
16 oz	500 mL

MEASURING DRY INGREDIENTS

U.S.	Metric
½ oz	15 g
1 oz	30 g
1½ oz	45 g
2 oz	60 g
2½ oz	75 g
3 oz	90 g
3½ oz	105 g
4 oz	125 g
4½ oz	140 g
5 oz	155 g
5½ oz	170 g
6 oz	185 g
6½ oz	200 g
7 oz	220 g
7½ oz	235 g
8 oz	250 g
8½ oz	265 g
9 oz	280 g
9½ oz	295 g
10 oz	315 g
10½ oz	330 g
11 oz	350 g
11½ oz	365 g
12 oz	375 g
12½ oz	390 g
13 oz	410 g
13½ oz	425 g
14 oz	440 g
14½ oz	455 g
15 oz	470 g
15½ oz	485 g
1 lb (16 oz)	500 g
1 lb 8 oz	750 g
2 lb	1 kg
3 lb	1.5 kg
4 lb	2 kg
5 lb	2.5 kg